FROM SCHOOL TO UNEMPLOYMENT?

LPL

Also by P. N. Junankar

THE COSTS OF UNEMPLOYMENT
MARX'S ECONOMICS
INVESTMENT: Theories and Evidence

From School to Unemployment?

The Labour Market for Young People

Edited by
P. N. Junankar
Lecturer in Economics
University of Essex

MACMILLAN
PRESS

First published 1987

Published by
THE MACMILLAN PRESS LTD
Houndmills, Basingstoke, Hampshire RG21 2XS
and London
Companies and representatives
throughout the world

Typeset by Latimer Trend & Company Ltd
Plymouth

Printed in Great Britain by
Anchor Brendon Ltd
Tiptree, Essex

British Library Cataloguing in Publication Data
From school to unemployment? : the labour
market for young people.
1. Youth—Employment—Great Britain
I. Junankar, P. N.
331.3′4′0941   HD6276.G7
ISBN 0–333–39842–4 (hardcover)
ISBN 0–333–39843–2 (paperback)

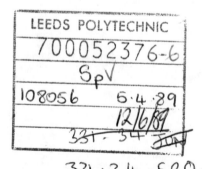

Contents

Notes on the Contributors

Patricia Dutton is a Research Fellow at the Institute for Employment Research. She has worked extensively on the engineering industry and on the youth labour market. She has published widely in several journals and contributed to *Mergers and Economic Performance* (K. Cowling *et al.*) and *Economic Change and Employment Policy* (edited by R. M. Lindley).

P. N. Junankar is a Lecturer in Economics at the University of Essex. He was a Principal Research Fellow at the Institute of Employment Research at the University of Warwick, 1984–5. He has been a Lecturer in Government at the University of Durham (1966–9), Visiting Assistant Professor at Northwestern University, USA (1972–3), Visiting Associate Professor at Queen's University, Canada (1978–9), Visiting Fellow at the Indian Statistical Institute, New Delhi, India and at the Australian National University in Canberra, Australia. He has worked on labour economics, macroeconomics, development economics and Marxian economics. He has published widely in several journals including *Economica, Economic Journal, Oxford Economic Papers* and *Journal of Development Studies*. He has published books on *Investment, Marx's Economics* and *Costs of Unemployment*.

Lisa M. Lynch is an Assistant Professor of Industrial Relations at the Massachusetts Institute of Technology and Faculty Research Fellow at the National Bureau of Economic Research, USA. Her previous appointments include Assistant Professor of Labor and Human Resources at Ohio State University (1983–5) and Lecturer in Economics, Bristol University (1982–3). Her publications in labour economics (mainly on youth unemployment) have appeared in the *Journal of Econometrics, Oxford Economic Papers*, and the *British Journal of Industrial Relations*.

Brian G. M. Main is a Reader in Economics at the University of Edinburgh. He has been a Visiting Associate Professor at the Graduate School of Business Administration, University of California Berkeley, USA (1980–1), Associate Fellow of the Institute for Employment Research, University of Warwick (1981–) and Member of the Centre for Educational Sociology, University of Edinburgh (1982–). He has published widely in the field of labour economics in several journals including the *American Economic Review, International Economic Review, Review of Economics and Statistics, Economica, Oxford Economic Papers, Journal of Human Resources*, and the *Scottish Journal of Political Economy*. He has recently published a research report with Peter Elias on *Women's Working Lives*.

David Marsden is a Lecturer in Industrial Relations at the London School of Economics. He has been Research Fellow at the Laboratoire D'Economie et de Sociologie du Travail, Aix-en-Provence (1973–5), a Senior Research Officer at the Department of Employment (1975–6), and Research Fellow at the University of Sussex (1976–80). He has published several articles and books including *Pay Inequalities in the European Community* (with C. T. Saunders), *The Car Industry; Labour Relations and Industrial Adjustment*, and *The End of Economic Man? Custom and Competition in the Labour Markets* (with T. Morris *et al.*).

Adrian Neale is a Research Officer at Nuffield College, Oxford. Prior to that he was Fellow at the Institute for Employment Research, University of Warwick (1980–4). His main research interests lie in the area of labour economics, econometrics and econometric computing. He has researched and published on the determination of employment, occupational structure and hours of work. Since 1984 he has been involved in a major econometric project at Nuffield College, designed to look at disequilibrium in economic relationships, the interaction of feedback and feedforward mechanisms, and on properties of long-run economic relationships.

David Raffe is a Reader in Education and Deputy Director of the Centre for Educational Sociology at the University of Edinburgh. He has worked extensively on the Scottish School Leavers' Survey, looking in particular at the youth labour market, secondary and further education and the transition from school. His publications include *Reconstructions of Secondary Education* (co-author), *Fourteen to Eighteen* (editor) and several papers and contributed chapters in books.

Amin Rajan is a Senior Research Fellow at the Institute of Manpower Studies, University of Sussex. Prior to that he worked as an Economic Adviser at the National Economic Development Office (1969–74), the Cabinet Office (1974–7), and Her Majesty's Treasury (1977–80). He has worked extensively on labour market problems and published several reports and papers on the subject.

Paul Ryan is a Fellow of King's College and Lecturer in Economics at the University of Cambridge. He has been an Associate Fellow of the Institute for Employment Research, University of Warwick, since 1983. He is a member of the Academic Reference Group on the Study of Funding of Vocational and Education Training, Manpower Services Commission (1968–). He was a Principal Economist at the Energy Resources Company, Cambridge, Mass., USA (1974–7). He has published several articles in books and journals (including the *British Journal of Industrial Relations*) and with G. Eliasson has written *The Development and Utilisation of Human Resources in the Context of Technological Change and Economic Reconstruction.*

William Wells is Economic Adviser at the Department of Employment. Prior to joining the government Economic Service he was a Temporary Lecturer in Economics at Queen Mary College, University of London (1976–7). He has worked on labour economics and published in the *Employment Gazette* as well as, in the Department of Employment working paper series, *Relative pay and Employment of Young People.*

Acknowledgements

The editor and publishers wish to thank the Controller of Her Majesty's Stationery Office for permission to reproduce the Crown copyright material in Chapters 3 and 5; also to IMS for permission to reproduce the questionnaire in the appendix to Chapter 12.

Preface

The chapters in this volume were first presented as papers to the 'Young Persons' Labour Market Conference' held at the Institute for Employment Research, University of Warwick in 1984. This conference was made possible by a generous grant from the Department of Employment to the IER, Warwick. This help is gratefully acknowledged. Neither the IER nor the Department of Employment is responsible for the views expressed in this volume. The volume includes a selection of the papers from this conference which were completely revised for publication in the light of referees' and editorial comments. Much new material has been added so that the volume is a free-standing contribution to the literature on youth labour markets, rather than being merely a conference volume.

I should like to thank Sheila Ogden and Pamela Keech for helping with the preparation of this book.

P. N. JUNANKAR

1 The Labour Market for Young People

P. N. Junankar

1.1 INTRODUCTION

The last few years have seen a dramatic worsening of the labour market for young people with increasing unemployment rates and increasing long-term unemployment. Young people leaving school face bleak prospects, with a very low probability of finding work. In some ways, the 1980s appear to be a repeat of the hopeless days of the 1930s but fortunately with better social security support. This book looks at some aspects of the labour market for young people: the relationship between wages of young people and their (un)employment; the probability of finding work being dependent on individual (personal) characteristics; and some government policies to attack the problem of growing youth unemployment. A common message of this book is that to tackle the problem of youth unemployment we need to reflate the economy. Other policies (e.g., training schemes) may have a small impact and could be used in conjunction with reflation.

The remainder of this chapter is structured as follows: section 1.2 gives a brief description of trends in unemployment in the OECD over the past few years, section 1.3 looks at the causes and consequences of youth unemployment, section 1.4 gives a preview of the papers in this volume, and section 1.5 concludes the chapter.

1.2 DESCRIPTION OF THE YOUTH LABOUR MARKET

Following a common convention, we define young people or 'youths' to be those people between 15 and 25 years of age. The 15 – 19 age group are referred to as teenagers and the 20 – 24 age group as 'young adults'. Before we proceed to a description of the trends it would be useful to provide a schematic presentation of the youth labour market. Figure 1.1 describes the different states the young can be in at different ages.[1] Assuming a school leaving age of 16 years (i.e.,

1

2

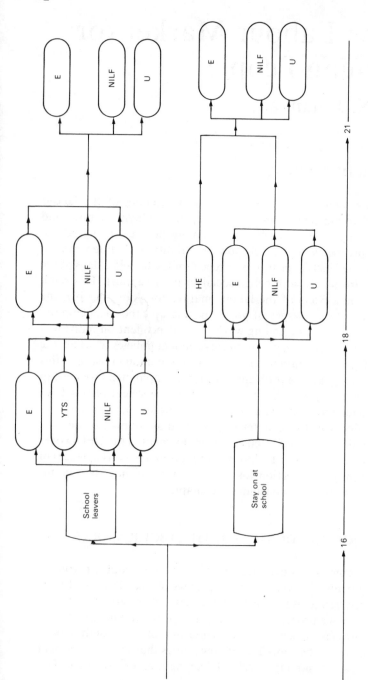

Key: E   Employment
YTS Youth Training Scheme
NILF Not in labour force
U   Unemployment
HE   Higher education

Figure 1.1   Schematic presentation of the youth labour market: alternatives at 16, 18 and 21

compulsory education up to 16), the pupils may decide to leave school or stay on at school. The school leavers may find employment (E), join a government training scheme (e.g., the Youth Training Scheme – YTS in Britain), not join the labour force (not-in-the-labour force – NILF), or become unemployed (U). Between 16 and 18 there may be some transitions between these states. After 18 (at least in Britain) the YTS option is no longer available so they can be in any of the remaining three states. Of those who stay on at school, at 18 (assuming they do not drop out earlier) they may go into higher education or join one of the other three states. Those who join higher education would at 21 have to choose (or attempt to choose) between the the three states – Employment (E), Not-in-the-labour force (NILF), or unemployment, (U). The rest may again remain in the same state or move to another state. In general, those who stay on at school *and* enter higher education are more likely to find employment, and their employment is likely to be more secure and long term. Those who leave school at 16 may find it more difficult to find work, and when they do they are more likely to enter menial, poorly paid, and short-term employment. Although the categories (states) of employment and unemployment are fairly clearly defined, the not-in-the-labour force category has 'fuzzy' boundaries with the unemployed state. Young people who cannot find work may opt out of the labour market for some time (discouraged workers) and then re-enter at a later stage. It may, therefore, be more appropriate to merge the unemployed and not-in-the-labour force categories and call it 'jobless' or 'non-employed'. There is evidence from the UK which supports this view – see Roberts, Duggan and Noble (1981).

Let us now turn to some of the evidence from OECD countries. Over the past few years youth unemployment has been rising in almost all the OECD countries. Table 1.1 illustrates the problem of growing unemployment. In particular (if we exclude USA and Japan) the problem is serious and growing, with about 1 in 5 youths unemployed. The pattern of unemployment is reflected in the pattern of employment. After several years of decline in youth employment there has been a slight increase, but this was mainly in the United States and Japan.

One of the worrying features of the youth labour markets has been the growth of long-term unemployment. Young people who have been unemployed for some length of time are likely to be discriminated against by employers. In addition, the long-term unemployed lose hope and hence give up actively searching for work. Finally,

Table 1.1 Youth unemployment in selected OECD countries (% of total youth labour force)

	Actual					
	1980	81	82	83	84	85
Youth unemployment rates						
United States	13.3	14.3	17.0	16.4	13.3	13.0
Japan	3.4	4.0	4.3	4.5	4.9	4.8
Germany	3.9	6.5	9.5	10.7	9.9	9.5
France	15.0	17.0	19.0	19.7	24.4	25.6
United Kingdom	13.9	18.1	23.1	23.2	21.8	21.7
Canada	13.2	13.3	18.7	19.9	17.9	16.5
Total of above Countries	12.2	13.7	16.4	16.6	15.4	15.3
Four major European countries	13.6	16.5	19.7	20.9	21.6	21.7
Youth unemployment levels (million)						
Seven major countries	6.8	7.7	9.2	9.2	8.5	8.4
Four major European countries	2.7	3.3	4.0	4.2	4.3	4.4

Note: See *Employment Outlook* and *Economic Outlook* for detailed definitions.
Source: OECD, *Employment Outlook 38*, 1985; *Economic Outlook 39*, May 1985.

unemployed young people are mainly unskilled and cannot go 'down the skill ladder' when looking for work. As a result there is likely to be 'state dependence': the probability of finding work is negatively related to the duration of unemployment. Of course, the longer the person is unemployed the more (s)he loses any skills or training previously acquired. One indication of the problem of youth unemployment is to look at the proportion of the youth unemployed who have durations greater than a year. Another is to look at the proportion of the young in the total long-term unemployment stock (durations greater than a year). Tables 1.2 and 1.3 illustrate the problem.[2]

Table 1.2   Youth long term unemployment (% of total youth unemployment)

	1979	81	82
France	2.1	22.6	31.1
Germany	6.8	6.2	10.3
Great Britain	9.3	12.9	21.2
United States	2.4	4.8	5.4

Source: OECD, *Employment Outlook,* 1983, Table 27.

Table 1.3   Youth share of total long-term unemployment (%)

	1979	81	82
France	28.1	27.8	30.8
Germany	9.0	11.5	14.8
Great Britain	16.8	24.4	25.8
United States	27.8	31.9	28.5

Source: OECD, *Employment Outlook,* 1983, Table 26.

Although more recent statistics are not published by the OECD, they state in the *Employment Outlook* (1985) that '[for eleven European countries] on average the share of youth in long-term unemployment has risen from 31.6 per cent in 1979 to 37.5 per cent in 1984. Virtually all of this increase was accounted for by young males' (pp. 21–3).

Another indication of the problem of growing long-term youth unemployment is to look at the mean duration of unemployment.[3] Table 1.4 illustrates the growth of the mean duration over the past few years in a sample of the OECD countries. In general, youths have lower durations than adults.

One problem with looking at unemployment duration data is that some people face recurrent unemployment, so that in a year the total number of weeks (months) of unemployment experience is much longer. There is evidence – see OECD (1985) – to suggest that the young are over-represented among those who have multiple spells of unemployment. It has been argued that these multiple spells represent 'job-shopping' by the young after leaving school and on entering the labour market. However, evidence in the study shows that the multiple spells are concentrated on only a few youths (rather than

Table 1.4   Mean average duration of unemployment in progress (months)

		Youths		Adults	
		Males	*Females*	*Males*	*Females*
France	1980	7.0	10.0	12.6	14.2
	1984	10.6	13.9	14.4	17.5
Germany	1980	3.5	4.2	8.6	8.2
	1984	6.7	6.6	12.6	11.9
United Kingdom	1980	4.0	3.7	12.2	9.1
	1984	11.5	9.2	19.4	13.4
United States	1980	2.4	2.0	3.6	2.7
	1984	3.4	2.6	5.8	3.9

Source: OECD, *Employment Outlook*, 1985.

being the norm). In addition, not only do some teenagers have multiple spells but so do a similar proportion of young adults. Evidence, therefore, points to some youths facing a 'hostile' labour market which leads to perpetual problems of unemployment. For some youths, a spell of unemployment is terminated not by finding work but simply by withdrawal from the labour market. The conclusion from this evidence is that youth unemployment is more serious than it appears, and policies should be introduced to alleviate the problem.

1.3   CAUSES AND CONSEQUENCES OF YOUTH UNEMPLOYMENT

The growing problem in the youth labour market is partly a reflection of the deep and long recession that most of the OECD countries have experienced over the past few years. In addition, because of various peculiarities of this market, young people have suffered disproportionately. The growth in unemployment has been explained in terms of a lack of aggregate demand,[4] an increased supply of young people (the 'demographic bulge'), a changing structure of the economy from industry to services, increased participation of (married) women taking on part-time work in the service sector, an increase in the relative costs of hiring young people (perhaps due to minimum wage legislation), and allegedly generous social security benefits. Although these provide macroeconomic causes of unemployment, on an individual level it has been observed that unemployment is highly concentrated on a segment of the youths: those who come from poor or deprived backgrounds and those from ethnic minorities. This also tends to hit the same group of people on several occasions (so-called recurrent unemployment) hence increasing the concentration of unemployment.

The consequences of unemployment on the unemployed youths are primarily a fall in current living standards and a fall in the future earnings profile. In addition there is some evidence of 'state dependence': unemployment in the current period depending on past unemployment. More importantly, unemployment leads to loss of self-respect. There is some evidence that unemployed youths are more likely to suffer from mental and physical illness (see Junankar, 1986, for a review of the literature). Youth unemployment has also been said to be responsible for an increase in crime and civil disorder (see Junankar, 1984). Youth unemployment (like unemployment overall) also leads to loss of real output. However, it is the young and the families of the young who suffer most in terms of an economic loss and social deprivation.

1.4 A PREVIEW OF THIS BOOK

The chapters in this volume cover a wide range of topics on the youth labour market. Part I focuses on the controversial issue of relative wages and (un)employment, Part II deals with microeconomic aspects of unemployment of youths, and Part III evaluates some policies that have been introduced in Britain.

Chapter 2 by David Marsden sets the scene for Part I on Relative Wages and Employment by providing comparative evidence on relative pay in some OECD countries. After a brief look at possible links between youth pay and youth employment, Marsden provides a detailed look at the differentials between youth and adult pay. In particular, he discusses the problem with data on relative pay and the differences that arise in making comparisons when apprentices are included or excluded. Various explanations for changes in relative pay are discussed, including market pressures, government policy, school leaving age, etc. The main conclusions of his paper are that: (i) there appears to be a weak link between relative pay and relative unemployment; (ii) the importance of vocational training (apprenticeships) in explaining relative pay in different countries; (iii) the *simultaneous* increase in relative pay in the 1960s and 1970s in the countries considered suggest some society-wide causes, rather than some particular factors in different countries.

Chapters 3, 4, 5 and 6 provide a stimulating debate on the (un)importance of relative wages in explaining the behaviour of the youth labour market. After the broad sweep of Marsden's contribution, Bill Wells in Chapter 3 (summarising Wells, 1983) looks in detail at the post-war British youth labour market using annual time-series data. The chapter begins with a close look at the movement of the earnings of young people relative to adults and argues that these can be explained (mainly) by institutional or non-economic factors. In particular, relative earnings do not adjust rapidly to equate the supply and demand for youths. He then makes out a case for a disequilibrium in the labour market for youths (males and females) and estimates models which suggest that earnings of young people relative to adults have a significant and large effect on the (un)employment level. He also finds that youth employment is disproportionately sensitive to the general level of demand.

The following chapter by Junankar and Neale (Chapter 4) provides a detailed look at the youth labour market in Britain using econometric models. The chapter begins with a critical review of the applied econometric literature on youth (un)employment and pays particular attention to the work by Wells (1983) which purports to explain the growth of youth unemployment in terms of increased relative wages of youths and a few other variables. They then discuss the importance of estimating disequilibrium ('switching regimes') youth labour market models by appropriate econometric methods. They find that the youth labour market was in excess demand for the earlier part of the period and excess supply for the latter part. They explain the growth of youth unemployment in terms of inadequate aggregate demand, structural change in the economy, and only marginally by relative wages. Overall, they recommend caution in interpreting the results because of the paucity and inadequacy of the time-series data.

Chapters 5 and 6 give a flavour of the controversy in this area. Wells in Chapter 5 replies to Junankar and Neale's criticisms and counter-attacks their disequilibrium model. Junankar and Neale in their Rejoinder in Chapter 6 highlight the points of agreement and disagreement. The readers are left to evaluate the debate. However, the combatants agree that the data on this subject are of poor quality, and that a disequilibrium model best represents the youth labour market.

Chapter 7 by Paul Ryan provides a fascinating analysis of why trade unions may have put pressure on employers to raise the relative wages of youths. The main plank of this hypothesis is that adult union workers protect adult pay being competed down by increased youth employment by insisting on increased relative pay for youths. Ryan then discusses the bargaining objectives of unions in the context of youth pay and youth employment. On the one hand adults are worried about competition by youths, but on the other youths are an interest group within unions as well as having family links with adult union members. In some preliminary work, Ryan tests the hypothesis linking unions to pay using British industry level data for a short time series. He finds that, in general, high pay for youths goes with high pay for adults, thus throwing some doubt on the 'competition' hypothesis. Overall, Ryan discusses an important issue and provides several interesting comments on unions' bargaining policies with reference to young workers. As he says, there is much more work that needs to be done to investigate this issue.

Part II of the book on Characteristics of the Youth Labour market begins with Chapter 8 by Brian Main on Earnings, Expected Earnings and Unemployment amongst School Leavers. This is an important econometric investigation of a data set of Scottish school leavers. The chapter investigates two issues: first, the earnings expectations of non-employed school leavers as compared to the actual earnings of employed school leavers, controlling for various personal and environmental characteristics. Using appropriate econometric methods to allow for a sample selection bias, it is found that the difference between the expected and market earnings may be due to experimental error because of a confusion between gross and net earnings. Second, an attempt is made to evaluate the effectiveness of the Youth Opportunities Programme (YOP) on the employment prospects of school-leavers. The results suggest only a modest beneficial impact of YOP. This work provides a rigorous analysis of a unique data set, and presents interesting results.

Chapter 9 by Lisa Lynch analyses the London youth labour market using a longitudinal data set. She estimates equations for the probability of being unemployed, participating in a government training scheme or returning to school. She also estimates earnings equations for those in employment. Her results show that personal characteristics (especially ethnicity and educational qualifications), environmental conditions (unemployment of other household members), and work experience variables are very important in explaining the probability of being unemployed, as well as the earnings of the employed. One of her most important findings is that unemployment may 'scar' young workers in their future employment and earnings prospects. This is one of the few econometric studies for Britain which studies the effect of race–ethnicity on employment prospects and hence deserves special attention.

Part III of the book focuses on policies introduced by the government to alleviate the problem of growing youth unemployment. Chapter 10 by Patricia Dutton takes a close look at (and evaluates) the British Youth Training Scheme (YTS). She provides detailed information about the setting up of YTS, its proclaimed objectives, the actual operation of the scheme and what happens to YTS leavers. In her study she emphasises the importance of training, especially as the recession led to a collapse of the apprenticeship schemes. Since YTS is still relatively young it is difficult to assess whether it has succeeded or not, but she concludes that job prospects for YTS leavers are primarily determined by the level of aggregate demand in the economy rather than by the merits or demerits of YTS. Overall, the paper provides an interesting perspective for looking at government training schemes.

Chapter 11 by David Raffe looks at the operation of YTS in Scotland using a sociology of education perspective. This analysis is based on Scottish school leavers' surveys. The chapter discusses the ambivalent nature of YTS: is it meant to alleviate unemployment or is it meant to provide training for all young people? YTS seemed to attract the less qualified labour market entrants who were either postponing job search or who hoped to increase the probability of employment. Interestingly, a large proportion (two-thirds) of the respondents of the school leavers' survey thought that YTS was 'just to keep unemployment figures down' and more than three-quarters agreed that it was 'a source of cheap labour'. The main conclusion of this chapter is that YTS operated largely as an unemployment-based scheme. This work provides food for thought, especially for policy-makers and cautions us not to expect too much of such government training schemes.

The final chapter in this volume by Amin Rajan (Chapter 12) provides a preliminary assessment of the young workers' scheme (YWS) introduced in Britain in January 1982. This is a scheme introduced by the government to 'interfere' with the labour market to reduce youth wages and to 'price the young workers into jobs'. On the basis of a survey of firms Rajan assesses the impact of YWS on adult – youth earnings differentials and its impact on employment. On the basis of this evidence Rajan concludes that the impact on earnings differentials was modest while the impact on employment was significant. However, the introduction of YTS in 1983 has led employers to prefer YTS to YWS. This is an interesting way of studying the impact of YWS (via questionnaires to firms), and complements our understanding of labour market analyses via econometric studies of time-series data.

1.5 CONCLUSIONS

This volume provides a multifaceted analysis of the youth labour market. The chapters in this book are based on original research which provide a unique source of empirical work on one of the most serious problems of present-day Western society – namely, growing youth unemployment. Although there are several minor differences of emphasis, the major conclusion is that growing youth unemployment is due to a lack of aggregate demand in the economy. Several policies to combat youth unemployment are discussed in the book, but a common theme is that they would work only in the context of a stimulation of the macroeconomy. On the basis of the microeconomic analysis, the conclusions are that youth unemployment is concentrated amongst a small group, those with poor educational qualifications, from poor backgrounds, and from ethnic minorities (black youths). An interesting finding was that current youth unemployment increases the probability of future unemployment and decreases future earnings. Thus youth unemployment is not only a problem today but has pervasive (negative) effects into the future. The social costs of this unemployment are likely to be with us for a long time.

Notes

1.   This presentation is based on the British educational system. There are obviously slight differences from country to country, but the broad outline would still apply. For purposes of simplicity, transitions between states have been ignored. (The British education system may

be more rigid than in other countries: if you leave school at 16 it is difficult to enter higher education at a later stage in your life.)

2   Unfortunately OECD do not publish these data annually. For Britain in April 1986, 27.7 per cent of unemployed youths had been unemployed for more than a year. At the same time, the share of youths in long-term unemployment was 24.3 per cent (MSC *Labour Market Quarterly Report,* Great Britain, June 1986).

3.   For a discussion of unemployment duration for youths in Britain, see Junankar (1986a). Note that due to ageing process the duration of unemployment of youths gets truncated as they become 25 years old. This may be one reason why youths have a shorter duration of unemployment.

4.   During a recession the first thing firms do is to reduce recruitment (hiring): the young being a new inflow to the labour market are immediately affected. The next step is to start firing workers: the young with least skills and training are the first to be fired. Employment protection legislation and last-in–first-out practices reinforce the problems for the young.

Part I

Relative Wages and Employment: Time-Series Studies

2 Youth Pay in Some OECD Countries since 1966

David Marsden[1]

2.1 INTRODUCTION

The Economic Significance of the Relative Pay of Young Workers

In the current recession, considerable attention has been fixed upon the earnings of young workers, and the possible relation between their relative pay and the current high levels of youth unemployment. Although the prime emphasis of this chapter is to examine the evidence relating to earnings, it is useful to set them in their wider context.

The argument that youth employment should be particularly sensitive to changes in young people's relative earnings stems from an application of standard microeconomic theory to the youth labour market. Like the demand for adult labour, that for young people's labour is also a derived demand, but there are several reasons for believing that the demand for youth labour may be more price elastic than that for adult labour as a whole.

First, many young workers are relatively unskilled and engaged in routine tasks and so can be the more easily replaced by other categories of adult worker or machinery. This may be particularly important in times of recession when employers may be reluctant to lay off some of their adult workforce. Moreover, the latter – fearing redundancy – may be more willing to accept redeployment to less skilled jobs otherwise done by less experienced and young workers.

Second, many young workers are concentrated in industries which might be thought to have a higher than average elasticity of demand for their product – such as textiles, wood, furniture etc. – and certain competitive services on account of the range of substitutes (e.g., competition from imports in the case of textiles and clothing, or competing types of retail outlet). On average, young workers may thus face a more elastic product demand than adults.

Third, young workers represent a sizeable proportion of the industrial labour force – those under 21, about one-tenth of the manual male labour force, and between one-tenth and one-third of the female manual labour force (see Table 2.3). In some industries which are major employers of young workers, this proportion is considerably higher; increases in young workers' costs can thus add a sizeable (if less than proportionate) contribution to total labour costs. This would be particularly important in industries in which the price elasticity of demand for the product is greater than the elasticity of substitution between young workers and adults, and (as has been suggested above) some industries employing large numbers of young workers may well face a relatively elastic product demand.

On three of the four Hicks–Marshall conditions determining the elasticity of derived demand, one might thus expect young workers' employment to be more sensitive to an increase in relative pay than that of many other workers. These surely are important reasons for concern about possible changes in the level of youth pay.

An additional factor, operating from the supply side of the labour market, is that an increase in youth relative pay could increase the cost in foregone earnings of continuing education, and hence lead a greater number of young people to decide to leave school and enter the labour market.

While this analysis may be appropriate to certain sections of the youth labour market, it has two principal limitations. First, it treats the source of movements in youth pay as exogenous – as, for example, might be the case if a youth minimum wage were introduced quite independently of labour market conditions. But it would be wholly inappropriate to the analysis of, for example, a demand-led increase in youth pay, or an increase resulting from the achievement of higher educational standards as compared with previous generations of workers.

Second, it takes no account of the importance of training and access to internal labour markets, which are very important processes in the youth labour market. For many young workers – as for many firms – the youth labour market is one in which a great deal of investment takes place both in the form of general training (such as apprenticeships and traineeships), and in seeking access to (and selecting recruits for) internal labour markets. While the cost of young workers relative to adults is still likely to be important, it has to be set in the context of the distribution of costs and returns from such investment over a much longer time period. This, of course, is not to deny that a great many young workers are in dead-end jobs conferring neither training nor marketable experience.

Nevertheless, taking the youth labour market as a whole – and thus not differentiating between the different types of labour market on which young people may be active – there has been some econometric work on the relation between changes in young workers' relative pay and their employment and unemployment, although the results are not wholly unanimous. Work on Britain by Layard (1982), Lynch and Richardson (1982), Junankar and Neale (Chapter 4 in this volume), and on France by Fourcans (1980) indicate a positive link between young workers' pay and their unemployment, but contrasting results have been obtained for Britain by Makeham (1980), and for France by Martin (1983) (see also Chapter 4 by Junankar and Neale in this volume). The British studies related directly to young workers' earnings, while the two French ones examined the impact of the minimum wage upon youth unemployment. A central problem under-lying the studies on both countries stems from the close relation between the trends in youth unemployment, youth pay or the mini-mum wage, and adult unemployment.

Of the British studies, Makeham found the coefficient on adult male unemployment completely dwarfed that on young men's relative pay which in all his reported results was insignificant. Both Layard, and Lynch and Richardson used vacancies as their measure of the general state of labour demand, the advantage being that vacancies display less of a trend than unemployment, although they cover only about one-third of all vacancies. Lynch and Richardson ran their analyses separately on both unemployment and vacancies, and achieved simi-lar results to those of Makeham on unemployment. A second element in Layard's analysis was to estimate demand elasticities for young workers and elasticities of substitution between young and adult workers in manufacturing, the dependent variable being the age composition of employment. He obtained a demand elasticity for young men's labour of -1.25, and for young women's labour of -0.31. He also found strong elasticities of substitution between young manual men and both young and adult manual women. In contrast, Hutchinson *et al.* (1984), while confirming that employers treated young men and women as substitutes, found that they treated young and adult men as complements. Wells has revised Makeham's earlier work, and obtained results more consistent with those of

Layard, and of Lynch and Richardson. However, as he points out, the results are to some extent dependent upon the particular time period chosen.

Fourcan's evidence on the effect of raising the minimum wage relative to average earnings upon young people's unemployment in France is consistent with that of Layard, and Lynch and Richardson for Britain, but (as Martin shows) once the trend factor is taken into account, any effect of the raising of the minimum wage upon youth unemployment disappears. However, Martin also points out that the level of the minimum wage compared to average earnings is low. His results may thus not be inconsistent with the majority of findings for Britain.

During the 1970s, young people's unemployment rates increased in all six countries, and they mostly rose faster than adult rates except in West Germany and the United States (Table 2.1). In the EEC countries, the steepest rise in youth shares of unemployment was in the early 1970s (mostly before 1973), and except in France and the Netherlands, young people's share of unemployment levelled off after about 1975. In Belgium, West Germany and the United Kingdom, this may have been exacerbated by an increase during the 1970s in young people's share of the total population.

The major exception was the United States, in which young people's unemployment share decreased during the 1970s, and where it fluctuated inversely to the overall unemployment rate. As will be seen in the section on trends in youth pay in the United States (p. 40), this was the only country which displayed a fairly long-term decline in young people's relative earnings. An apparent inverse relationship between fluctuations in the youth unemployment shares (for both those under 21 and those under 18) and the overall unemployment rate may indicate different lay-off and recruitment policies among American employers as compared with their European counterparts.

Some Questions on Comparative Levels and Trends of Youth Pay Raised by Research on Youth Unemployment

The focus of this chapter is on comparisons of levels of – and trends in – young people's relative earnings in Western European countries (and, where possible, with the United States). The policy interest in young people's relative pay has been largely engendered by concern that increases could adversely affect young people's employment opportunities. A number of questions will be examined in greater detail in this chapter:

1. What is the differential between young and adult workers in different countries, and do those countries with a smaller differential have high rates of youth unemployment?
2. What have been the trends in the differential between young workers and adults in these countries?
3. Do the time series for individual countries cast any light on trends in youth unemployment?
4. How representative are the aggregate series on youth pay used in the empirical studies already mentioned of the experience of individual industries?
5. How important are composition effects on average earnings for young workers arising from such changes as the raising of the school leaving age?

The plan of this chapter will broadly follow the outline of these questions, beginning with a comparison of the differential between young and adult workers in the six West European countries, followed by a comparison of changes between 1966 and 1978. These two analyses will be based upon Eurostat's structure of earnings surveys for 1966, 1972, and 1978, matching results for Britain from the NES and the EMO (the statistical acronyms and sources used in this analysis are listed in the Appendix on p. 48). The next section looks at some of the principal causes of changes between 1966 and 1978, including changes in the school leaving age, changing expectations, government and union wage policies, and labour market pressures. This is followed by a brief discussion of the US experience.

Analysis of Young Workers' Relative Pay

Ideally, a study of young workers' pay would disaggregate earnings for individual years, as the conditions affecting each age group are different, and it would treat young people on different labour market career paths differently because in many respects these are only partial substitutes for each other. Unfortunately, the data available impose a much cruder analysis based mostly on the conventional distinction between those on adult rates of pay and those not. In the past this has usually meant that statistical convention divides off those under 21 from those aged 21 and over (and sometimes for women, those under

Table 2.1   Unemployment Rates (by Sex and Age 1973–81)[a]

	Males			Females			age 14-19 as % of unemployed	
	14–19	*20–24*	*All ages*	*14–19*	*20–24*	*All ages*	*Males*	*Females*
Belgium								
1973	2.9	2.0	1.2	5.5	3.4	2.6	9.3	16.5
75	7.3	5.5	2.2	13.0	8.6	5.5	12.6	16.1
77	8.4	6.4	3.1	16.7	16.1	10.9	9.2	8.5
79	10.8	7.0	3.9	19.9	18.2	12.9	9.0	7.5
81	23.3	13.0	7.5	32.2	24.8	13.1	12.9	10.7
France								
1973	4.5	3.0	1.5	7.9	4.0	2.6	13.7	18.6
75	8.8	5.9	2.6	16.7	6.4	4.3	14.2	21.1
77	13.5	6.9	3.3	24.5	11.6	6.1	15.5	18.9
79	14.8	8.8	4.1	32.7	14.1	7.4	12.7	18.8
81	20.7	9.4	4.9	38.6	16.9	9.5	17.8	22.5
West Germany								
1973	1.2	0.6	0.4	1.4	0.7	0.8	20.0	19.4
75	6.3	5.1	2.8	6.7	3.7	3.2	14.4	20.0
77	5.2	4.4	2.4	7.1	5.1	3.8	13.0	16.5
79	4.0	2.5	1.8	6.3	3.7	3.5	13.3	14.9
81	4.6	3.7	2.3	6.6	4.5	3.9	13.8	17.1
Italy								
1973	18.8	12.2	3.3	18.7	13.2	6.1	26.5	31.8
75	15.2	10.7	2.7	17.0	12.2	4.9	23.7	29.0
77	18.8	14.6	3.3	25.0	17.8	7.0	25.2	29.4

79	20.3	16.8	3.8	32.6	20.7	8.6	23.0	28.5
81	21.2	16.1	3.9	32.9	21.8	9.3	28.2	33.5
Netherlands								
1973	3.3	3.5	1.9	3.5	1.8	1.7	7.9	33.4
75	8.1	7.2	3.4	5.9	2.7	2.9	9.0	27.4
77	7.1	6.1	3.3	8.7	3.6	3.3	6.5	25.2
79	7.2	5.4	3.0	13.3	5.2	4.1	6.5	25.8
81	17.2	10.3	5.2	15.5	6.7	5.5	12.4	27.5
United Kingdom								
1973	4.5	3.2	2.4	2.9	2.4	1.7	10.8	14.4
75	8.8	7.1	4.2	9.3	6.9	5.2	10.9	12.7
77	10.4	8.0	4.8	10.7	7.0	4.4	12.1	18.7
79	9.1	5.9	3.8	8.4	5.4	3.1	14.4	22.3
81	21.2	14.7	9.0	18.2	9.5	6.2	16.7	27.6
United States[b]								
1973	12.8	6.4	4.0	15.2	8.4	6.0	28.9	28.1
75	18.7	12.8	7.6	19.6	12.6	9.3	21.8	23.1
77[c]	17.3	10.7	6.2	18.3	11.2	8.2	24.0	23.9
79[c]	15.8	8.6	5.1	16.4	9.6	6.8	26.3	23.9
81[c]	20.1	13.2	7.4	19.0	11.2	7.9		24.9

Notes:

[a] Ratio of unemployed persons to the labour force, restricted concept (excluding non-active persons seeking paid employment, included in US data).

[b] Ages 16–19.

[c] Annual averages.

Sources: Eurostat Labour Force Sample Survey, and US Bureau of Labor Statistics, Employment and Earnings.

18 from those aged 18 and over). The greater part of the analysis will thus focus on young workers under 21, using finer age breakdowns wherever possible. Inevitably, using such a large age group will mean that problems of assessing the importance of composition effects in changes in average earnings for the whole group will arise frequently. These will be discussed as they occur.

A good deal of the comparisons will be based upon Eurostat's structure of earnings surveys, which record the gross earnings of employees in establishments with 10 or more employees. In 1966 coverage was confined to manual workers in industry. In 1972 it was enlarged to include non-manual workers in industry, and in 1978 (after a special survey in 1974) it was further enlarged to include distribution, banking and insurance. Details are recorded on gross hourly earnings (manual workers) and monthly earnings (manual and non-manual workers) before deductions for income tax and employees' social insurance contributions. The reporting unit is the establishment, and returns are made for selected individual workers. The survey month is October. The survey covers workers with a contract of employment, and hence excludes apprentices, unless the national statistical offices make their own provision for including additional questions.

The term young people's 'relative pay' is used to denote their pay relative to that of adults of the same sex, unless otherwise stated.

2.2 COMPARISON OF YOUTH RELATIVE PAY IN EEC COUNTRIES IN 1978

Comparisons of relative earnings of young workers in different countries have recently received a certain amount of attention (for example in Jones, 1982 and OECD, 1980), and an attempt will be made in this section to compare the relative earnings of workers aged below 21 in France, West Germany, the Netherlands and the UK (data were not available on a suitable basis for Belgium). Such comparisons should be treated with a great deal of caution for both economic and for statistical reasons.

The Treatment of Apprentices

Becker (1975) and Mincer (1974) have stressed the importance of the distribution of the costs and returns of different types of training over a worker's career for the understanding of earnings differentials between different age groups. A central distinction is that between the distribution of costs and returns for 'general' and for 'specific' training. General training gives rise to skills which are useful to a large number of employers – a good example being craft apprenticeships – while specific training produces skills which are often useful only in the firm in which such skills are developed. With general training, there is always the danger that firms which have not trained their own workers will seek to 'poach' skilled labour from those which have. This has always been a problem in Britain, especially before the Industrial Training Act 1965. Because firms cannot prevent skilled workers they have trained from leaving, there is a strong incentive to make trainees bear some (or all) of the cost of general training. This can be done by paying a trainee rate which is lower than the trainee's marginal product, and thus likely to be considerably below the rate paid to other workers of the same age. In actual practice, poaching can be reduced if – as in Britain – apprenticeship training is partly financed by means of levies on all employers to fund grants to those undertaking training, or – as in West Germany – where there is a strong belief among the great majority of employers in their wider responsibility to provide training.

For specific skills, the danger of losing skilled workers through 'poaching' by other employers is much smaller, and because employers can recoup their investment in training by paying specifically skilled workers less than their marginal product after the training period, there is less pressure to push training costs onto trainees. One might thus expect the earnings differential between trainees and skilled workers to be markedly greater for general than for specific skills.

The relevance of this to international comparisons lies in differences in the organisation of vocational training in different countries. In the UK – and especially in West Germany – apprenticeships play the major part in vocational training for young manual workers (and in West Germany also for clerical workers). These give rise to general skills for which there is a wide market. In contrast, in France, greater reliance has been placed upon specific training organised by the enterprise, and this (together with the system of job classifications based on a hierarchical rather than a craft principle and which makes greater use of upgrading) means that the external labour market for skilled workers in France is more restricted than in either Britain or

West Germany. One might thus expect to find a smaller differential between trainees and skilled workers (and thus between young workers and adults) in France than in either Britain or West Germany.

The apprenticeship system covers a larger proportion of young workers in West Germany, and is thought to provide a better technical training (Prais, 1981, Jones and Hollenstein, 1983). Moreover, there is some indication that West German skilled workers receive a slightly bigger differential over semi-skilled workers than do their British counterparts – 13.4 per cent greater than semi-skilled in Germany in 1972, compared with 10.0 per cent in Britain (Saunders and Marsden, 1982, Table 4.2), and in 1978 11.3 per cent and 9.6 per cent respectively.[2] Moreover, during much of the 1970s, skill differentials were considerably reduced in much of British industry, recovering their levels of the early 1970s only in 1979. One might thus expect West German trainees to be prepared to invest more (and thus to accept a comparatively lower trainee rate) than in Britain.

Comparisons in 1978

Table 2.2 compares the relative earnings of workers aged under 21 in industry (excluding construction) in France, the Netherlands, West Germany and Great Britain. A striking feature is the similarity in young workers' earnings relativities in Britain, France and Germany for non-manual workers, for female manual workers, and once adjustments are made for apprentices, for male manual workers. The notable exception was the Netherlands in which youth pay was between 5 and 15 percentage points below that of the other countries. This appears to be due to a higher proportion of young workers under 18, but mostly due to lower relative pay for both those aged under 18 and those aged 18–20. Tables 2.3 and 2.4 (see pp. 30 and 33) show that youth relative pay in Belgium was similar to that in France and Germany in 1978, but that that in Italy was somewhat higher.

Among *non-manual* workers, the differences between France and West Germany lie within the range of statistical and rounding errors. If account is taken of the much smaller sample on which the British data are based, the same can be said of British non-manual men. The exception is British non-manual women, but this appears to be confined to industry, which represents only about one-quarter of female non-manual employment. If instead one takes industry and the

Table 2.2 Relative monthly earnings of young workers in industry in France, West Germany, the Netherlands and the UK in 1978 (earnings of workers under 21 as a % of earnings of all ages, full-time, production industries excluding construction)

	France (October 1978)	West Germany (October 1978)	Nether-lands (October 79)[a]	United Kingdom[b] (April 79)	
				Apprentices	
				Included	Excluded
Manual workers					
Men	75.8	76.9	59.1	63.7[c]	(i) 74.1[e]
					(ii) 68.0[e]
Women	87.3	83.3	67.6	85.8[d]	
Non-manual workers					
Men	47.5	47.9	41.9	46.1[d]	
Women	67.8	67.6	59.1	76.3[d]	
All workers					
Men	61.2	68.4 (39.6)[c]	50.1	59.0[c]	(i) 65.4[e]
					(ii) 61.8[e]
Women	77.9	76.6 (63.0)[c]	62.6	81.4[d]	

Notes:

[a] Including apprentices and trainees.

[b] New Earnings Survey 1979 (Great Britain only).

[c] Including apprentices, only included in German data for comparison with the United Kingdom.

[d] Numbers of female and non-manual apprentices in industry are very small.

[e] Upper and lower estimates of effect of excluding apprentices.

Sources: SEI 1978: France – INSEE/SSIS; West Germany – *Statistisches Bundesamt GLS;* Netherlands – data from Eurostat SEI sample, provided by CBS; UK Department of Employment NES.

main service sectors together, the youth differential for this group in all three countries lies between 67 per cent and 69 per cent. The reason may be that in Britain there are relatively fewer women in managerial positions in industry than in services sectors (see Saunders and Marsden, 1981, Table 4.4, p. 141) thus depressing the average earnings of adult non-manual women.

In the industrial sector, among *manual men* (the largest of the four groups examined), comparisons between the countries need to take account of differences in the treatment of apprentices. In both Britain and West Germany, apprenticeships constitute the principal method of training skilled labour for industry, while in France they play a much smaller role. The Netherlands is in an intermediate position with school-based vocational training supplemented by short apprenticeships. In 1978, of manual workers in industry, in West Germany 5.1 per cent were apprentices, in the UK 4.2 per cent, and in France 0.4 per cent, Belgium 0.7 per cent, Italy 1.3 per cent, and the Netherlands between 0.8 per cent and 1.0 per cent (Eurostat LCI Tables A1/123, and A1/125, establishments with 10 or more employees). France and Italy have apprenticeships but their main importance lies outside the industrial sector, and in small firms. An attempt has therefore been made to estimate relative pay both including and excluding apprentices.

Excluding apprentices
Relative earnings of young male workers under 21 are roughly similar in France and Germany. However, the groups of workers referred to in either country are not identical. In France, they include both future skilled and future semi-skilled workers, while in Germany, many will be future semi-skilled, future skilled workers having been excluded by the exclusion of apprentices. Nevertheless, some workers attain skilled status before the age of 21. Despite a recent expansion in their number, skill training in France still relies relatively little on apprenticeships, and because skills are in consequence less transferable, there is less reason for employers to seek to share training costs by means of a special trainee rate. There is therefore less reason for the pay of future skilled and future semi-skilled workers to differ greatly, so one can conclude that the figures in Table 2.2 give a fair picture of the pay of young semi-skilled workers in either country relative to adults.

Two estimates are given for the earnings differential in Britain excluding apprentices, the higher (74.1 per cent) being based on the unrealistic assumption that half of manual men under 21 are apprentices, and the lower (68.0 per cent) on the assumption that 30 per cent are apprentices. In the mid-1970s about half of male 16 year old school leavers started apprenticeships, but there is a considerable drop-out rate, so that 30 per cent or below is probably a more realistic estimate.

These adjustments suggest that the pay of male manual workers under 21 compared with all ages is a little lower in Britain than in either France or West Germany once apprentices are excluded, but the size of the difference should not be exaggerated.

Including apprentices

France emerges as the country in which the relative earnings of manual males under 21 are highest, but (as already suggested) this may primarily be a reflection of the organisation of industrial training in that country. Comparison between Britain and Germany is a little more problematic. Using estimates kindly provided by the Statistisches Bundesamt, it has been possible to obtain a figure for the pay of all males and all females under 21 compared with all ages (39.6 per cent and 63.0 per cent respectively). It should be stressed that the remuneration of German apprentices is strictly speaking a training allowance (*Ausbildungsbeihilfe*) and not a wage, although determined mostly through collective agreements. For Britain, the same adjustments applied above to the earnings of manual men were applied to all men combined. Comparing Britain and Germany, it is clear that young men's relative pay is somewhat lower in Germany, this being a reflection both of the greater proportion who are apprentices, and apprentices' lower relative pay. Again, it has to be remembered that apprenticeships are on the whole of somewhat shorter duration in Germany than in Britain, the standard apprenticeship in the engineering industry in Germany being three years as against four years in Britain. While this does not affect the overall statistical comparison just made, the greater duration of apprenticeships in Britain would correspondingly reduce the difference in gross foregone earnings between the two countries.

Despite the difficulty of making direct comparisons between apprentices' remuneration in West Germany and the UK some broad comparisons can be made. Compilations from regional agreements in Germany by the Federal German Ministry of Labour on apprentices' allowances in December 1982 compared with the equivalent results from the Federal German Statistical Office's quarterly earnings survey indicate that manual apprentices in their first year receive about 20 per cent of average male manual earnings, increasing to about 30 per cent in their fourth year. Compared with the UK, these figures are both lower overall, and show a smaller increase during the course of the apprenticeship than the corresponding basic wage rates of apprentices relative to adult rates for Britain. However, if the UK apprentices' rates are compared to adult earnings (as was done for

West Germany), then the difference decreases. In Britain – in engineering the apprentices' rate increases from about 30 per cent of adult
earnings in the first year to about 55 per cent in the fourth year, and in
vehicle building from about 30 per cent to about 60 per cent.
Comparing apprentices' average earnings to those of all workers
combined in the 1975 labour cost survey gives a figure for apprentices
and trainees in manufacturing industry of 55 per cent, or 84 per cent
of the earnings of all those aged under 21.[3]

For manual women levels of youth relative pay are broadly similar in
France, West Germany, and Britain. Comparison with the UK may
be slightly misleading because of the large number of part-time older
women who are not covered in Table 2.2. Again, the Netherlands is
the exception. The reason seems to be that despite the low labour
force participation of married women in that country, a higher
proportion of manual women are classified in skilled and semi-skilled
jobs than in other countries (Saunders and Marsden, 1981).

While such international comparisons should be treated with
caution, the similarity in the levels of youth relative pay in industry in
these countries contrasts with the differences in terms of both of youth
unemployment rates and shares indicated in Table 2.1. One of the
prime causes of youth unemployment apart from pay highlighted in
the econometric studies in Britain was the level of overall labour
demand as indicated by adult unemployment or by vacancies. Rough
and ready allowance for differences between the countries in this
respect can be made by comparing ratios of youth to overall unemployment rates. Comparing the results in Tables 2.1 and 2.2 reveals
little overall correspondence between these ratios and youth relative
pay, which suggests that other factors are also important.[4]

Second, it has often been suggested that (in Britain as compared
with West Germany) the level of young workers' relative pay has been
a cause of their comparatively higher unemployment, and that too
high levels of apprentice remuneration has made this form of training
less attractive to employers. It would appear that the income foregone
by apprentices undergoing training is markedly smaller in Britain
than in West Germany, but this should be set against the possibly
smaller gross return on such investment in Britain, and the slightly
longer duration of apprenticeships in Britain.[5]

2.3 YOUNG MANUAL WORKERS' PAY

Description of the Changes

A longer perspective on young workers' relative pay between 1966 and 1978 can be obtained using results from the earlier Eurostat wage structure surveys for Belgium, France, Germany, Italy and the Netherlands, and from the EMO for Britain, shown in Table 2.3. The most striking point is the overall improvement in the pay of young men relative to adult men in all countries, and the generally more limited changes in the pay of young women relative to adult manual women.

Between 1966 and 1972, young men's relative pay increased in all six countries, and continued to do so between 1972 and 1978 except in France and Germany. Young manual women between 1966 and 1972, in contrast, experienced little change in their relative pay in Belgium, Italy and the Netherlands, a decline in the UK, a small increase in West Germany, and a sizeable increase only in France. In the second period, young women experienced an improvement except in France and Germany. Over the whole period between 1966 and 1978, young manual women's relative pay improved, except in Germany and Britain, where it remained near its 1966 levels (see Table 2.3).

On the whole, there has been a decline in the percentage of young workers under 21 in the industrial labour force since 1966, but there is no straightforward link between countries and periods in which youth relative pay rose and the youth employment share declined. Indeed, the greatest declines in employment share were among young manual women, yet this was the group for which there was the smallest net change in relative pay between 1966 and 1978. A fuller investigation would of course require analysis of demographic trends, as of patterns in lay-offs and early retirements, although the big employment 'shake-out', did not start until after 1979.

The decline in youth employment in industry has had a small effect on *average* pay for those aged under 21 as, on the whole, the youngest members of the group have been the most affected. For four countries, it was possible to calculate average youth pay in 1978 using the proportions aged under 18 and aged 18–20 in 1972. The results, in parentheses under the simple 1978 figures in Table 2.3 show that (except for young women in Belgium and the Netherlands) such compositional changes accounted for only a part of the increase in youth pay, at least up to 1978.

Table 2.3 Relative earnings of manual workers under 21 in industry 1966 – 78 (Hourly earnings, October)

Year	Earnings of workers <21 as % of:				Workers <21 % of all ages	
	Males ≥ 21		Females ≥ 21		Males	Females
Belgium						
1966		67.4		78.4	10.2	29.1
72		70.6		79.2	10.1	27.4
78		77.4		83.3	7.7	17.0
1972 age composition[a]		(74.5)		(80.0)		
France						
1966		71.9		77.9	10.8	30.4
72		77.7		86.4	9.6	20.8
78		75.7		86.1	6.2	13.0
1972 age composition[a]		(75.2)		(85.5)		
West Germany	all ages		all ages			
1966	78.3	77.1	84.0	81.8	6.3	14.0
72	79.1	78.2	85.5[b]	83.9	5.2	12.1
78	81.1[b]	n.a.	85.1[b]	n.a.	4.4	12.2
1972 age composition[a]	76.6[b]	(n.a.)	83.7[b]	(n.a.)		

	Males≥21	Females≥18	<21	<18
Italy				
1966	77.0	84.4	4.9	19.9
72	77.9	84.3	4.2	16.8
1978	84.8	89.9	3.3	9.4
1972 age composition[a]	(85.0)	(89.8)		
Netherlands				
1966	50.9	63.6	12.4	51.6
72	54.0	63.3	9.1	34.8
79	59.7	66.8	9.8	24.6
1972 age composition[a]	(58.1)	(64.0)		
United Kingdom[c]	Males≥21	Females≥18	<21	<18
1966	51.2	66.4	10.1	11.5
72	53.3	63.3	8.2	10.8
78	61.6	65.8	9.0	8.1
1972 age composition[a]	(n.a.)	(n.a.)		

Notes:

[a] Constant age composition based on under 18 and 18–20 age groups in 1972 applied to 1978 results.

[b] Estimates of hourly earnings derived from monthly averages. Hours estimates were made for those aged 18–20. Higher earnings estimate assumes 18–20 group worked same hours as <18, and lower estimate, same hours as ≥18.

[c] Includes apprentices.

Sources: Belgium, France, Italy and the Netherlands – Eurostat.SEI; West Germany – Eurostat SE; 1966 and 1972, and GLSE for 1978; UK – EMO.

Finally, Pearson correlation coefficients calculated on young workers' earnings in 1966 and 1972, and on changes in the percentage differential between young and adult workers, indicate that the overall reduction in the differential shown in Table 2.3 was indeed reflected in the experience of most industries. There was a greater diversity of experience between individual industries between 1972 and 1978.

Young Non-manual Workers' Monthly Earnings 1972–8

Changes in young *non-manual* workers' relative pay between 1972 and 1978 were more uniform than for manual workers, and increased in all countries for both men and women except in West Germany, and among young women in Belgium. More detailed age breakdowns show that for France the improvement affected both those under 18 and those aged between 18 and 20, as do the more detailed analyses for Britain (Wells, Chapter 3 in this volume). Such age breakdowns were not available for the other countries.

More detailed time-series data for France and Britain show that the greater part of the increase in relative pay had occurred in France by about 1974, and in Britain by about 1975–6 (Marsden, 1983).

The percentage of non-manual workers under 21 declined considerably in all countries for both men and women, the one exception being the small increase in employment share of young non-manual men in Britain. This was also found among manual men in that country, a change which occurred in nearly all two-digit industries between 1972 and 1978.

As for manual workers, comparisons across the countries reveal no simple correlation between changes in relative pay and employment share at the aggregate level, although again more systematic investigation of other factors (notably changes in the supply of young workers, in training provisions, and in the overall demand for labour) is needed before any firm conclusion can be drawn.

2.4   FACTORS BEHIND THE CHANGES IN YOUNG WORKERS' RELATIVE PAY

Changes in the School Leaving Age

The school leaving age was raised from 15 to 16 in France from

Table 2.4 Monthly earnings of young non-manual workers in industry (1972 and 1978) (average monthly earnings (full-time) as % of workers aged 21 and over (October))

	Men		Women	
	1972	78	1972	78
Belgium				
<21	46.4	48.0	62.6	61.1
France				
<18	36.2	39.7	54.5	57.2
18–20	43.9	47.3	63.7	67.0
All <21	43.3	46.8	63.1	66.6
Clerical only <21	63.4	66.9	70.5	73.9
(% of clerical ≧ 21)				
West Germany				
<21	49.3	47.8	67.1	65.0
Italy				
<21	48.5	61.3	65.6	78.0
Netherlands				
<21	35.2	42.7	54.4	59.4
United Kingdom[a]				
<21	35.6	44.1	(<18) 52.1	57.0

PERCENTAGE OF WORKERS UNDER 21

	Men		Women	
Belgium				
<21	0.9	0.5	12.8	6.3
France				
All non-manual				
18–20	1.3	0.5	9.8	4.5
<21	1.4	0.6	10.7	4.6
Clerical only <21	5.2	2.4	12.6	5.8
West Germany				
<21	1.2	0.5	13.1	9.7
Italy				
<21	0.9	0.4	13.1	5.5
Netherlands				
<21	2.2	1.1	32.5	26.7
United Kingdom[a]				
<21	4.2	4.6	(<18) 6.6	5.6

Notes:
[a] Great Britain only, April 1973 and 1979, weekly earnings.
Sources: Belgium, France, Italy and the Netherlands – SEI 1972 and 1978; West Germany – SEI 1972 and GLSE; UK – NES.

January 1967, and in Britain from September 1972. As yet it remains at 15 in West Germany, but the majority of 15 year old school leavers follow formally-organised vocational training. In both France and Britain, the change was partly anticipated by parents and pupils as the number of 15 year olds in full-time education had been increasing steadily for some years before. In both Belgium and the Netherlands there was a substantial increase in the percentage of 15 and 16 year olds remaining in full-time education between 1972 and 1975.

The effect of changes in the school leaving age on young workers' relative pay can be analysed into three main components. The first is purely arithmetic – that it removes from the labour market a number of the lowest-paid young workers, thus causing the average for the whole age group under 21 to rise. This may be tempered by a desire on the part of employers to adapt age-related scales to take account of the lesser experience of 16 year olds after the change, but 16 year olds' pay expectations (combined with pressures from collective bargaining or the simple lack of flexibility of administrative rules governing pay systems) is likely to make this difficult. The practical effect may have been spread over several years as parents and pupils anticipated the change.

The second effect is more complex, and relates to the quality of the additional training received in school, and thus its value on the labour market. Whether or not the extra year in school increases workers' productive potential on leaving (and thus the appropriateness of higher pay levels than for former 15 year old leavers) depends upon the quality of education received. In the early years after the raising of the leaving age, it appeared that many young people felt that the extra year had been imposed on them, and lack of motivation compounded the effects of administrative improvisation in many schools. Initially, many employers may thus have felt that the extra year in school was a poor substitute for a year's work experience. However, as the changes have been digested, it is likely that many of these problems have diminished, although there is still considerable debate in most countries as to the appropriateness of school training for jobs outside. Moreover, the decision to raise the leaving age in France in 1967 was taken as early as 1959 (*Ordonnance*, 6 January 1959). However, any resulting composition effect in France and the UK does not explain the whole change, as can be seen in more detailed age breakdowns which show that those aged between 18 and 20 also benefited from an increase in relative pay (Marsden, 1983, Wells, 1983).

The third is the effect upon the supply of young workers on the labour market generally, and upon entry into vocational training schemes within the enterprise. Even in fairly casual labour markets, employers are geared to operating with a certain type of labour, and need time to adjust to changes in its supply. The reduction in the supply of young workers could thus have created a seller's market for a short time. In cases where firms' recruitment decisions are more geared towards the attraction of longer-term employees whom they might train, the outcome would be more complex, but it is conceivable that this could also involve pressure to increase starting rates of pay in order to continue to attract the same quality of job applicant.

On the whole, as the increase in youth relative pay was not confined to those under 18 when suitable data were available, it is fair to conclude that the prolongation of secondary education was only one factor affecting youth average pay. Moreover, its effect was uneven. In Britain, for example, whereas its effect upon young manual men's relative pay was fairly permanent, its effect upon young women's was reversed within two years.

Changing Expectations Among Young People

Although these are likely to be affected by the state of the labour market, they are also likely to have been affected by the widespread belief in the 1960s and 1970s in the value of extending education beyond the limits of previous generations, and by the lowering of the age of majority from 21 to 18 (in Britain, for example, it was lowered in 1969, and in France and West Germany a little later). In particular, the lowering of the age of majority may have influenced the movement (to be described more fully later) in Britain and West Germany to lower the age at which young workers move onto adult rates of pay.

Government Policies on Pay

The countries most affected were Britain, France, and the Netherlands. Two major incomes policies in Britain, the second and third stages of Mr Heath's pay policy between April 1973 and early 1974, and the period of the Labour government's Social Contract between August 1975 and August 1977 made express provision for bigger pay increases for the lower paid, and one probably unintended consequence may have been to help younger workers at the expense of older ones. Although rates of increase in wages mostly exceeded the pay norms, there was nevertheless a reduction in pay inequalities, especially during the early period of the Social Contract.

The other major element of pay policy in Britain during the period was the implementation of the Equal Pay Act between 1970 and 1975, anticipated somewhat in the public services. This would not have affected young workers' pay relative to that of adults of the same sex, but it would have raised young workers' pay relative to adults when both sexes are combined because a greater proportion of women workers are under 21. In addition, during the periods of incomes policy, increases resulting from the implementation of the Act were exempt from the incomes policy restrictions, so that adult manual men's pay dropped back relative to both women and young workers. This would seem to explain, in part, why there was a reduction in the youth–adult differential among manual men but not among manual women. However, there is a discrepancy between the two principal British series over the date of the cessation of the increase in young men's relative pay: the NES series placing the change after April 1975, and the EMO series after October 1976. There is, therefore, some doubt as to whether it occurred before or during the special provision for lower-paid workers under the Social Contract between 1975 and 1977. Since 1983, the government's Young Workers' Scheme (YWS) and Youth Training Scheme (YTS) have fostered lower rates of pay for young workers, and may have contributed to the decline in young workers' relative pay in the 1980s.

In France, the two main such policies were the raising of the minimum wage relative to average earnings (notably in 1968 and in 1973), and the element of pay restraint in M. Barre's austerity package introduced in late 1976. However, the effect of the pay restraints were mostly felt by the highest paid, and so are unlikely to have had much effect upon youth relative pay. Data on year-to-year changes (DAS) indicate that the slight decline in youth relative pay between 1972 and 1978 mostly took place after 1974, the period of increase extending from 1966 to about 1974.

Although the minimum wage strictly applies only to workers aged 18 and over, changes have repercussions on the pay levels of workers under 18. First, French collective agreements do not, as a rule, now specify special rates for young workers (unlike agreements in either West Germany or the UK). The Grenelle agreements of 1968 either suppressed altogether, or raised the age rates of pay in collective agreements to 70 per cent of the full adult rate for 16–17 year olds, and 80 per cent for 17–18 year olds, and a government decree in 1971 raised the minimum rate for those under 17 and those aged 17–18 to 80 per cent and 90 per cent respectively of the full adult rate. Second, the minimum remuneration of apprentices is linked by law to the minimum wage, starting at 15 per cent of the SMIC for the first half-year of the apprenticeship, and rising to 60 per cent in the final year. Additional evidence of the impact of the raising of the minimum wage (and, in particular, of the subsequent adjustments to minimum youth rates) is that between 1966 and 1972 the percentage point change in the youth–adult differential was greatest in the lowest-paid industries, giving a Pearson correlation coefficient of -0.68 (on 26 branches), compared with one of -0.01 for 1972–8 (on 33 branches).

As a result of the Grenelle agreements in June 1968, there was an immediate 35 per cent increase in the minimum wage, and from 2 January 1970, legislation providing for periodic adjustments in the minimum to allow for increases in the purchasing power of average earnings. However, its effect upon youth pay may have been limited because of the extent to which the minimum had fallen behind average earnings during the 1960s. Saunders and Marsden (1981) found that this increase had a relatively small effect upon either inter-industry dispersions or skill differentials even in lower-paying industries. Nevertheless, despite being a smaller increase, that of July 1973 appears to have had a bigger effect upon industry and skill differentials because of the initially higher level of the minimum (Marsden, 1980, p. 115). The increase in the minimum wage of 10 per cent in June 1981 may also have boosted young workers' relative pay.[6]

In the Netherlands, a special youth minimum wage for those aged under 23 was introduced in January 1974 specifying the rate for young workers as a percentage of the adult minimum wage. Initially the rate was 7.5 per cent below the adult rate for those aged 22, and an additional 7.5 per cent below that for each additional year below dropping to 47.5 per cent of the adult rate for those aged 15. The rates for each age group were reduced in December 1980 dropping to 35 per cent for those aged 15. According to the CBS, about 25 per cent of young workers aged 15–22 were on the minimum wage, compared with 5.3 per cent of those aged 23–64 (CBS, 1981 and 1983). While this provides strong *prima facie* evidence that minimum wage changes affected youth relative pay, it should be noted that much of the increase for young manual women can be explained by age compositional changes. Moreover, Crone (1986) argues that (particularly in recent years) minimum wage changes have to some extent adapted to labour demand changes.

In view of the fairly high proportion of young workers receiving it (Table 2.5), one might have expected the increase in youth relative pay after 1972 to have been greater that it was. Among women workers the effect on the youth–adult differential may have been partly offset by a rather faster improvement in women's relative pay.

Table 2.5 Netherlands, percentage of young workers receiving the minimum wage in November 1979

Industry SBI (1974)	*Age*	
	16–19	20–22
0 Agriculture and fisheries	17.7	13.0
2/3 Industry	28.8	14.7
6 Distribution, hotels, etc.	66.5	41.7
7 Transport	21.6	8.9
8 Banks and insurance, etc.	19.0	18.0
All activities	37.1	18.0

Source: CBS1981.

Pressures from Collective Bargaining

Pay scales in wage agreements do not just reflect union preferences. They are the outcome of both union and employer aims; changes in young workers' wage rates in collective agreements probably thus include a number of the influences already discussed, plus the effect of labour market pressures. But unions can also to some extent develop their own independent influence. For Britain, at least, the importance of institutional pressures in raising youth relative pay in the 1970s is highlighted by the high levels of excess supply of young workers then prevailing (Wells, 1983). One reason for union pressure to raise youth relative pay (and in particular trainee pay) suggested by Ryan (Chapter 7) is to discourage employers from seeking to substitute youth and especially trainees for adult labour.

In both West Germany and the UK, basic wage rates for young

workers have increased. In West Germany, special rates for workers under 18 in many regional industry agreements were either increased, or abolished altogether in the early 1970s (D/TLTG). For Italy, Mariani (1986) argues that union pressures to reduce differentials of all kinds in the early 1970s, and the pressures from the system of flat-rate wage indexation operative from the middle 1970s contributed greatly to reducing youth/adult differentials in that country

For the UK, also, there is some evidence that (over roughly the same period) young workers' basic rates increased, and the age at which the full adult rate was obtained was reduced in a large number of collective agreements (see UK/TRHW). Whereas these changes in basic rates appear to have affected relative earnings, the changes in youth basic pay in West Germany apparently have had little effect upon relative hourly earnings.

In all these countries, there is a considerable amount of negotiation over pay at plant and company level, so it would appear that individual German employers and their works councils did not pass this change on to gross earnings. It is of note that a number of West German collective agreements also reduced the basic rates for skilled relative to unskilled workers in the same period, and that these changes are also barely reflected in gross earnings (Marsden, 1981).

Labour Market Pressures

Full testing of the labour market pressures on young workers' relative pay would require a fuller examination of the determinants of young people's employment trends which is beyond the scope of this chapter. There have, however, been a number of recent studies of the relationship between young workers' relative pay and youth aggregate unemployment discussed earlier. An important factor affecting youth unemployment appears to have been general economic conditions, but Layard (1982) and Lynch and Richardson (1982) found some evidence that the increase in Britain in young manual men's relative earnings has contributed to their levels of unemployment (although it should be noted that their method of testing assumed that changes in relative pay were exogenous). This can be interpreted in two ways. First, it could suggest that some of the 'institutional' and social factors reviewed above (as distinct from an increase in demand relative to supply) caused the increase in youth pay in Britain; otherwise one might equally expect an increase in youth pay to coincide with an increase in youth employment in the short run. Alternatively, it could mean that young workers' relative earnings (although increasing initially in response to demand pressures) have not been sufficiently flexible to respond to the subsequent drop in demand for their labour. The latter view receives some support from Wells (1983), who argues that there was excess demand for youth labour until about 1969–70 and excess supply thereafter. However, such findings have to be treated with caution on account of the parallel increase in youth and adult unemployment. Moreover, because of the high training component in many young people's work, and the importance of gaining access to internal labour markets, there are many sections of the labour market in which the conventional short-run analysis of an employer's demand for labour is inappropriate.

2.5   TRENDS IN THE UNITED STATES 1967–81

The decline in young workers' relative pay throughout most of the 1970s offers a striking contrast to the pattern in the Western European countries. Figure 2.1 shows the median weekly earnings of young workers (aged 16–24) as a percentage of those aged 25 and over for the second quarter of each year.[7] Comparisons with Western Europe should be made with care because of the different age range used, and especially because of the difference in coverage: the US figures include additionally workers in the services sector, and those in small establishments.

A second notable feature of the US experience is that the fluctuations about the declining trend in youth relative pay coincide with fluctuations in young people's share of unemployment. Youth relative pay fell when young people's share of unemployment fell. One interpretation is that in the US youth relative pay is affected by the state of demand for their labour relative to adults, which appears in contrast with Western Europe. However, in view of the differences in coverage between the data for the two continents, it is possible that the greater flexibility of youth relative pay in aggregate in the US reflects events in the casual type labour markets of many small firms in the services sector.

An additional factor is that young people's share of unemployment in the US has varied inversely with the overall rate of unemployment. The increases in young workers' relative pay may thus reflect a

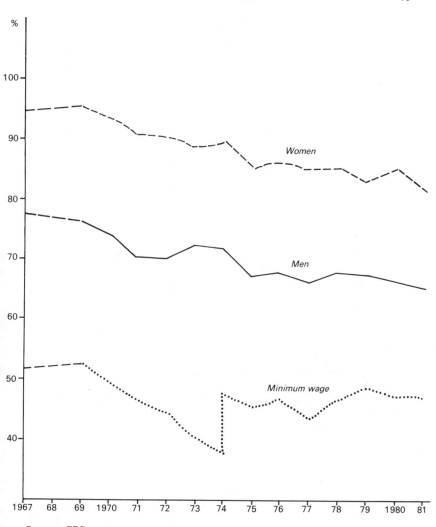

Source: CPS.
Figure 2.1   Relative weekly earnings of young workers and the minimum wage 1967–81, United States, full-time workers in all sectors. See notes to Table 2.6, p. 42.

deterioration of the demand for older workers. In contrast with several Western European countries, the youth unemployment share decreased when the overall unemployment rate increased. This may reflect the lay-off practices among many US firms where agreements

Table 2.6   United States: relative weekly earnings[a] of young workers and the minimum wage of 1967–1981 (full-time workers in all sectors)

	Males[b] %	*Females[c]* %	*Minimum wage[d]* %
1967	77.6	94.9	51.4
68	–	–	–
69	76.1	95.3	52.9
1970	74.2	93.6	49.2
71	70.4	91.0	46.4
72	70.2	90.6	44.4
73	72.3	88.8	40.3
74	71.6	89.5	47.3
75	67.4	85.4	45.4
76	67.9	86.2	46.7
77	66.4	85.3	43.4
78	68.0	85.5	46.7
79	68.4	85.9	47.9
1980	66.8	83.5	47.5
81	65.0	84.0	47.0
82	62.3	81.2	44.4
83	58.7	78.5	43.5

Notes:
[a] May, or second quarter of each year.
[b] Males aged 16–24 compared with males aged 16 and over.
[c] Females aged 16–24 compared with females aged 16 and over.
[d] Minimum wage, converted to 40-hour week basis, compared with median weekly earnings of male and female full-time workers.
Source: CPS (various years).

on lay-offs according to seniority may make shedding labour in a recession easier than in Western Europe. In contrast, the first reaction of many European firms is to cut recruitment, which hits young workers disproportionately.

Finally, changes in the minimum wage may have affected youth pay. However, its effects are hard to gauge on account of the numerous exemptions for particular groups of young workers, problems of enforcement. Figure 2.1 includes the Federal minimum wage as a percentage of the weekly earnings of all full-time workers covered by the CPS converted into a weekly equivalent (based on a 40-hour week). The minimum wage declined sharply as a percentage of average weekly earnings between May 1969 and May 1974, but after a big increase in May 1974 it continued at roughly the same level thereafter. The increasing gap between the minimum wage and average earnings between 1969 and 1974 may have allowed youth pay to fall behind adult pay, at least up until about 1973, and the stabilisation of the minimum after 1974 may have slowed the decline in young workers' relative pay in the middle and late 1970s.

2.6   CHANGES SINCE 1978

Evidence of changes in youth relative earnings since 1978 is fragmentary for most of these countries. In Britain, by 1983, the pay of young compared to adult men (and of young compared to adult women) had declined almost every year since 1978, reversing some of the advances of the early 1970s. In the Netherlands – perhaps reflecting the reduction of the youth minimum wage – weekly earnings of workers aged 16–20 increased only half as much as those of workers of all ages (NL/ HYS). In West Germany, wage rates for unskilled young workers showed little change since the middle 1970s suggesting that there has been no further pressure in industry–regional level collective agreements to raise youth relative pay (D/TLTG). In contrast, in France, the increase of the minimum wage in 1981 and the exemption of minimum wage increases from the government's wage and exemption of minimum wage increases from the government's wage and price freeze in late 1983 may have given a boost to youth relative pay. Nevertheless, young workers may have lost out in subsequent attempts by union bargainers to restore differentials. Where there is some evidence, it would thus seem that youth relative pay has not increased since 1978 (and in some cases has fallen a certain amount), but probably not yet back to the levels of the early 1970s. One important factor increasing the gap between young workers and adults, has been the increase in the pay of higher-paid occupations in which there are few young workers (particularly in Britain since 1979). Occupational differentials increased between 1978 and 1984 in Britain, Germany and the United States, but not in France (Marsden, 1985).

2.7   SUMMARY AND CONCLUSIONS

The comparisons of differentials between young and adult workers in

France, West Germany, and the UK in 1978 revealed a broad similarity in the levels of pay of young workers relative to adults in all three countries for all four major groups (manual and non-manual men, and manual and non-manual women). Although there were differences between the three countries, no country emerged as consistently giving higher or lower levels of relative pay to young workers. Among manual men (if we exclude apprentices), West Germany gave the highest relative pay, and the UK the lowest. If we include apprentices, then West Germany has the lowest relative pay for young workers, but it should be stressed that apprentices' pay in both France and Germany has a different legal status from wages. The difference between Britain and Germany lies in the larger proportion of young men who are apprentices and their lower relative remuneration in Germany. But this may be a reflection of the slightly bigger differential between skilled and semi-skilled workers in Germany, and the higher reputation of their technical vocational training. The Netherlands were the exception with a significantly lower level of youth relative pay.

Among manual women, France has the highest relative pay for young workers and the Netherlands the lowest, but with the exception of the Netherlands, the differences between the countries are small. Among non-manual men, West Germany has the highest youth relative pay, and the Netherlands the lowest, and among non-manual women, the UK has the highest. The higher relative pay of young non-manual women in the UK is probably the result of the smaller proportion of women in managerial positions in industry than in either France or Germany.

Between 1966 and 1972, the relative earnings of young manual men increased in all six European countries – as they did between 1972 and 1978, except in France, and possibly West Germany. For manual women, the picture was more complex. Their relative pay by comparison changed less between 1966 and 1972 (falling significantly only in Britain), but increased in the second period, except in France and Germany. Much of the increases between 1972 and 1978 may have occurred in the earlier part of the period: in Britain and France (for which there is direct evidence), youth relative pay rose until about 1975, after which there was some decline. Changes in wage rates of West Germany suggest a similar pattern. The changes in relative earnings appear to have been widespread across all industries between 1966 and 1972, but more varied between 1972 and 1978, possibly on account of the ending of the increases after 1974–5.

An important factor behind the changes in relative earnings was the change in nationally- and regionally-determined wage rates. Evidence from collective agreements and legal provisions indicates that a number of changes occurred in all three countries in the late 1960s and early 1970s.

Three broad conclusions can be drawn from this picture. The first relates to the timing of the changes in youth pay and the increase in youth unemployment; the second to the importance of vocational training systems in understanding inter-country differences; and the third to the factors behind the changes over time, and why they should have occurred at a broadly similar time in all three countries.

Simple comparison of trends in youth relative pay and the share of the unemployed under 21 would indicate some relation between the two. The proportion of the unemployed under 21 did indeed increase in the early 1970s in most countries, and then either slowed or levelled off after about 1975–6. The major exception was the US, in which the percentage of the unemployed under 21 fluctuated about a declining trend through the 1970s, and this was the one country in which young workers' (aged 16–24) relative earnings declined throughout the late 1960s and 1970s. It is clearly important to know whether the apparently greater responsiveness of young workers' relative pay in the US has contributed to their declining unemployment share, but the difference in coverage between the US and the continental European data has to be resolved before the question can be answered properly.

Why should the share of the unemployed under 21 increase with aggregate unemployment in many of the European countries, whereas the opposite usually happened in the US? One possible reason is that owing to legislation and collective agreements regulating lay-offs in many European countries, and the absence of the type of agreement common in the US which enables employers to lay off workers in bad times in a fairly routine fashion, the first reaction of European employers to recession is to cut recruitment. Only later do they negotiate short-time working or lay-offs: the fall in the youth unemployment share in a number of countries thus occurs after the initial rise in unemployment.

While there may be some (albeit diffuse) link between *trends* in young workers' relative earnings and youth unemployment, there does not appear to be any obvious link between *levels* of youth relative pay in different countries and their respective levels of youth unemployment at least for 1978 – nor indeed should there be unless allowance is made for differences in general economic conditions between the countries. A rough and ready allowance for this can be made by comparing the ratios of youth to adult unemployment rates. But there is not much correspondence between the ranking of countries according to youth relative unemployment rates for 1979 and the levels of youth relative pay in 1978–9 for males, and even less for females.

The second broad conclusion relates to the importance of the organisation of vocational training in different countries to an understanding of young workers' pay relative to adults. The pattern of general or transferable training in British and West German apprenticeships does indeed carry a lower rate of pay for the apprentices as compared with young workers undergoing specific or non-transferable training as is more the case in France. This factor would seem to be the major source of differences in the youth–adult differential between the three countries for manual workers.

The third conclusion relates to the factors behind the changes. That the increase in young workers' relative pay should have occurred at roughly the same time (namely the late 1960s and the early 1970s) in all the European countries itself calls for some explanation, as might the different position in the US. Moreover, the reflection of the increases in collective agreements (and in France also in legal changes) and their spread across a wide range of industries (at least between 1966 and 1972) rules out the influence of one or two exceptional industries. It also rules out the accumulation of a large number of unrelated factors. Indeed, these facts point towards economy-wide – or at least labour market-wide – and society-wide causes.

High rates of economic growth through the 1960s and the resulting tightening of labour markets may have played an important role. For Britain, Merrilees and Wilson (1979) and Wells (1983) have suggested that until the late 1960s there was excess demand for youth labour which would have enabled young workers' relative earnings to increase without damaging their employment prospects, but that conditions changed after the end of the 1960s. For the first period, Wells found little evidence of a relation between youth pay and youth unemployment, but in the second, one emerges. One could thus argue that the increase in young workers' relative pay in the UK was partly caused by an increase in demand for youth labour although aggregate unemployment rates were already rising by the late 1960s some time before the big increases in youth relative pay of the early 1970s. Moreover, although this type of argument might appear to work for

Britain and West Germany, it fits less well to France where youth relative pay was falling through the middle 1960s up to 1967–8 (Marsden, 1983).

One additional factor may have been the social and industrial unrest of the late 1960s. In France at least, Reynaud *et al.* (1971) has argued that the strikes of May–June 1968 were in some respects a more dramatic form of the normal pattern of French industrial relations, under which grievances and union demands accumulate until the dam breaks. In West Germany (and also in Italy) young workers played an important part in the 'spontaneous strikes' of 1969 and the early 1970s, feeling that the established systems of workplace representation was not taking adequate account of their particular interests. Subsequently, the West German works councils and unions reacted to give a greater voice to young workers, and this may have partly taken the form of the faster increases in basic rates noted earlier. One interpretation of the increase in youth relative pay in the early 1970s is thus that it was a delayed reaction to the tightening of the youth labour market during the 1960s, and the increased self-awareness of young people catalysed by their role in the events of May–June 1968. This is not to deny the importance of labour market pressures, merely to suggest that they did not immediately take the form of increased relative pay. One could argue that many young people first experienced the power given by the increase in the demand for their labour as greater freedom to change jobs (or to use this as a threat to their employers), and a greater freedom to undertake the responsibilities associated with adult status. Adults may have resisted such developments on pay for longer because of the importance of established pay structures and pay norms. After this period, the higher levels of relative pay may have exacerbated the effect on youth employment on the decline in demand for their labour caused by the recession, and the climate of economic uncertainty from the middle 1970s, which made firms more cautious about recruitment.

APPENDIX   A NOTE ON TERMINOLOGY AND SOURCES

Terminology

1. *Relative pay* is used to denote the pay of young workers compared either to that of workers of all ages, or that of adults. The precise age group is made clear in the text.

2. *Earnings* consist of the basic wage or salary plus any amounts received for overtime or bonus work, before deduction of tax and employees' social insurance contributions.
3. *Wage rates* are the basic rates of pay determined in collective agreements, by law, or by an employer, and exclude payments for overtime and bonuses.
4. *Employees* denote all people with a contract of employment, and other assimilated categories (e.g., apprentices and trainees) but exclude those working on their own account, and working proprietors.
5. *Manual workers* denote skilled, semi-skilled and unskilled workers, often referred to also as blue-collar workers, operatives, or wage earners.
6. *Non-manual workers* denote administrative, technical, clerical and managerial staff.
7. *Workers* denote people who work, and is used as a generic term.

Abbreviations

SEI   Eurostat's survey of the structure of earnings in industry.
LCI   Eurostat's survey of labour costs in industry.
LFSS   Eurostat's labour force sample survey.
NACE   Economic activity classification used by Eurostat.
SSIS   INSEE's publication of the 1978 results of the Community's structure of earnings survey (SEI) – *La structure des salaires dans l'industrie et les services en 1978.*
DAS   INSEE's annual survey of annual earnings – *Les salaires dans l'industrie, le commerce, et les services.*
GLSE   The Federal German Statistical Office's publication of the Community's structure of earnings survey (SEI) results – *Gehalts- und Lohnstrukturerhebung 1978.*
TLTG   The Federal German Statistical Office's compilation of data from collective agreements – *Tariflöhne und Tarifgehälter.*
HYS   The Netherlands half-yearly earnings survey carried out by the Centraal Bureau voor de Statistiek.
NES   The British Department of Employment's new earnings survey.
EMO   The British Department of Employment's survey of the earnings of manual workers in October.
TRHW   The British Department of Employment's compilation of wage rates from collective agreements – Time Rates and Hours of Work.
EESC   The British Department of Employment's survey of earnings in engineering, shipbuilding and chemicals.
CPS   The United States Department of Labour's current population survey.

Principal Statistical Sources

Eurostat's SEI survey records the gross earnings of employees in establishments with 10 or more employees. In 1966 coverage was confined to manual workers in industry. In 1972 it was enlarged to include non-manual workers in industry, and in 1978 (after a special survey in 1974) it was further enlarged to include distribution, banking and insurance. Details are recorded on gross hourly earnings (manual workers) and monthly earnings (manual and non-manual workers) before deductions for income tax and employees' social insurance contributions. The reporting unit is the establishment, and returns are made for selected individual workers. The survey month is October. The survey covers workers with a contract of employment, and hence excludes apprentices, unless the national statistical offices make their own provision for including additional questions. The sample fraction, except for Britain, is upwards of 10 per cent.

The Department of Employment's NES records gross weekly and hourly earnings before tax and employees' social insurance contributions for employees in all activities and in establishments of all sizes. It has been carried out annually on a 1 per cent sample since 1970.

The Department of Employment's EMO provides gross weekly and hourly earnings of manual workers before tax and employees' social insurance contributions in most activities. Employers in firms with more than 10 employees provide information of the gross earnings bill and the numbers of workers employed.

For other EEC statistical sources see Marsden (1984).

Notes

1. The author would like to thank Eurostat, the INSEE, the Statistisches Bundesamt, and the Department of Employment for considerable help in making available additional statistical material, and for advice on use of some of the data. He would also like to thank L. Hake, I. Jones, J. Martin, P. Paterson, A. Rajan, R. Richardson, P. Schwansee, W. Wells and G. Wurzberg for extensive comments on earlier drafts. A version of this chapter was presented at a conference funded by the European Commission on 'Youth pay and employers' recruitment practices for young people in the Community' held at Farnham Castle in June 1985. My thanks are also due to participants at the conference.

   Thanks are also due to the Organisation for Economic Co-operation and Development and the European Commission for financial support. The views expressed are those of the author.

2. Direct comparisons of skill differentials between the two countries for 1978 still await publication of the full Eurostat results. In West Germany the differential between skilled and semi-skilled workers had declined by 1978 to 11.3 per cent in both hourly and weekly earnings. In Britain, in the engineering industries the differential in weekly earnings increased from 8.8 to 9.6 per cent between 1972 and 1978 (EESC), but this followed a period of considerable compression of skill differentials in the middle 1970s. An additional factor possibly affecting youth employment in West Germany has been the increase in the

cost of training places (Noll *et al.*, 1983), although this may have been offset by a widespread belief among West German employers that there is a collective responsibility incumbent upon them to train young workers (Edding Commission, 1974).

3. Eurostat LCI Tables A1/123, and A1/125. The figures for Britain in LCI appear to be a little higher than that in other UK sources. The Department of Employment's survey 'New Entrants to employment' (*Department of Employment Gazette*, September 1980: 943–53) gives apprentices and trainees as 3.9 per cent of all workers (manual and non-manual) in manufacturing in 1978, equivalent to about 5.5 per cent of manual employees. About two-thirds of these are apprentices.

4. France has a slightly smaller proportion of the male labour force aged under 18, possibly a reflection of the greater emphasis on technical education in schools. This could push up the estimate of youth relative pay compared to Britain and Germany. Recalculating the relative pay of French manual men aged under 21 for 1972 using the British age weights for those aged under 18 and between 18 and 20 (from the 1974 NES) caused the French figure to drop by about $2\frac{1}{2}$ percentage points.

5. Recently, however, the differences between the two countries have decreased, as a number of German apprenticeships (especially in engineering) have increased to $3\frac{1}{2}$ years, while some EITB apprenticeships can now be completed after $3\frac{1}{2}$ years on the apprentice's 20th birthday. I am grateful to Ian Jones for drawing this to my attention. Nevertheless, according to *Wirtschaft und Statistik* (1981) as late as 1980 only a relatively small proportion of West German apprenticeships extended into a fourth year.

6. The impact of the SMIC on low-paid groups may have been temporarily enhanced by the government's decision to make increases in the minimum wage exempt from the wage and price freeze in force between June and October 1982.

7. The figures are from the CPS. A number of changes in the survey were introduced in 1979, notably the quarterly collection of earnings data. This may reduce comparability with earlier years. The data from 1967 until 1979 relate to May of each year.

3 The Relative Pay and Employment of Young People

William Wells

3.1 INTRODUCTION

This chapter is a summary of research which is set out more fully in Wells (1983). It examines how the earnings of young people have moved relative to those of adults over the post-war period. The reasons for these movements are then considered, and it was found that the relative wages of young people do not appear to adjust rapidly in response to changes in the level of their demand or supply. Rather, it appears that most of the movements that occur can be attributed to 'institutional' or non-economic factors such as the effect of the lowering of the age of majority in 1969 on the reduction in the age at which adult rates of pay are paid. In such a situation movements in the young person–adult relativity cannot be regarded as an equilibrating force to balance supply and demand for young people and, thus, there exists the possibility of shortage or surplus in the labour market for young people.

To test this possibility the approach first outlined in Merrilees and Wilson (1979) was used, and the conclusions reached were very similar. In particular, the period until 1969 for young males (a year or two later for young females) tended to be one where young people in the labour force were in short supply (or at least not in surplus) and the level of their employment determined largely by the size of the relevant demographic cohort and the decisions of young people to enter further education or employment. Subsequently, there has been a surplus of young people and, in this period, their employment appears to have been determined both by the general demand for labour and the cost of their labour relative to other groups. The effect of changes in the general level of demand and relative labour costs in this later period cannot be quantified exactly because of inadequacies in the data. However, it does appear that the level of youth employment (especially for under 18 year old males) is inversely related to changes in their relative labour costs and positively related to changes in the general level of demand for labour. Also, the effects of relative labour costs changes appear to be large and the changes in youth employment in response to changes in the general level of demand more rapid than for the labour force as a whole.

3.2   RELATIVE EARNINGS OF YOUNG PEOPLE: SOURCES AND POST-WAR MOVEMENTS

Sources

Information on earnings by age group is drawn from two main sources. The first is the annual survey carried out in October of each year into the earnings and hours of manual workers in establishments in manufacturing and certain other industries and services. This provides information on average earnings by broad age category for the period 1948–79 and as such covers virtually all the post-war period. However, its coverage is not comprehensive, as it is confined to manual workers and excludes some non-manufacturing industries. Also, the age classifications are broad and differ for each sex: the survey distinguishes the average earnings of males under 21 and females under 18 from those of other employees. For the period as a whole relative movements in average earnings of these age categories may thus not be a complete reflection of the experience of young people in the labour market, and some of the movements in the relative earnings of young people may be masked by the breadth of the age classification.

The second source, the New Earnings Survey (NES) is a sample survey of the earnings of employees in employment in Great Britain in April of each year covering employees in all occupations in all types and sizes of businesses in all industries. Since 1973 consistent figures have also been provided in finer age details than that given in the October survey. The drawbacks of the NES in this context is that it has been running for a comparatively short period of time (it has been carried out in its present form only since 1970). Also, there were changes in the sampling methods in the early years of the NES which affected the measurement of average earnings, especially of young people. However, taken together the two sources do complement each other in that the October survey conveys the broad movements in the relative earnings of young people over the post-war period until 1979 whilst the NES provides more detailed information on the more recent past and the period after 1979.

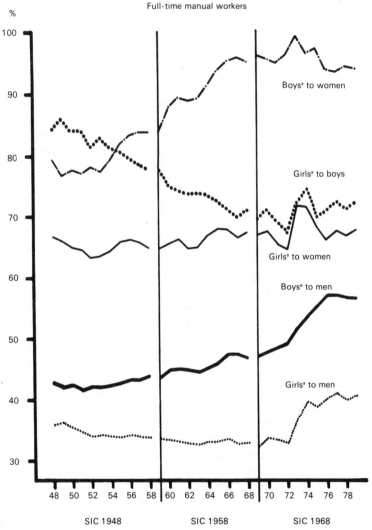

Figure 3.1   Age/sex weekly earnings relativities (%) from the October earnings Survey.

 [a] See notes to Table 3.A1, p. 67.

Post-war Movements

The estimated relative earnings of young people obtained from the October survey are depicted in Figure 3.1 (with the figures given in Table 3.A1 of the Appendix, p. 67). From these it is apparent that until 1972 the average earnings of youths and boys under 21 rose relative to those of adult men and women and girls under 18. Over the same period the earnings of girls aged under 18 were little changed relative to those of both adult men and adult women. Subsequently there was a sharp increase in the average earnings of young people of both sexes relative to adults of both sexes. This increase was maintained relative to adult men but not adult women. A similar increase in the average earnings of young females aged under 18 relative to those of young men aged under 21 occurred in the early 1970s. This too was (partially) reversed. By 1976 all the changes seemed to have worked their way through and from 1976 until the age information in the survey ceased in 1979 there was little change in the average earnings of young people relative to adults of both sexes or in the relativity between young males and young females.

The estimated relative earnings of young people (manual, non-manual and all employees) obtained from the NES relative to adult males and females for all employees are depicted in Figures 3.2 and 3.3 (with the figures given in Tables 3.A2 and 3.A3 of the Appendix). These figures indicate that the same pattern emerges for virtually all age and sex groups when comparing the average earnings of young people relative to adult males aged 21 and over. There is a strong increase in the relativity of each group in the years 1973–5 for young males and 1973–7 for young females. For the rest of the decade the average earnings of young people relative to adult males has remained at roughly the levels of the mid-1970s. Thereafter, there has been a fall concentrated mostly in the most recent period 1982–4. However, the current level is still above what it was before the rapid increase of the early 1970s.

The picture that emerges when comparing the average earnings of young people with those of adult women aged 18 and over is slightly different. Here, the rapid increase in the relative average earnings which occurred after 1973 was swiftly reversed for young males and by 1976 they were generally at (or below) the level of 1973. For young females, the reversal of the sharp increase in relative earnings was more gradual and more marked among the younger ages and the manual workers. Further falls in the average earnings for young

%

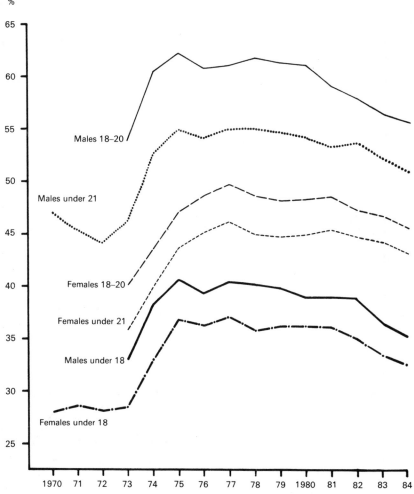

Figure 3.2 Average gross weekly earnings[a] of full-time employees under 21[b] as a % of the corresponding figure for males aged 21 and over (all workers).

[a, b] See notes to Table 3A.2, p. 70.

people of both sexes have occurred since 1979 with a particularly large fall occurring in 1982–4.

In summary, the evidence from the NES is very similar to that from the October survey for the comparable periods. There was a sharp increase in the average earnings of young people relative to those of adults in the early 1970s which was reversed relative to adult women

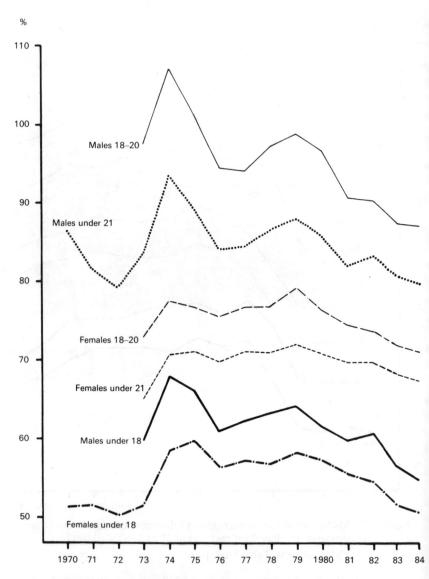

Figure 3.3   Average gross weekly earnings[a] of full-time employees under 21[b] as
a % of the corresponding figure for all females aged 18 and over
[a, b] See notes to Table 3.A3, p. 72.

but not adult men. This was followed by a period of relative stability which persisted until recent years. Since then there is evidence of a fall, particularly in 1982–4.

3.3 FACTORS AFFECTING THE TRENDS IN RELATIVE AVERAGE EARNINGS OF YOUNG PEOPLE

Any change in the average earnings of young people relative to those of adults can be allocated between a change in the composition of employment and a change in earnings for the same employment. Compositional changes appear to have been the more important factor until the end of the 1960s. Thereafter, there were a number of factors tending to increase relative pay for the same employment coupled with a further compositional change when the school leaving age was raised to 16 (ROSLA) in September 1972. These factors explain most, if not all, of the movements in the average relative earnings of young people in the post-war period (until the early 1980s at least) with the level of supply and demand for young people's employment having at best only a marginal effect.

The October survey was considered to see whether, in the period until 1979, compositional changes in either the industrial distribution or the number of hours worked could explain the movements in relative average earnings. However, neither of these factors appears to have been important.

On the other hand, changes in the age structure of young people in employment do account for some of the movement. In particular, a large part of the movement in young people's relative average earnings until the end of the 1960s can be attributed to changes in the average age of young people in employment. Several factors contributed to an increase in average age over this period. (This in turn increased relative average earnings because the average earnings of young people tend to increase with age.) One was the gradual increase in the proportion of young people in post-compulsory education. Another was the phasing out of National Service from 1959 onwards which returned many 18–20 year old males to the civilian labour market. The passing through of the post-war baby boom also resulted in the average age of young people under 21 growing over the period 1962–7 after causing an initial dip as they entered the labour force. The other major age compositional change was the raising of the school leaving age to 16 (ROSLA) in September 1972 which produced a further increase in the average age of young people in the labour market and contributed to the rapid increase in the relative average earnings which is evident in both the October survey and the NES.

Apart from these compositional influences there were also factors tending to increase relative pay for the same employment. However, most of these factors seem to have occurred since the late 1960s. The most direct effect on the relative earnings of young males under 21 has arisen from reductions in the age at which adult rates of pay are payable (this change affected young males more, as females were generally in occupations where adult rates were already payable at 18). Although such changes have occurred in a piecemeal fashion throughout the post-war period there was an acceleration of this tendency in the early 1970s following the lowering of the age of majority to 18 in 1969 (see Table 3.1). Nor was the effect restricted to those aged 18–20 which were now more frequently paid at adult rates.

Table 3.1   Cumulative percentages of those in industries receiving adult rates of pay

Age	April 1970	April 1975	April 1980
18	12	42	53
19	14	46	59
20	28	84	90
21	99	100	100
22	100	100	100

Source: Department of Employment, Economic and Social Division, 'Time Rates of Wages and Hours of Work.

An analysis of a sample of agreements in 'Time Rates of Wages and Hours of Work' (reproduced in Table 3.A4 of the Appendix) shows that the pay of those remaining on non-adult rates was generally shifted upwards when the age of adult rate payment was lowered, presumably to facilitate a gradual transition to adult rates. These increases in relative earnings appear to have been perverse because the labour market position of young people was deteriorating at the time.

There was also a further increase in relative pay for the same employment as well as a compositional effect at around the time of ROSLA. This, too, occurred at a time when the youth labour market was not buoyant and at least part of the increase was due to the effects of the prevailing incomes policies which tended to compress differentials generally (see Ashenfelter and Layard, 1983).

The other movements in the relative average earnings of young people are the fall relative to adult women in the mid-1970s and the decline relative to adults of both sexes in the 1980s, especially between 1982 and 1984. The first of these was due, in part, to the Equal Pay legislation whilst the latter is (as yet) unexplained, but is worthy of further consideration. It could be due to the effect of market forces on differentials. However, analyses of collective agreements by the Labour Research Department (LRD) (1983), IDS (1985) and IRRR (1985) suggest that this is not the case as there is not much evidence of widening differentials in negotiated pay rates. Another possibility is that the Young Workers' Scheme (YWS) may have had some effect especially since its introduction (in January 1982) coincided with the start of the period when youth differentials showed their largest fall. The YWS scheme will tend to reduce young people's relative earnings both because of its wage-stop provision and because any job created as a result of the subsidy will tend to be for the youngest and lowest-paid, thereby imparting a downward compositional effect.

3.4 THE CASE FOR DISEQUILIBRIUM IN THE YOUTH LABOUR MARKET

The previous section provides evidence for the contention that the relative earnings of young people do not adjust quickly to balance demand and supply because most of the relativity movements can be attributed to non-market force explanations. There thus exists the possibility of shortage or surplus in the youth labour market. Merrilees and Wilson (1979) present a convincing case for the assertion that young people were in short supply until the late 1960s, whilst the opposite is true thereafter. Their approach was to examine movements in economic variables in order to isolate periods of potential shortage and surplus and then test this hypothesis econometrically by fitting labour demand functions during periods of predicted surplus and supply functions during periods of predicted shortage then testing for structural breaks. The approach was replicated and extended in Wells (1983) and there was broad agreement on the conclusions. In particular, the period until 1969 for young males (a year or two later for young females) appears to be one where young people in the labour force were in short supply both in absolute and relative terms. Subsequently, there has been a surplus of young people. (The method is discussed in Junankar and Neale, Chapter 4, in this volume.)

Further indirect evidence supporting this contention is provided by the inconsistency between the results of studies estimated largely in the earlier period (see Abowd *et al.*, 1981, Hutchinson *et al.*, 1979 and Makeham, 1980; 1981). These attempted to fit demand functions in a period where, if it was a period of shortage, supply functions would be more appropriate. The results would then differ according to differences in their formulations. This does in fact appear to be the case. Further support for this hypothesis is given by the fact that formulations based on these studies when estimated solely in the latter period do provide consistent results.

3.5 EXTENSIONS OF THE ANALYSIS

Merrilees and Wilson concentrated on teenagers of both sexes. An improved data set enabled a division into finer age groups. In particular under 18 and 18–19 year old age groups are considered (a selection of results are presented in Junankar and Neale in Chapter 4). There is also a concentration on the later period when there is a surplus of young people in the labour market.

Finer Age Groups

The division of young people into finer groups confirm the results of the analysis for teenagers as a whole for the earlier period. The numbers of young people in employment in each age group appear to be determined primarily by the size of the relevant population cohort and the decisions of young people to enter either further education or employment. Increases in real disposable income seem to have stimulated the entry of young people into the workforce, suggesting that the substitution effect dominates the income effect for these groups of workers.

In the later period there is a difference in results between the two finer age groups. For the under 18 groups there are well-defined demand functions with expected signs on the variables and a collapse of the explanatory power of the supply equations. For the 18–19 age groups even in this later period the supply functions work better than the demand functions, which perform badly. In fact, for 18–19 year olds it was not possible to identify a structural break, and the supply function estimated over the whole period is statistically indistinguishable from the estimates for the sub-periods. It thus appears that much of the excess supply of young workers is concentrated in the under 18 category and the 18–19 year olds are relatively unaffected. This is, perhaps, because they are close substitutes for adults and the labour costs differentials are sufficiently large to sustain their attractiveness to employers. Alternatively, as possibly the closest substitutes for under 18 year olds, their employment may benefit if the employment of under 18s suffer.

The Situation Since the End of the 1960s

The non-recognition of the possibility of excess demand for young workers may have led to results based on coincidence in Abowd *et al.*, Hutchinson *et al.* and Makeham. However, the formulations of demand equations used in these studies provide a useful basis for studying the robustness of the results in the later period using a variety of formulations. Therefore, for the period 1969–81 for young males and 1971–81 for young females demand equations based on the four studies were estimated. The analysis below concentrates on the under 18 age groups, as it was again not possible to obtain well-defined demand functions for 18–19 year olds. This suggests that their experience even in this latter period was different than that of the younger age group.

Table 3.A5 in the Appendix gives the results of one set of equations for under 18s of both sexes based on these formulations and Table 3.3 the estimated elasticities for the relative labour costs and cyclical terms as an example of the results obtained. The results for each sex are discussed below.

Young Males Under 18

The results for young males are best expressed with reference to two equations set out below. (These equations should be taken as indicative of the forces at work rather than as preferred equations.)

Table 3.2 Estimated elasticities of cyclical and relative labour costs variables for young people under 18 (first difference equations)

Equation no.	Dependent variable	Cyclical variable	Relative labour cost variable				$\bar{R}^2$	DW
			YM/AM	YF/AF	YM/F	YF/M		
Males								
D2	$\text{Log}(N_{YM}/N_M)$	−0.02	−2.71**		−1.39*		0.87	2.1
D2a	$\text{Log}(N_{YM}/N_T)$	−0.01	−2.90**		−1.45*		0.87	2.0
D3	$\text{Log}(N_{YM})$	−0.90*	−2.52**		−1.36*		0.81	1.4
D4	N_{YM}/N_M	−0.02	−1.72**		−1.58**		0.85	1.9
D4a	N_{YM}/N_T	−0.01	−1.82**		−1.20*		0.86	1.8
D5	N_{YM}	−0.01	−1.98**		−1.26*		0.84	2.0
D6	$\text{Log}(U_{YM})$	+1.00**	+10.10*		+2.83		0.76	2.3
Females								
D2	$\text{Log}(N_{YF}/N_F)$	+0.05		+2.54		−2.10*	0.31	2.0
D2a	$\text{Log}(N_{YF}/N_T)$	+0.05		+2.53		−2.00*	0.31	2.1
D3	$\text{Log}(N_{YF})$	−0.05		+2.08		−1.88**	0.33	1.7
D4	N_{YF}/N_F	+0.08		+2.25		−1.35*	0.43	1.8
D4a	N_{YF}/N_T	+0.06		+2.77		−1.64*	0.42	1.9
D5	N_{YF}	+0.06		+2.47		−1.51*	0.34	1.8
D6	$\text{Log}(U_{YF})$	+0.55		−2.34		+5.21	0.57	1.9

Notes: All equations were in first differences (see Table 3.A5 in Appendix, pp. 74–5).
*, ** denotes significance at 5 per cent and 1 per cent respectively.
M, F, T denotes males, females and total; a prefix of $Y(A)$ denotes young (adult) – e.g., YF = young females under 18.
Cyclical variable is the male unemployment rate (excluding school leavers).
Source: Wells (1983).

Estimating period 1969–81

$$N_{YM} = 0.01 + 1.17 \ N_T - 2.97 \ RLC_{YMAM} - 1.46 \ RLC_{YMF} - 0.05 \ ROSLA \tag{3.1}$$

$$(0.09) \ (3.1) \quad (-5.2) \quad\quad (-2.6) \quad\quad (-1.3)$$

$\bar{R}^2 = 0.85 \ RSS = 0.0042 \ DW = 2.17$

$$U_{YM} = -0.01 + 1.00 \ UX_M + 10.10 \ RLC_{YMAM} + 2.8 \ RLC_{YMF} - 0.75 \ ROSLA \tag{3.2}$$

$$(-0.1) \ (3.7) \quad\quad (2.3) \quad\quad\quad (0.7) \quad\quad (-2.2)$$

$\bar{R}^2 = 0.76 \ RSS = 0.2552 \ DW = 2.33$

The equations are in first differences of natural logarithms except for the constant and the *ROSLA* dummy. The figures in brackets are *t*-statistics.

N, *U*, *UX* are respectively employees in employment, unemployment rate and unemployment rate excluding school leavers.

RLC is the relative labour costs (labour costs are defined as gross weekly earnings plus employers' National Insurance contribution and surcharge paid in respect of the employee).

ROSLA is a dummy variable used to reflect the effect of the raising of school leaving age to 16 in September 1973; it is defined as 1 in 1973, 0 elsewhere.

Subscripts *YM*, *AM*, *M*, *F* refer respectively to young males, adult males, all males and all females.

The employment equation (3.1) is representative of the formulation for young males under 18, with a strong negative relationship between the labour costs of young people relative to adult males and their (relative) employment with estimated elasticities generally over 2. Similar negative relationships exist between the labour costs of young males under 18 relative to all females and their (relative) employment with estimated elasticities around 1.4. These results are consistent throughout all the formulations.

The exact extent of the effect of the general level of demand on the employment of young males is difficult to determine because there are problems in choosing an appropriate cyclical variable. However, on balance it does appear that young males under 18 are affected disproportionately by changes in the general level of activity. For example, the estimated elasticity of this group's employment with respect to changes in total employment in equation (3.1) is greater than one (1.17). Although this is not a significant difference, it is also likely to be an underestimate of the disproportionate cyclical effect for two reasons. First, the counter-cyclical 'special employment measures' dampen any cyclical response, and as these are concentrated amongst young people they will mask the actual effect on young people more than that for adults. Second, the formulations used in the econometric work are likely to understate the level of the cyclical effect on young people because they look at proportionate changes. As the unemployment rates for young people are above those of adults, and equiproportionate increase in young and total unemployment rates will thus lead to an increase in the absolute differential between the two rates.

Comparison between equations (3.1) and (3.2) also enable some indirect inferences to be drawn about the effect of the general level of demand on the supply response of young males under 18. In particular, it appears that the 'discouraged' worker effect predominates for this group, and their activity rates fall in times of recession.[1] (This conclusion is consistent with the research carried out in the OECD by Martin, 1983). The basis for this contention is that it appears that the proportionate decrease in young male employment is greater (1.17 in equation 3.1) than the equivalent proportionate increase in young male unemployment (1.00 in equation 3.2) when total employment decreases and total unemployment increases.[2] It should be noted, however, that part of the estimated difference is due to the differential effect of special employment measures on employment and unemployment. These measures (especially those aimed at young people such as the Youth Opportunities Programme (YOP) and the Youth Training Scheme (YTS)) have a greater effect on the numbers registered as unemployed than they do on the numbers in employment. As the schemes are more concentrated among young people this may, therefore, provide some of the explanation.

Finally, it is possible to consider the effect of changes in relative labour costs on total rather than relative employment. So far, the analysis has focused on the share of total employment taken by young people but changes in relative labour costs will also have an effect on average labour costs and possibly, therefore, the size of total employment. Estimates elicited from the formulations based on Abowd *et al.* (1981) suggest that increases in relative labour costs appear to be associated with decreases in total as well as young people's employment although the effect is much less (20 per cent of the decrease in young people's employment would be a very broad estimate of the fall in total employment). This result is, however, even more uncertain than the rest of these results in this section. As well as the data problems discussed below there is also a fairly free adaptation of the Abowd *et al.*

methodology and these adaptations may invalidate the estimation even if the original methodology is legitimate.

As well as the specific problem described above, it is necessary to enter a cautionary note about the analysis in this section. There are problems with both the shortness of the estimating period (13 observations) and the quality of the data. The consistency of the employment data and the applicability of the earnings data are uncertain, even though considerable care has been taken to improve the data and ensure consistency. The ending of the National Insurance (NI) card count of employees in 1972 removed the prime source of data on employees in employment by age. Although the Labour Force Survey (LFS) provides consistent biennial information from 1975 on the proportion of employees in employment by age there exists not only the problem of interpolation between LFS estimates but also the possibility that the LFS and the NI card count are not consistent with each other and the problem of bridging the gap between the two sources in 1973–4. This period is crucial because of the effect of *ROSLA*, and although information from a number of sources was used to try to obtain figures for these two years they generally give different answers and the estimates, therefore, lack certainty. The main source of the earnings data is the October enquiry because it provides information on the period before the NES. However, this does mean that there was no alternative to using the earnings of manual males under 21 in certain industries as a proxy for the earnings of young males as a whole. This also increases uncertainty about the results.[3]

Young Females Under 18

The results for females from Tables A.3.4 and A.3.5 are not as well established. There remains strong significant negative relationships between the labour costs of young females under 18 relative to males (of all ages) with an elasticity of about 1.5–2.0, but relative to adult women the results suggest that their (relative) employment is positively related. (The elasticity of around 2 is not, however, significant in any of the formulations.) Other formulations tried do, however, find negative and significant relationships. There are, also, problems discerning a cyclical effect.

It is likely that at least part of the problems of inconsistency are due to the problems of the data. The employment data problems are discussed above, but a main cause of uncertainty would appear to be the source of earnings information. The coverage of the October survey is unrepresentative of the employment of young females as it is concentrated in manual occupations and the production sectors. Another problem which may have had an effect are the secular increase in female activity rates which makes it difficult to obtain an adequate proxy for the general level of activity for young females (the unemployment rates of adult males (excluding school leavers) was generally used, but it is not completely satisfactory). Finally, it may be that the labour market experience of adult females changed during this period, and this may in turn have affected the employment of young females independently of the factors modelled here. For example, Zabalza and Tzannatos (1983) have suggested that over this period adult females experienced an increase in relative demand which could not be attributed to factors such as changes in their costs.

Summing up the results for young people under 18 of both sexes it does appear that, on balance, in the recent past their share of total employment has fallen both because the cost of their labour has risen relative to adults and because they are particularly affected by falls in employment. The size of these effects are difficult to determine because of problems with the data. However, the evidence suggests that the effect, especially of the increasing relative labour costs, is large. This is, perhaps, not surprising as over the period a combination of the lowering of the age at which adult rates of pay were paid and *ROSLA* has meant that the period on non-adult rates of pay was drastically shortened. At the turn of the 1970s a young man leaving school at the statutory minimum leaving age (15) would have up to 6 or 7 years' labour market experience before he received adult rates and a young woman generally up to three years'. By 1975 (and certainly by 1980), school leavers at 16 would in the (increasingly general) case where adult rates were paid at 18 have a maximum of two years' experience. Not only that but the rate of non-adult pay relative to adult pay also increased substantially.

APPENDIX A   EARNINGS STATISTICS

Table 3 A1   Earnings relativities by age and sex (%), average gross weekly earnings at October each year, all industries and services covered by the enquiry

	Boys[a] to men[a]	Girls[a] to men[a]	Boys[a] to women[a]	Girls[a] to women[a]	Girls[a] to boys[a]
Year					
	Industry groups according to the 1948 SIC				
1948	42.6	35.8	79.2	66.6	84.1
49	42.1	36.2	76.5	65.8	86.0
1950	42.4	35.5	77.4	64.9	83.8
51	41.6	34.9	76.9	64.5	83.8
52	42.0	34.0	77.9	63.2	81.1
53	41.7	34.3	77.1	63.4	82.3
54	41.9	34.0	79.1	64.2	81.1
55	42.2	33.9	81.6	65.6	80.4
56	43.0	34.2	83.0	66.0	79.5
57	43.1	33.9	83.5	65.6	78.6
58	43.6	33.8	83.5	64.7	77.5
59	43.4	33.4	83.5	64.2	76.9
	Industry groups according to the 1958 SIC				
59	43.3	33.5	83.4	64.5	77.3
1960	44.7	33.3	87.6	65.3	74.5
61	44.9	33.2	89.2	66.0	74.0
62	44.7	32.8	88.1	64.7	73.4
63	44.4	32.6	88.4	64.9	73.4
64	45.1	33.0	91.1	66.6	73.1
65	45.9	33.1	93.7	67.5	72.0
66	47.2	33.4	95.2	67.4	70.8
67	47.2	32.7	95.5	66.3	69.4
68	46.6	32.9	94.9	67.0	70.6
69	46.9	32.4	96.2	66.4	69.0
	Industry groups according to the 1968 SIC				
69	46.9	32.5	96.2	66.6	69.2
1970	47.6	33.6	95.4	67.3	70.6
71	48.4	33.3	94.7	65.1	68.7
72	49.0	32.8	95.9	64.3	67.0
73	51.4	37.0	99.3	71.5	72.0
74	53.5	39.5	96.3	71.2	74.0
75	55.5	38.7	96.8	67.4	69.6

Table 3 A1 cont.

76	56.7	40.0	93.4	65.7	70.4
77	56.7	40.8	93.2	67.1	72.0
78	56.3	39.7	93.9	66.3	70.6
79	56.2	40.4	93.6	67.3	71.9

Notes: 'Men' = males 21 years and over: full-time manual workers.
'Women' = females 18 years and over: full-time manual workers.
'Boys' = youths and boys under 21 years: full-time manual workers.
'Girls' = girls under 18 years: full-time manual workers.
Source: October Enquiry into the earnings and hours of manual workers.

Table 3 A2 Average gross weekly earnings[a] of full-time employees under 21 as % of the corresponding figure for males aged 21 and over (at April each year).

	Males under 21[b]	Females under 21[b]	Males 18–20[b]	Females 18–20[b]	Males under 18[b]	Females under 18[b]
All employees						
1970	47.1					28.0
71	45.3					28.6
72	44.1					28.1
73	46.1	35.8	53.7	40.1	32.9	28.4
74	52.6	39.8	60.2	43.6	38.2	32.9
75	54.8	43.6	62.0	47.0	40.6	36.7
76	53.9	44.9	60.6	48.5	39.2	36.2
77	54.7	45.9	60.8	49.6	40.3	37.0
78	54.7	44.8	61.4	48.4	40.0	35.7
79	54.4	44.6	61.0	48.0	39.7	36.1
1980	54.0	44.7	60.8	48.1	38.8	36.1
81	52.9	45.2	58.7	48.3	38.8	36.0
82	53.3	44.5	57.6	47.0	38.7	34.9
83	52.4	44.2	56.7	46.7	36.4	33.3
84	50.9	42.9	55.6	45.3	34.9	32.3
Manual employees						
1970						
71	51.7					33.7
72	50.3					32.2
73	52.2	39.9	63.0	45.9	37.0	33.3
74	60.1	46.1	70.4	50.9	42.7	38.8
75	62.1	48.5	71.8	51.4	45.2	43.1
76	61.1	50.1	69.9	54.7	44.2	41.5
77	61.5	49.5	69.8	54.4	45.2	41.5
78	61.8	49.3	70.6	54.2	44.7	41.4
79	61.1	49.0	69.9	53.2	44.1	41.7
1980	61.2	49.6	70.4	53.8	43.5	41.0
81	61.5	49.9	69.2	53.9	45.0	40.4
82	62.3	48.6	67.9	51.5	45.2	39.7
83	62.0	49.2	67.8	52.2	43.0	40.0
84	60.3	47.9	66.5	51.4	40.6	38.0
Non-manual employees						
1970						
71	36.3					23.5

Table 3 A2 cont.

72	35.2					22.8
73	36.6	31.0	40.1	34.5	26.0	23.7
74	41.0	34.2	44.9	37.3	30.1	27.9
75	44.3	38.6	48.0	41.8	33.8	31.7
76	43.9	39.2	48.0	42.3	31.4	31.5
77	45.4	40.8	48.8	43.9	33.4	32.4
78	45.3	39.6	49.1	42.6	33.3	30.9
79	45.2	39.8	48.8	42.8	33.5	31.5
1980	45.4	39.4	49.2	42.4	33.6	31.4
81	44.5	39.4	47.9	41.9	32.4	31.3
82	44.9	39.1	47.5	41.1	32.1	30.3
83	43.5	38.5	46.1	40.6	30.2	28.2
84	42.8	37.4	45.6	39.2	30.5	27.6

Notes: [a] Excluding those whose pay was affected by absence.
          [b] For 1974 and later years age was measured in the survey in terms
               of completed years at 1 January. For 1973 and earlier years age
               was measured in terms of completed years at the time of the
               survey.
Source: NES.

Table 3 A3 Average gross weekly earnings[a] of full-time employees under 21 as % of the corresponding figure for females aged 18 and over (at April each year)

	Males under 21[b]	Females under 21[b]	Males 18–20[b]	Females 18–20[b]	Males under 18[b]	Females under 18[b]
All employees						
1970	86.4					51.2
71	81.4					51.4
72	79.0					50.2
73	83.5	64.9	97.4	72.7	59.7	51.5
74	93.3	70.6	106.7	77.3	67.7	58.4
75	89.0	70.9	100.8	76.5	66.0	59.6
76	83.8	69.7	94.2	75.3	60.8	56.3
77	84.3	70.8	93.7	76.5	62.2	57.1
78	86.3	70.7	97.0	76.4	63.1	56.4
79	87.6	71.7	98.3	77.3	64.0	58.1
1980	85.3	70.6	96.1	76.0	61.3	57.1
81	81.3	69.5	90.2	74.2	59.6	55.4
82	83.2	69.5	89.9	73.3	60.4	54.4
83	80.6	68.0	87.3	71.9	56.1	51.2
84	79.4	66.9	86.8	70.7	54.4	50.3
Manual employees						
1970						
71	99.3					64.7
72	96.5					63.7
73	101.0	77.2	121.8	88.8	71.6	64.5
74	111.0	85.2	130.1	94.1	78.8	71.6
75	107.8	84.1	124.6	89.1	78.5	74.8
76	101.0	82.7	115.5	90.4	73.1	68.5
77	100.7	81.0	114.2	89.0	73.9	68.0
78	101.0	80.6	115.4	88.5	73.1	67.6
79	103.1	82.6	117.8	89.7	74.3	70.3
1980	100.6	81.5	115.6	88.4	71.5	67.5
81	100.7	81.6	113.3	88.2	73.7	66.0
82	104.0	81.1	113.4	86.0	75.5	66.3
83	101.3	80.3	110.8	85.2	70.2	65.3
84	100.2	79.7	110.6	85.4	67.6	63.3
Non-manual employees						
1970						
71	71.7					46.5

Table 3 A3 cont.

72	68.9					44.6
73	71.3	60.3	78.1	67.2	50.6	46.2
74	78.0	65.0	85.3	71.0	57.3	53.1
75	76.5	66.7	82.8	72.2	58.3	54.8
76	73.4	65.6	80.3	70.7	52.5	52.7
77	75.1	67.5	80.7	72.5	55.2	53.5
78	77.2	67.5	83.6	72.6	56.7	52.6
79	77.4	68.2	83.5	73.3	57.4	53.9
1980	77.5	67.4	84.0	72.4	57.4	53.7
81	75.0	66.5	80.8	70.7	54.6	52.8
82	76.5	66.7	81.0	70.2	54.7	51.7
83	73.6	65.2	78.1	68.7	51.2	47.7
84	73.6	64.3	78.4	67.5	52.4	47.4

Notes: [a] Excluding those whose pay was affected by absence
[b] For 1974 and later years age was measured in the survey in terms of completed years at 1 January. For 1973 and earlier years age was measured in terms of completed years at the time of the survey.

Source: NES.

Table 3 A4   Percentage of adult rates paid to young workers in a sample of private sector national agreements (males 1966–82)

Year	Age		
	15 Year Old	*17 Year Old*	*18 Year Old*
1966	42.4	48.9	57.4
67	40.9	47.2	55.4
68	41.8	48.1	56.5
69	42.2	48.1	59.2
1970	43.6	49.9	62.8
71	45.7	52.5	62.8
72	44.2	50.8	60.7
73	45.8	51.0	61.3
74	–	56.1	65.7
75	–	57.0	67.4
76	–	56.5	66.7
77	–	58.3	68.6
78	–	56.4	66.8
79	–	60.2	70.8
1980	–	60.0	70.9
81	–	60.3	71.7
82	–	60.2	71.7

Source: Department of Employment, Economic and Social Division, based on 'Time Rates of Wages and Hours of Work'.

Table 3 A5 Employment of young people under 18
a Males under 18 for period 1969–81
b Females under 18 for period 1971–81

Equation no.	Dependent variable	Constant	Cyc	Male RLC
a **Males**				
D2	dLog(NYM/NM)	+0.01	−0.02	−2.71**
		(1.5)	(−0.6)	(−4.7)
D2a	dLog(NYM/NT)	+0.01	−0.01	−2.90**
		(0.9)	(−0.5)	(−5.1)
D3	dLog(NYM)	+0.01	−0.90*	−2.52**
		(0.9)	(−2.3)	(−3.8)
D4^{c1}	d(NYM/NM)	+0.00	−0.00	+0.03**
		(0.9)	(−0.4)	(4.3)
D4a^{c1}	d(NYM/NT)	+0.00	−0.00	+0.02**
		(0.5)	(−0.3)	(4.6)
D5^{c2}	d(NYM)	+0.00	+0.00	+0.02**
		(0.5)	(0.1)	(4.5)
D6	dLog(UYM)	−0.01	+1.00**	+10.10*
		(−0.1)	(3.7)	(2.3)
b **Females**				
D2	dLog(NYF/NF)	−0.01	+0.05	−2.10*
		(−0.3)	(0.3)	(−2.2)
D2a	dLog(NYF/NT)	+0.00	+0.05	−2.00*
		(0.0)	(0.3)	(−2.2)
D3	dLog(NYF)	+0.00	−0.05	−1.88*
		(0.1)	(−0.3)	(−2.2)
D4^{c1}	d(NYF/NF)	−0.00	+0.00	+0.03*
		(−0.6)	(0.4)	(2.1)
D4a^{c1}	d(NYF/NT)	−0.00	+0.00	+0.01*
		(−0.3)	(0.4)	(2.2)
D5^{c2}	d(NYF)	−0.00	+0.00	+0.01*
		(−0.2)	(0.0)	(2.1)
D6	dLog(UYF)	+0.02	+0.55	+5.21
		(0.2)	(0.7)	(1.4)

Source:　Wells (1983)

Notes:

C1, C2　In order to obtain comparable formulations to those in Abowd *et al.*
(1981), all the independent variables have been divided by the average labour
costs of full-time young people of that sex under 18 and multiplied by: (i) the
average labour costs of all full-time workers of both sexes (in equations
marked *C1*) and (ii) total labour costs of all full-time workers of both sexes (in
equations marked *C2*).

Female RLC	ROSLA	Residual sum of squares	DW	$\bar{R}^2$
−1.39* (−2.5)	−0.06 (−1.4)	0.0042	2.09	0.86
−1.45** (−2.6)	−0.05 (−1.3)	0.0042	2.04	0.87
−1.36* (−2.1)	−0.08 (−1.5)	0.0056	1.41	0.81
+0.03** (2.6)	−0.00 (−1.1)	0.0000	1.86	0.85
+0.02* (2.3)	−0.00 (−1.0)	0.0000	1.82	0.86
+0.02* (2.3)	−0.00 (−0.9)	827.87	1.96	0.84
+2.83 (0.7)	−0.75* (−2.2)	0.2557	2.33	0.76
+2.54 (1.3)	−0.20 (−1.1)	0.0349	2.04	0.31
+2.53 (1.4)	−0.20 (−1.2)	0.0317	2.06	0.31
+2.08 (1.2)	−0.18 (−1.2)	4077.64	1.74	0.33
−0.04 (−1.3)	−0.00 (−1.2)	0.0001	1.78	0.43
−0.02 (−1.4)	−0.00 (−1.2)	0.0000	1.86	0.42
−0.02 (−1.4)	−0.00 (−1.4)	435.06	1.80	0.34
−12.34 (−1.6)	+0.31 (0.5)	0.5403	1.94	0.57

All independent variables except *ROSLA* and the constant are first differences of natural logarithms. All dependent variables are in first differences (*d*) with some also in natural logarithms (Log). The figures in brackets are *t* statistics.

Independent Variables

CYC   A cyclical variable (the unemployment rate of males excluding school leavers)

RLC   Relative labour costs

In the equations for young males, this is the labour costs of full-time young males under 21 as a proportion of: (i) the labour costs of full time males 21 and over (male *RLC*); (ii) the labour costs of full-time females of all ages (female *RLC*). In the equation for young females, this is the labour costs of full-time young females as a proportion of: (i) the labour costs of full-time males of all ages (male *RLC*); (ii) the labour costs of full-time females aged 18 and over (female *RLC*).

ROSLA   A dummy to capture the effect of the raising of the school leaving age to 16 in September 1972: it is 1 in 1973, 0 elsewhere.

Dependent Variables

N   Employees in employment

U   Unemployment rate

Subscripts M = Male
F = Female
T = Total $(M + F)$
Y = Young (under 18)

APPENDIX B   DATA AND ABBREVIATIONS

N   Employees in employment (000): mid-year GB

The all age count for the period 1959–75 was taken from the estimates of employees in employment on a continuous basis (see *Department of Employment Gazette*, 1975). Thereafter the estimates were based on the censuses of employment (at the time of estimation the 1978 Census was the latest available). For the period before 1959 the figures from the NI card count were adjusted by a grossing factor equal to the ratio of the 1959 estimate of employment on the continuous basis to the estimate from the NI card count.

N_i Employees in employment (000) by age/sex: mid-year GB

The estimated proportions of total employees in employment in any age/sex group were applied to the total number of employees in employment. The proportions were derived until 1972 from the 1 per cent NI card count of employees (employees in employment plus the unemployed). From 1975 the estimates were derived from the biennial labour force survey, with the intervening years calculated as an average of the two surrounding years. The figures for 1973 and 1973 were derived from a number of sources.

u_i Unemployment (000) (mid-year GB (adjusted)) by age/sex

The mid-year count was held in June until 1961, July thereafter. Partly to overcome this problem and partly to avoid school leaver seasonality problems the mid-year estimate of school leavers was replaced by the annual average.

ux_i Unemployment (000) (mid-year GB (adjusted)) by age/sex excluding school leavers

U_i Unemployment rate (mid-year GB (adjusted)) by age/sex (per cent)

Defined as $100*(u_i/N + u_i)$

UX_i Unemployment rate excluding school leavers (mid-year GB (adjusted)) by age/sex (per cent)

Defined as $100*(ux_i/N + ux_i)$

POP_i Population of working age (000) (mid-year GB) by age/sex

Defined as between ages 15 and 64 for males (15–59 for females) until 1972; 16–64 (16–59) thereafter.

$PPOP_i$ Potential population of working age (000) (mid-year GB) by age/sex

Defined as $POP_i - ED_i - AFi$ where ED_i is the number in post-compulsory education by age/sex; AF_i is the number in the Armed Forces (including National Servicemen (by age/sex))

Subscript i Y = Young M = Male T = Total
A = Adult F = Female

The subscripts M and F can be used either singly to refer to all people of that sex or together with subscripts from A/Y to denote a finer breakdown. For example, AM refers to adult males. What age group is being considered will be indicated in the text.

Earnings/ labour costs variables   All of the variables are measured in pounds and for young males refer to under 21, young females to under 18, adult males 21 and over, adult females 18 and over. The basis for the earnings/labour costs data is the October Earnings Survey which considers the gross average weekly (and hourly) average earnings of manual workers in Index of Production and certain other industries. The figures in this chapter refer to full-time workers. Between 1948 and 1979 the earnings figures are taken directly from the OES but, for 1980–1 they are estimated by comparison with figures for equivalent manual age/sex groups in the NES.

$WAGE_i$ Real disposable income (£) by age/sex

Defined as $GW(1 - TAX)/P$ where GW is the gross average weekly earnings; TAX is the average rate of tax and National Insurance paid by someone earning GW pounds per week. P is the retail price index.

RW   Relative weekly earnings (per cent)

Defined as $100* GW_Y/GW_A$ where Y and A refer to the young and adult age groups respectively. For example, RW_{YMAF} is the relativity between young males (under 21) and adult females (18 and over).

RLC   Relative weekly labour costs (per cent)

Defined as $100* (GW_Y)1 + N1R_Y)(/GW_A)1 + NIRA))$ where NIR is the employers' National Insurance contribution (and surcharge) for an employee earning GW pounds per week.

ROSLA Dummy variable to reflect effect of raising of the school leaving age to 16 in 1972.

In the first difference equation this is defined as 1 in 1973, 0 elsewhere.

Notes

1. More precisely, the effect for young males is larger than for the population as a whole.
2. The reported equations are actually on a slightly different basis as equation (3.1) considers total employment of both sexes whereas equation (3.2) considers male unemployment only. However, the result still stands when the employment equation is run using male rather than total employment.
3. It should be noted that the uncertainty caused by the data problems affects all of the results, not just those concerning relative labour costs. The cyclical effects are thus also problematical.

4 Relative Wages and the Youth Labour Market

P. N. Junankar and A. J. Neale[1]

4.1 INTRODUCTION

The dramatic rise of youth unemployment in recent years in most OECD countries has led to the introduction of various policies targetted at youths. Although there are competing explanations of this phenomenon (as of aggregate unemployment), the British government (in particular) has been seduced by the explanation that the growth in youth unemployment is due to a rise in the relative wages of youths. The Prime Minister stated in Parliament (Hansard 27 July 1981, Cols 835–6) '[b]ecause the wages of young people are often too high in relation to those of experienced adults, employers cannot afford to take them on'. The Department of Employment produced a research paper (Wells, 1983) allegedly providing econometric evidence for this view. *The Times* gave this favourable publicity, and entitled an article 'Pay Cuts Would Create Jobs for Young People' (20 December 1983). In this chapter we review some of the evidence on the relationship between relative wages and youth (un)-employment in Great Britain and then estimate a disequilibrium model of the youth labour market.

The rapid growth of youth unemployment has been viewed with concern by the young, by their parents, by economists and by politicians. Unemployment in the early years of a potential working life may have permanent 'scarring' effects, and affect the future prospects of employment and/or the future earnings profiles.[2] In addition, there is concern that youth unemployment may have harmful social consequences in terms of violence and crime.[3] This has led to massive government intervention (by an allegedly *laissez-faire* government) in this market by the introduction of various schemes like the Youth Opportunities Programme (YOP), Youth Training Scheme (YTS), Young Workers' Scheme (YWS), etc.[4] It is worth noting that young people on these schemes are not treated as being unemployed (or employed). It is, therefore, a (politically) convenient method of lowering the monthly count of the unemployed: it is a method of 'massaging the unemployment figures'.

Most explanations of the rise in youth unemployment stress the peculiarities of this particular sub-group of the labour market. If employers believed that youth and adult labour was homogeneous, youth labour would be hired in preference to adult (since youth wages are lower). For several reasons, employers have a demand for youth labour as distinct from adult labour: typically because young people are inexperienced and need training. Similarly, youth labour supply is clearly different from adult labour supply. Employers could substitute adult for youth labour on the demand side, while youths supplying labour have an option of supplying labour, remaining in education, or not participating in the labour market at all. It has been argued that the youth labour market is a 'secondary' labour market:[5] workers are hired on short-term contracts with low wages and poor working conditions, promotion prospects are limited, there is a large pool of new employees available, etc. Changes in aggregate demand lead firms to use this secondary labour market as a buffer: it is easier to hire and fire in this labour market. Given the higher turnover of young people, employers can also rely on natural wastage to tide them over difficult times.

An alternative view of the labour market (which has some common elements with the 'secondary' or 'dual' labour market hypothesis) explains the growth of youth unemployment in terms of the recession (a fall in aggregate demand), with employers preferring experienced adult workers and firing on the basis of last-in-first-out (LIFO) inexperienced youths. The existence of employment protection legislation also makes it more expensive to fire older workers (employees with longer service). However, LIFO is an agreed industrial relations procedure which predates employment protection legislation. Another explanation is in terms of structural change in the economy, leading to a fall in production in youth-intensive industries. A factor emphasised by neoclassical economists is that a rise in the relative wages of youths leads to a decrease in demand (and an increase in supply) for them, hence increasing unemployment. Allied to this is an argument (based on a *competitive* model) that the imposition (or raising) of minimum wages has led to a decrease in demand for youths. From the supply side, the increase in youth unemployment is explained by a demographic bulge in this age group, by youths preferring to live on (allegedly generous) social security benefits, or by youths preferring to hustle in the informal economy rather than accept 'legitimate' but poorly-paid work. Finally, for various reasons youths have higher turnover and quit rate, so that in a slack market they would have higher unemployment rates. In their earlier years in the labour market they spend time 'sampling' jobs and searching for better paid (or more satisfying) jobs. It is worth noting that youths are a large proportion of the total flow of people who are looking for work, although they are a relatively small proportion of the stock of employment.

The remainder of this chapter is structured as follows: section 4.2 discusses alternative methods of modelling youth (un)employment and reviews the evidence from British time-series studies. Section 4.3 evaluates Wells (1983). Section 4.4 provides some results using a disequilibrium estimation method, and Section 4.5 concludes the paper. To anticipate our conclusions, we find that the youth labour market is best described by a disequilibrium model, that the growth of youth unemployment is primarily due to the recession, and that the effects of relative wages are relatively small.

4.2 ECONOMETRIC MODELLING AND EVIDENCE

In this section we review the alternative methods of modelling the youth labour market using British time-series data. Before we turn to the econometric modelling, let us briefly look at the data sources. The data on employment by age are readily available (on an annual basis for June–July) until 1972 and were obtained from the National Insurance (NI) card count. However, after the abolition of NI cards this vital source of data was destroyed. After 1972 data can be obtained from the biennial (now annual) Labour Force Surveys (LFS) which began in 1973 (although for various reasons the first 'reasonable' estimates are available in 1975). Data on employment by age are also available (on an annual basis) from the General Household Survey from 1971. However, as this is a relatively small sample the numbers of young people in it are very small and may not be very good indicators of youth employment overall. In other words, we do not have a reliable annual time-series of employment of young people.

The data on youth unemployment are (relatively speaking) good. They are available on a quarterly and annual basis, although various legislative changes make comparisons over time difficult. In particular, the ending of National Service (conscription) in 1959, the raising of the school leaving age (ROSLA) in 1972, various changes in regulations about how soon after leaving school the young could register as unemployed, and in recent years various government schemes like the YOP and YTS make comparisons over time hazardous. A key problem with this data series is that it understates the true level of youth unemployment, as it includes only those young people who *register*, and after 1982 only those in receipt of benefits.[6] There is much evidence from surveys that many young people do not register as unemployed (see, for example, Roberts *et al.*, 1981 and Lynch, 1985). Although the data on the *numbers* unemployed are readily available, the data on percentage *rates* of unemployment are based on *estimates* of employment by age.

The data on youth earnings – a key variable (especially) for neo-classical economists – are fairly limited. The main source until 1979 for these data were the (annual) October Earnings Enquiry carried out by the Department of Employment. These provide information on earnings for males under 21, and 21 and over, and for females under 18, and 18 and over. The October Earnings Enquiry is a survey of establishments in the UK with more than 10 employees and covers *manual* workers in manufacturing, mining and quarrying (except coal mining), construction, gas, electricity and water, transport and communication (except railways and sea transport), certain miscellaneous services and public administration. To the extent that the young work in small establishments, non-manual occupations, and the services sector (in particular) these earnings data are misleading. In general, these data are unrepresentative for young females and as the industrial sector has declined, the data are becoming less and less representative of young male employees as well. Since 1970 (on an annual basis) a rich source of earnings data are the New Earnings Survey (NES). This survey is carried out in April of *individual employees* in *Great Britain* in all occupations/establishments/industries. In 1974–5 the sampling frame changed to include only employees in the PAYE system, thereby excluding low-income (and hence often young) people. However the advantage of the NES data is that it has a more comprehensive coverage, as well as giving a finer breakdown of earnings (for example, under 18s for males and females as well as under 21s for males, etc.). However, the time series is relatively short.

To summarise, the different data series have different coverage (geographical, industrial, age, etc.), are collected at different months in the year, and are not available on a *consistent* basis for the whole post-war period. It is important to keep in mind this problem of data limitation when we review some of the conflicting evidence.

Let us now turn to the formal (econometric) modelling of the youth labour market and a review of British time-series evidence. There are three different approaches:

1. Unemployment functions
2. Employment functions
3. Labour demand and supply functions:
   (i) Equilibrium
   (ii) Disequilibrium.

For the purposes of this chapter we shall concentrate our attention on one research study which 'typifies' each approach.

Unemployment Functions

A common approach is to estimate youth unemployment *stock* (either as *numbers* unemployed or as an unemployment *rate*) as a function of variables which are selected on a more or less *ad hoc* basis. Any variable which affects youth labour demand or supply is introduced in the unemployment function: it is a quasi-reduced form.[7] Examples of this approach are Collier (1978), Makeham (1980), Layard (1982), Lynch and Richardson (1982) and OECD (1980). This approach can be formalised as follows.[8]

$$L^D = L^D(Z_1) \tag{4.1}$$
$$L^S = L^S(Z_2) \tag{4.2}$$
$$U = L^S - L^D = L^S(Z_2) - L^D(Z_1) \tag{4.3}$$
$$U = f(Z_1, Z_2) \tag{4.4}$$

where:

L^D and L^S are labour demand and supply, U is unemployment and Z_1 and Z_2 are vectors of (allegedly) exogenous variables (a common element in Z_1 and Z_2 may be wage rates).

In this approach it is assumed that there is always an excess labour supply and that Z_1 and Z_2 are exogenous variables. Implicitly it is assumed that wage rates are exogenous and do not adjust (at least in that period) to clear the labour market – i.e., they are predetermined. In addition, it is implicitly assumed that the 'min' condition applies – that is, employment equals the minimum of L^D, L^S which by assumption is always L^D. (Note that if equations (4.1) and (4.2) were in logs, equations (4.3) and (4.4) could be treated as unemployment *rates*.)

Equation (4.4) is usually estimated in linear or log-linear form after adding a white noise random error term.

If the demand and supply functions are derived from an optimisation process then the components of the vectors Z_1 and Z_2 are determined by the precise specification of the maximand and the constraints. For example, if the demand function is derived from a cost-minimising model (subject to an exogenous output level, and input prices) then Z_1 would contain the output level and relative input prices. In a profit-maximising model of a competitive firm output is endogenous and would be *excluded* from Z_1. If the supply function was derived from utility maximisation subject to exogenous wage rates and unemployment benefits, then the supply function would contain these variables. However, as most of the work using unemployment functions does not set out a formal model the variables included in equation (4.4) are purely *ad hoc*. In most cases the unemployment function is estimated with some index of aggregate demand (often the male unemployment rate or vacancies), a relative (youths to adults) earnings or labour cost variable, a potential population variable (as an index of labour supply), and assorted variables like replacement ratios (benefit–income ratios), dummies to capture legislative or other changes, etc. Note that if we derive equation (4.4) from the underlying demand and supply equations we should have unemployment depend on relative labour costs (from the demand side) *and* the *level* of youth wages (from the supply side).

A general finding of this genre of studies is that aggregate demand is an important determinant of youth unemployment – see Makeham (1980), Layard (1982), Lynch and Richardson (1982), OECD (1980), Wells (1983). In contrast, the relative wages (or earnings, or labour costs including national insurance) variable has a very mixed outcome. Makeham (1980)[9] using annual data (1959–76) and the OECD (1980) using annual data (1959–79) find no significant effect of relative wage costs. However, Layard (1982) using annual data (1959–76), Wells (1983) (using annual data 1969–81 for males and 1971–81 for females) and Lynch and Richardson (1982) using annual data (1950–78) find significant (or almost significant) effects of relative wage costs.

Let us take the Lynch and Richardson (1982) research as 'typifying' this approach. They estimate an equation for the *proportion* of the *numbers* of young male (female) unemployed to the *numbers* of total unemployed males (females). The young are defined as 'aged less than 20 years' (p. 371). (It is worth noting that others have often estimated equations with the dependent variable as the *level* of the young unemployed.) The independent variables they tried out in their equations were an index of 'general business conditions' (which they proxied by the male unemployment rate and by total vacancies),[10] employment costs of young workers relative to adults (implicitly ignoring other input costs), a measure of supply of young workers, an index of demand conditions in 'youth intensive' industries, a replacement ratio, and a dummy. The equations were estimated in log-linear form using a Cochrane–Orcutt estimation method for males and females using the January (July) annual time series from 1950–78. The results for the January equations are reported, although they state that similar results were obtained for the July data. It is curious that the data were not pooled (that is, biannual data) as most variables (except the relative employment costs) are available on (even) a quarterly basis. The main findings are that for males the aggregate demand *indices* are statistically significant, but that the replacement ratio and the supply of young workers variables are *not* significant. The employment cost variable (lagged one period) is not significant ($t = 0.74$) when using the male unemployment rate as an index of aggregate demand. However, when vacancies are used instead of the male unemployment rate, the relative employment cost variable increases in significance ($t = 1.98$), but is still poorly determined. For females the results are similar except that relative employment costs are significant (whichever aggregate demand index is used), as are aggregate demand, labour supply, and the youth-intensive industry index. Overall these results are 'better', but there is evidence of structural instability in 1979–80 (unlike for males) which they explain in terms of changes in NI legislation which increased registration of females. However, they neglect the possible impact of special employment measures.

The main conclusions to be derived from these studies are that the estimated equations are very sensitive to the exact dates of the sample data and to the inclusion (or exclusion) of variables. However, in all studies aggregate demand is a significant variable while relative wages (costs) are significant only in some studies. Overall, these results are a useful step in formulating a rigorous model of the youth labour market but the results should be treated with caution.

Employment Functions

Following in the footsteps of Brechling (1965), employment is postulated to adjust slowly towards an equilibrium stock due to increasing marginal costs of adjustment. The equilibrium employment stock is usually derived from a cost-minimising model and hence depends on output and relative input prices.[11] In this model labour is treated as a quasi-fixed input with convex costs of adjusting labour stock. Note that in a certain world if we did not have *increasing* marginal costs of adjustment we would have a 'bang bang' solution: firms would adjust instantaneously. With uncertainty firms may respond slowly to exogenous changes in demand to 'wait and see' if the changes are 'permanent'.

Hutchinson, Barr and Drobny (1984) follow this approach in their investigation of the male youth labour market. They explicitly assume (p. 188) that there is disequilibrium (excess labour supply) in this market (in their estimation period, 1952–72), with employers always on their demand functions. Assuming cost-minimising firms, optimal employment stock is determined by the exogenous output level and the wage costs of male youths relative to other groups, and a quadratic time trend to proxy (exogenous) capital stock growth. They write

$$L_y^* = g(Q, t, t^2, W_y/W_1, W_y/W_2, \ldots W_y/W_n) \tag{4.5}$$

where:

L_y^* is the demand for male youths, Q is output, $t,\ t^2$ a quadratic time trend and W_y/W_i are the wages of male youths relative to male adults, female adults, etc.

A partial adjustment equation where actual employment L_y adjusts slowly is postulated:

$$L_y(t) - L_y(t-1) = a(L_y^*(t) - L_y(t-1)) \tag{4.6}$$

The model (substituting equation (4.5) in equation (4.6)) is estimated in log-linear form on annual data (1952–72). The authors follow recent econometric methodology to find an appropriate dynamic specification. The results (using autoregressive least squares) are robust (for that period) and suggests that youth labour is a *substitute* for female labour. They find that the relative labour cost elasticities are significant and relatively large. The output elasticity is greater then (but not significantly different from) unity, which supports the view that youths suffer proportionately more in cyclical downturns.

Unlike much of the work on young people, the Hutchinson *et al.* research is a careful piece of systematic and rigorous econometric modelling. However, not too much weight should be put on these results for four reasons:

1. The data are from an early period prior to changes in the age of majority (which happened towards the end of their sample), the introduction of various government policies aimed at the youth labour market, etc. The results may, therefore, be misleading for the present time.

2. At least part of the sample period is widely believed to be a period of excess demand in the labour market. As such, they may be observing points on a supply function (assuming a 'min' condition) – so that, for example, the finding of complementarity with adult males may be misleading. On the other hand, if this was a period of equilibrium they may have estimated a 'mongrel' relationship.

3. Strictly speaking, equation (4.5) is one of a system of equations with similar equations for young females, adult males, and adult females. Similarly, equation (4.6) should be specified with a matrix of adjustment coefficients so that the adjustment of *one* input depends on deviations from optimal levels of *all* inputs (*à la* Nadiri and Rosen, 1969).

4. As other input prices are excluded the estimated parameters may be biased. However, most other research in this field also ignores other input prices.

Labour Demand and Supply Equations

An obvious way to model the youth labour market is to set up demand and supply functions and to estimate the model by appropriate methods. In this framework we can either assume market clearing or not. In a market clearing model, if the identification conditions are satisfied, we can obtain the parameters of the structural equations. Some authors simply specify a demand equation assuming away problems of identification and treat wages as exogenous. This is analogous to the employment functions approach, except that it assumes complete adjustment within the unit period. For most non-market clearing models it is usually assumed that the quantities transacted are determined by the short side of the market: the so-called 'min' condition. These models can be estimated by either:

1. Assuming *a priori* which period is a demand- (supply)-constrained regime (see, for example, Merrilees and Wilson, 1979 and Wells, 1983).

or

2. Maximum likelihood estimation methods and letting the data determine the switching point(s) (see, for example, Rice, 1986 and section 4.4 below). The advantage of this method is that we use *all* the data to estimate the supply and demand functions, and that we can allow for more than one switch in regimes.

In an interesting study, Layard (1982) estimates a demand system (derived from a translog cost function) using data for manual workers in the British manufacturing sector (biannual 1949–69). Assuming that wages are exogenous and that the demand function is identified he estimates a system of equations for four inputs (boys, girls, adult males, adult females) using Zellner's (1962) SURE methods imposing symmetry restrictions.[12] Layard finds significant and negative own-price elasticities (girls do not have a significant coefficient) and finds that there is a high degree of substitutability between the different kinds of labour. In parentheses, it is worth noting that only half of the wage terms are significant at usual levels. These results should be treated with caution for four reasons:

1. The data are for manufacturing only. The evidence suggests that a large proportion of youths (especially females) work in the services sector. The data are very old and the manufacturing sector has declined substantially since 1969.
2. Although the use of duality theory is valid under the assumption of exogenous wages and cost-minimising behaviour, there is no guarantee that the stochastic equations are dual. There is some evidence of misspecification in the low Durbin–Watson statistics reported. Note also that he does not allow for any dynamics but assumes instantaneous adjustment.
3. If – as we shall argue – there was a disequilibrium in the labour market, it is invalid to estimate a labour demand system over his sample period. Many people would argue that the period 1949–69 was one of excess demand, and hence the observations may be coming from a supply function. Even in an equilibrium framework, the demand function may not be identified.
4. The estimated elasticities may be sensitive to the use of alternative cost shares. Many of the elasticities have relatively large standard

errors. With a high proportion of females working in the services sector, these elasticities cannot be extrapolated to the whole economy.

Overall, although this is an interesting application of duality theory to the labour market, it ignores the supply side of the market and the results should therefore be handled carefully.

We now turn to recent attempts which treat the youth labour market as being in disequilibrium. An important study using this approach was by Merrilees and Wilson (1979), using annual data from 1952 to 1978. The authors use *a priori* information to separate the sample into excess demand (supply-constrained) and excess supply (demand-constrained) regimes. In their study they evaluate the evidence on unemployment and vacancies and reports from the Youth Employment Service to determine that the period 1952–69 was a period of excess demand for males and the period after that one of excess supply. For females they consider the period 1952–71 as one of excess demand and the period 1972–8 as one of excess supply. They also use (Chow) stability tests to confirm their 'professional judgement'.[13] They find that an equilibrium model performs poorly compared to a disequilibrium model: the supply equation is identified for the earlier period and the demand equation for the latter period. Further, they find that real wages do not adjust to clear the market. Overall, the study is an important first step in estimating a disequilibrium model. Their results suggest an important role for aggregate demand, a significant relative wage coefficient, and a positive effect on employment of government policies.[14] As we shall argue in the next section, OLS estimation of this model with *a priori* sample separation leads to truncated error terms and hence inconsistent parameter estimates.

In a recent study Rice (1986) estimates a disequilibrium model using annual data for 1953–79.[15] Using the Maddala–Nelson (1974) approach she finds that for teenage males the period until 1972 was one of excess demand and after 1972 one of excess supply. For teenage females she finds the period until 1963 one of excess demand, excess supply until 1966, excess demand until 1970 and excess supply thereafter – in other words, multiple switches. She finds that – although relative wages are significant in explaining the rise in unemployment – the aggregate demand effects are quantitatively more important for males. This study is a significant contribution to the literature and is impressive in the way that she carried out a

sequence of hypothesis tests. Unfortunately, her data set ends just
before the sudden increase in unemployment.[16]

4.3   A CRITIQUE OF WELLS (1983)

In this section we evaluate Wells (1983) using his model as a vehicle
for investigating various aspects of the youth labour market. We
begin this section by an outline and evaluation of Wells's theoretical
model and a summary of his conclusions, followed by a battery of
tests of dynamic specification, error specification, stability tests, and
tests of robustness.

The Model

Following in the footsteps of Merrilees and Wilson (1979) (henceforth
M–W) Wells sets up in Chapter 7 a log-linear disequilibrium model.
Wells uses several different aspects of the labour market to justify the
view that relative wages are exogenously determined. However, he
does not attempt to formulate an econometric model to justify these
conclusions. His model is specified as follows:

$$\ell n \, L_i^S = a_0 + a_1 \ell n(PPOP)_i + a_2 \ell n(WAGE)_i + \varepsilon_1 \tag{4.7}$$

$$\ell n L_i^D = b_0 + b_1 \ell n(UX_M) + b_2 \ell n(RLC)_i + \varepsilon_2 \tag{4.8}$$

$$\ell n L_i = \min(\ell n L_i^S, \ell n L_i^D) \tag{4.9}$$

where:

L_i^S is labour supply of the ith group

L_i^D is labour demand of the ith group

$PPOP_i$ is the population of the relevant age group less the number in
          full-time education, *less* the number in the armed forces
          (including National Service)

UX_M is the male unemployment rate excluding school leavers

$WAGE_i$ is the real average weekly earnings *less* tax and national
          insurance of full-time manual workers of the relevant group
          (strictly speaking, a supply function should use a *wage rate*
          and not earnings)

RLC_i are the relative labour costs (gross earnings *plus* the
          employers' national insurance contribution) of youths
          (males under 21, females under 18) relative to adults.

This specification (estimated in first differences of logs) and the sample separation (1969 for male, 1971 for females) is taken directly from M–W.[17] In general he also includes a lagged relative labour cost term. The model is presumably based on usual neoclassical maximising theory. To justify an aggregate demand (cyclical) variable in the labour demand function we need to assume cost-minimising firms. This implies that the appropriate variable should be an index of production (for example, GDP or industrial output): the unemployment rate is a 'lazy indicator' of cyclical movements. Although the study emanates from the Department of Employment, there is no attempt to model the impact of various Special Employment Measures (SEM). There are, however, numerous references to SEMs to explain poor or conflicting results. A priori we would expect the SEMs to affect the demand for youths, perhaps by altering the elasticity with respect to RLC (since the SEMs are implicit subsidies to employers).

The labour supply function is specified in such a manner (in the definition of PPOP) that individuals have no choice to stay on in education or to join the armed forces.[18] There is also no attempt to study the impact of social security benefits on labour supply, and so the estimated wage elasticity may be biased.

One final comment on the specification: the model is estimated separately for males and females, for under 18 year olds, 18–19 years olds, and under 20 year olds. This assumes a heterogeneity of labour with employers demanding each kind of labour. Presumably the demand for 18–19 year olds will be derived from the previous employment of under 18 year olds, since they would have acquired relevant skills and experience. The unemployed 18–19 year olds would not be competing in the same market. It is worth stressing that the labour market is not an auction market where the entire labour supply is thrown on the market in each period: there are several existing contracts (implicit or explicit). This suggests that aggregation over the different age groups is a hypothesis to be tested. In particular we would expect the results of the under 18 year olds to be affected by the SEMs. This suggests that Wells's model needs to be respecified differently for different age groups.

The Data and Wells's Results

Wells uses annual data from 1953 to 1981 and estimates supply functions for 1953–69 (for males) and 1953–71 (for females) and demand functions for 1969–81 (males) and 1971–81 (females). In other words, his regressions are run on 17 and 13 observations for males and 19 and 11 for females which means there are very few degrees of freedom and the usual caveats for small samples apply. Perhaps more importantly, the data for the crucial dependent variables (employment by age groups) are obtained from the NI card count up to 1972 and after that by extrapolation (for 1973 and 1974) and interpolation (as an arithmetic mean) between the biennial Labour Force Surveys. In other words, *for the latter period approximately half the observations for the dependent variables were crudely interpolated data.* Similarly, a key (for Wells) right hand side variable – the wage or relative cost variable – was obtained from the October Enquiry until 1979 and *the data for 1980 and 1981 were estimates obtained from the New Earnings Survey.*[19] This was obtained by regressing the October Earnings data on the New Earnings Survey (NES) data from 1971–9. Again, this makes the estimates for the latter period shaky: no sensitivity analysis was carried out. The data are for mainly the industrial sector and exclude many services and hence are (in particular) inappropriate for females. (It is also worth noting that the employment data are mid-year estimates while the wages (costs) data are for October. We have centred these data and report our results later.)

Let us now summarise Wells's findings:

1. The disequilibrium approach (with *a priori* sample separation) is superior to the equilibrium approach
2. The results for the under 18 year olds allegedly support his model, while the results for 18–19 year olds and under 20 year olds are recognised to be inadequate
3. Labour supply is positively related to wages (earnings) and *PPOP*
4. Labour demand is negatively related to relative labour costs and to the unemployment rate which is an index of aggregate demand (the cyclical factor); however, the cyclical variable is not significant for females[20] – it is this result which has given much joy to *The Times* editorial writer (20 December 1983) and to the Thatcher government.

Before we provide a detailed critique it is worth noting that the only 'reasonable' results he obtains are for males under 18 years old. However, the wage variable is a relative wage of *under 21* to the 21 and over group. In general his Durbin–Watson statistics are in the indeterminate range which may suggest a misspecified model. Although Wells often treats the incidence of a structural break as supporting a (disequilibrium) switch point, it is worth stressing that this too could also reflect a misspecified model.

A Critique

Although we are sympathetic to the view that we should treat the youth labour market in terms of a disequilibrium model, we find that Wells's work is inadequate on several grounds. First, although he provides a plethora of results, he does not carry out any specification tests to compare alternative models. In particular, although he estimates numerous models (especially in Chapter 9) there are no tests provided which would show the superiority of one model over the others.[21] Second, there are no tests of dynamic specification of the model. On p. 71 he argues that some alternative lag structures were tried and 'if the explanatory power of the equation collapses with a different lag structure, it may cast suspicion on the results'. Again, this is an unusual approach. Third, there are no tests of the error specification implied by the first differencing of the equations. Finally, OLS estimation leads to inconsistent results when the sample is separated (because of truncated error distributions).

In our work we first replicated Wells's results, and then carried out various hypotheses tests:

1. Dynamic and error specification
2. Stability tests
3. Tests of robustness.

Dynamic and error specification

Wells estimates his model in terms of first differences of logarithms without any justification. To test his specification we carried out the following tests on the data for the sub-periods. Let:

$$y_t = a'_o + \Sigma a'_i X_{it} + u_t \qquad (4.10)$$

and

$$u_t = \rho u_{t-1} + \varepsilon_t \qquad (4.11)$$

where the ys and Xs are logged variables except one X variable which is a time trend. First differencing (4.10) gives:

$$\Delta y_t = a_o + \Sigma a_i \Delta X_{it} + \varepsilon_t \qquad (4.12)$$

which is the form of equation estimated by Wells. We could test the error specification by estimating equation (4.10) by autoregressive least squares and test the hypothesis $\rho = 1$. Another test of error specification is to use a Lagrange Multiplier (LM) test for residual autocorrelation in equation (4.12). We find that Wells's equations do fairly well on an LM test except for the female labour supply equations for the under 18s and the 18–19 year old groups. However, when we estimate equation (4.10) and test for $\rho = 1$ we find that we reject the hypotheses *in all cases* for males but accept the hypothesis for half the cases for females (case = age/demand/supply).[22]

A summary of these results is presented in Table 4.1.

A further test was to rewrite equation (4.12) as:

$$y_t = a_o + \lambda y_{t-1} + \Sigma a_i X_{it} + \Sigma \beta_i X_{it-1} + \varepsilon_t \qquad (4.13)$$

and test the restrictions: $\lambda = 1$ and $a_i = -\beta_i$ for all i. A likelihood ratio

Table 4.1   Test results

	Hypothesis	$\rho = 1$	U_i not auto-correlated	$\lambda = 1, a_i = -\beta_i$	Parameter stability*
Males					
Demand	< 18	Reject	Accept	Accept	Accept
equations	18–19	Reject	Accept	Accept	Accept
1969–81	< 20	Reject	Accept	Accept	Accept
Supply	< 18	Reject	Accept	Accept	Accept
equations	18–19	Reject	Accept	Reject	Accept
1953–69	< 20	Reject	Accept	Reject	Accept
Females					
Demand	< 18	Accept	Accept	Reject	Reject 1972
equations	18–19	Reject	Accept	Accept	Accept
1971–81	< 20	Reject	Accept	Accept	Accept
Supply	< 18	Accept	Reject	Accept	Accept
equations	18–19	Reject	Reject	Reject	Reject 1965
1953–71	< 20	Accept	Accept	Reject	Reject 1969
Rejection frequency (%)	75		17	42	25

Notes: All tested at 95% level.
*Equations estimated over the *whole* period, by Recursive least squares.

test rejected the restrictions for all the supply equations (the earlier period) except for the under 18s. For the demand equations (the latter period) the restrictions were rejected only for the females under 18 (see Table 4.1).

Overall these results provide only partial support for the dynamic specification adopted by Wells.

Stability tests

As mentioned earlier, tests of the parameter stability provide us with information about the robustness of the model and may also indicate switches in regimes. We used Brown, Durbin and Evans's (1975) recursive residuals Cusum Square test for this purpose.[23] Interestingly, this method suggests a significant break *only for females*. The significant breaks are for under 18 year old females at 1972 (demand equation), 18–19 year old females (supply equation) at 1965, and under 20 year old females (supply equation) at 1969. The absence of any obvious 'switch' point (especially for males) suggests that Wells's model may be inadequate to detect disequilibrium behaviour. This issue is discussed further in section 4.4 below.

Tests of robustness

In this sub-section we estimated Wells's model with an alternative definition of the cyclical variable and with alternative wage (cost) variables. We argued earlier that – if the labour demand function is derived from cost-minimising behaviour – an appropriate aggregate demand (cyclical) variable is an index of GDP (excluding North Sea Oil) and not the unemployment rate.

The results – with the difference of the log unemployment being replaced by the difference of the log of GDP (*less* oil, *MLH 104*) in Wells's demand equations – led to some changes. The significance of the relative labour cost terms (RLC, RLC_{t-1}) increased for males but decreased for females (see Table 4.2). In addition, the absolute value of the output elasticity increased with this specification, although still not significant. See Appendix Table 4.A1 for Wells's results with the unemployment rate.

In an earlier section we commented on the fact that while the employment data were for June, the wages (costs) data were for October. For consistency, we used a weighted average of the wages variable:

$$\bar{W}_t = 0.75 W_t + 0.25 W_{t-1}$$

Table 4.2   Wells's demand equations: tests for robustness

	Constant	Relative labour costs	Relative labour costs (*t*-1)	GDP	R^2	DW
Males 1969–81						
< 18	− 0.008 (0.58)	− 3.993 (4.54)	1.682 (1.99)	0.359 (0.81)	0.73	2.52
18–19	− 0.032 (1.55)	− 0.870 (0.63)	1.808 (1.35)	0.882 (1.26)	0.25	2.17
< 20	− 0.022 (1.68)	− 2.264 (2.62)	1.823 (2.20)	0.628 (1.45)	0.44	1.65
Females 1971–81						
< 18	− 0.060 (2.35)	− 0.781 (0.93)	− 0.938 (1.56)	0.562 (0.43)	0.36	0.69
18–19	− 0.007 (0.40)	− 0.118 (0.23)	0.004 (0.01)	0.303 (0.38)	0.02	1.41
< 20	− 0.031 (2.04)	− 0.472 (0.93)	− 0.414 (1.15)	0.430 (0.55)	0.27	0.54

Notes:
1. All variables are first differences of logs.
2. Absolute *t*-statistics in parentheses.
Overall, Wells's model is poorly specified and his results are not robust.
They should, therefore, not be used for any policy purposes.

Introducing this weighted average wages term in the labour supply equations leads to a decrease in the coefficients and an increase in its significance.[24] We then estimated the demand equations with a GDP index and with weighted relative labour costs. As before, the GDP index was not significant for any group but the weighted labour cost terms were significant only for males under 18.

As a further test of the sensitivity of Wells's results we estimated his labour demand equations with a relative labour cost variable for the under 18s to the 21 and over group for males (females) to correspond with the dependent variable (employment of under 18s). This relative labour cost variable was constructed from NES data (which we believe is more representative for the young) and then following Wells's procedure to obtain estimates for the pre-1970 (in some cases pre-1974) data.[25] It is interesting to note that these data series are very

Figure 4.1   Relative labour costs: males

different for males but very similar for females (see Figures 4.1 &
4.2).[26] For Wells, the male relative labour cost series is upward
trended (more or less) throughout the period, which picks up the
declining trend in employment since the 1960s. Using the NES data we
have a declining trend for males until the early 1970s, rising due to the
raising of school leaving age and then declining again (except for a
minor blip in 1979).

The results with our NES-based series (Table 4.3) suggest that
Wells's model breaks down completely for males with *no* significant
parameters, poor R^2s and very low DWs. The female equations,
although slightly better, suffer from problems of serial correlation.

Table 4.3 Alternative models of employment: A reworking of Wells's Tables 13 and 14 (dependent variables: employment males (females) under 18)

	Estimating Period	C	NES RLC	NES RLC(t-1)	CYC	R^2	DW
Males under 18	(1)	−0.0222 (1.10)	−0.4308 (0.48)	−0.5300 (0.54)	−0.0388 (0.76)	0.1264	0.6154
	(2)	−0.0396 (1.81)	0.0384 (0.09)	−0.0487 (0.12)	0.0332 (0.32)	0.0245	0.8080
	(3)	−0.0200 (1.69)	0.0231 (0.08)	−0.1012 (0.35)	−0.0249 (0.54)	0.0234	0.7225
Females under 18	(4)	0.0035 (0.25)	−0.0319 (0.04)	−1.3304 (1.73)	−0.0728 (1.19)	0.2692	0.6617
	(5)	−0.0557 (2.24)	−0.8236 (1.90)	−0.4324 (0.97)	0.0119 (0.12)	0.4254	0.6345
	(6)	−0.0150 (1.26)	−0.7632 (2.19)	−0.3315 (1.01)	−0.0692 (1.46)	0.2186	0.6253

	Estim- ating Period	C	NES RLC	NES RLC(t-1)	GDP	R^2	DW
Males under 18	(1)	-0.0434 (1.63)	-0.2661 (0.29)	-0.8858 (1.01)	0.0085 (0.81)	0.1316	0.4892
	(2)	-0.0334 (1.58)	0.0340 (0.07)	-0.0047 (0.01)	-0.0029 (0.29)	0.0229	0.8388
	(3)	-0.0244 (1.74)	0.0015 (0.00)	-0.1484 (0.53)	0.0013 (0.19)	0.0143	0.7021
Females under 18	(4)	-0.0079 (0.28)	0.6613 (1.02)	-0.9991 (1.18)	0.0008 (0.07)	0.2001	0.5462
	(5)	-0.0509 (2.34)	-0.8743 (2.15)	-0.5034 (1.18)	-0.0054 (0.64)	0.4563	0.7445
	(6)	-0.0283 (1.92)	-0.5756 (1.74)	0.3279 (0.94)	0.0047 (0.79)	0.1726	0.5167

Notes:

1. All variables are first differences of logs.
2. *NES RLC* is a relative labour cost variable derived from NES data (see Appendix). *CYC* is the male unemployment rate.
3. All equations were estimated by OLS.
4. Estimating periods are: (1) 1953–69; (2) 1969–81; (3) 1953–81; (4) 1953–71; (5) 1971–81; (6) 1953–81.
5. Parentheses contain absolute value of *t*-statistics.

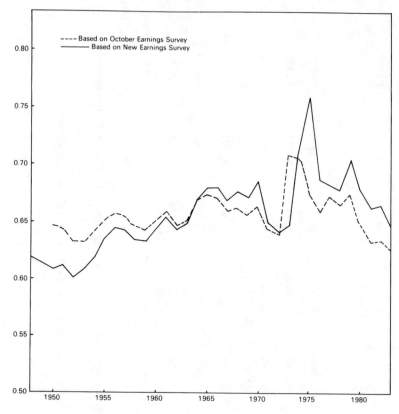

Figure 4.2   Relative labour costs: females

4.4   A DISEQUILIBRIUM MODEL OF THE YOUTH
LABOUR MARKET

In this section we outline a disequilibrium model of the youth labour
market taking account of some of the criticisms we made of earlier
work. We estimate this model by maximum likelihood methods using
the density functions provided by Maddala and Nelson (1974, Model
1). Before we turn to our model and estimates we list our four
objections to the *a priori* sample separation assumed by M–W and
Wells (1983).

1.   Their method is extreme in classifying regimes with probability 1
2.   They assume a single switch point

3. It removes from the field of empirical study what is perhaps the most interesting phenomenon in this area, namely the timing and extent of disequilibrium
4. When used in combination with OLS, even if the assumed sample separation is correct, it will give rise to inconsistent estimates.

As M–W and Wells estimated their models in first differences of logs it would not make sense to estimate their model with a min condition. We are therefore unable to provide a set of comparable disequilibrium estimates.

We propose the following model:

$$L_t^D = L^D(\bar{Q}_t, \ WRLC_t, \ SMD, \ t, \ L_{t-1}) + \varepsilon_1 \tag{4.14}$$

$$L_t^S = L^S(Pop_t, \ W_t, \ SB_t, \ NSD, \ t, \ UR_t) + \varepsilon_2 \tag{4.15}$$

$$L = \min(L^D, \ L^S) \tag{4.16}$$

where:

$$\bar{Q}_t = \sum_{i=1}^{40} \left(\frac{e_i}{E} q_i \right) = \text{an employment weighted output index}$$

e_i = employment in the ith industry

q_i = output of the ith industry

L = aggregate employment

$WRLC$ = weighted relative labour cost

SMD = a zero–1 special measures dummy

t = time trend

L_{t-1} = lagged employment

Pop = population of males (females) under 18

W_t = earnings

SB = supplementary benefits

NSD = a zero–1 National Service dummy (for males only)[27]

UR_t = adult unemployment rate.

The labour demand function is derived from a cost-minimising model with partial adjustment. $\bar{Q}_t$ is an index of aggregate production which takes account of changing industrial structure. A time trend is included to proxy for the growth of capital stock and changes in technology. The labour supply function allows for supplementary benefits to affect the decisions of the young and a time trend allows for changing preferences. The male unemployment rate is included to allow for any 'discouraged worker' effect.

The model was estimated (in log-linear form) by maximum likelihood methods on annual data 1953–81, and the results are presented in Table 4.4; the notes to Table 4.4 give details of the optimisation method. Using Kiefer's (1980) classification technique we find that there was excess supply for males for the period 1960–81 and for females for the periods 1956–63 and 1974–81. The labour demand

Table 4.4   A disequilibrium model: Maximum likelihood estimates

	Males < 18	Females < 18
Demand		
CONSTANT	0.47 (0.41)	− 17.41 (0.49)
$\ell n\overline{Q}_t$	0.19 (0.06)	2.16 (0.06)
$\ell n WRLC_t$	−0.23 (0.13)	−3.92 (0.02)
SMD	0.14 (0.02)	0.11 (0.01)
t	−0.02 (0.002)	−0.05 (0.002)
$\ell n E_{t-1}$	0.71 (0.04)	0.87 (0.006)
σ_D^2	0.0009 (0.0002)	0.0001 (0.00002)
Supply		
CONSTANT	−2.64 (0.04)	−2.56 (0.30)
$lnPOP_t$	1.43 (0.004)	1.17 (0.02)
$lnWAGE_t$	0.29 (0.006)	0.65 (0.06)
$lnSUPBEN_t$	0.33 (0.02)	0.04 (0.04)
NSD	− 0.001 (0.0008)	
t	0.01 (0.0002)	−0.003 (0.002)
$lnUR_t$	− 0.15 (0.0006)	−0.15 (0.004)
σ_S^2	0.00001 (0.000002)	0.001 (0.0002)
R_D^2	0.93	0.94
R_S^2	0.90	0.93
R_{min}^2	0.99	0.99
log likelihood	86.50	75.80
Periods of excess supply		
	M 1960–1981	
	F 1956–1963, 1974–1981	

Notes:
Asymptotic standard errors in parentheses
Optimisation was carried out by quasi-Newton methods using NAg routine EO4LBF on a Burroughs 6800 machine, using an analytical Jacobian and Hessian. The Hessian was also used to derive asymptotic standard errors of the parameters. Despite 'flattish' likelihood functions, the converged estimates are virtually invariant to the parameter starting values chosen, although from certain points the algorithm would crash first and, of course, the number of iterations involved could vary considerably.

function has plausible signs and magnitudes for most of the estimated parameters. The aggregate demand variable is significant but has a fairly small (large) elasticity for males (females). The relative labour cost variable has a small and insignificant (large and significant) coefficient for males (females). The SEM dummy turns out to be *positive* and significant.[28] The supply function also has plausible signs and magnitudes in most cases. There is evidence of a discouraged worker effect and the sign on supplementary benefits is 'perverse'.[29] Overall, these results are fairly encouraging. To reiterate, we find aggregate demand a significant variable in determining employment and relative labour costs are not well defined for males. It is interesting to note that the switch point(s) are very different from those that were chosen *a priori* by M–W and Wells. These results are very encouraging, and we feel that further work should investigate such models.

4.5 CONCLUSIONS

In this chapter we have reviewed some of the literature on relative wages and the youth labour market. Our major finding is that the youth labour market is best described as being in disequilibrium, with some periods of excess demand and some of excess supply. We argued that much of the earlier work which assumed an equilibrium to estimate demand or employment functions should be treated with caution. We paid particular attention to Wells's work and found that his model is poorly specified, theoretically and econometrically. In particular, we find that cyclical or aggregate demand variables are important in explaining the growth of unemployment. The impact of relative wages on youth employment is often not significant (in some models) and even when significant is quantitatively small. In our chapter we have pointed out several problems with the data, especially key variables like employment and relative wages. We would like to stress that the limited number of observations in an annual time series model when we use *a priori* sample separation makes the results very sensitive to the particular specification of the model. We argue that a way forward is to investigate the youth labour market using disequilibrium estimation techniques. Future work should also pay particular attention to SEMs.

APPENDIX   RELATIVE LABOUR COSTS

The New Earnings Survey (NES) based data on relative labour costs (*NES RLC*) used in the text were derived in the following way.

A. The NES manual earnings were regressed on the October Earnings Enquiry (*OEE*) data and a raising of school leaving age (*ROSLA*) dummy. The results obtained are presented below:

1. **Males**

   (a) Under 18
   $$NES = 0.674 + 0.748 \ OES(<21) - 1.921 \ ROSLA$$
   $$(0.47) \quad (22.89) \qquad\qquad (-2.46)$$

   $$R^2 = 0.998 \qquad DW = 2.19$$
   (Estimated on annual data, 1973–81)

   (b) 21 and over
   $$NES = -2.210 + 1.002 \ OES(\geqslant 21) - 1.798 \ ROSLA$$
   $$(-1.96) \quad (56.39) \qquad\qquad (-1.87)$$
   $$R^2 = 0.998 \qquad DW = 2.19$$
   (Estimated on annual data, 1970–81)

2. **Females**

   (a) Under 18
   $$NES = -0.439 + 1.017 \ OES(<18) - 2.225 \ ROSLA$$
   $$(-0.76) \quad (47.22) \qquad\qquad (-4.59)$$

   $$R^2 = 0.998 \qquad DW = 1.49$$
   (Estimated on annual data, 1971–81)

   (b) 18 and over
   $$NES = -0.240 + 0.971 \ OES(\geqslant 18) - 1.491 \ ROSLA$$
   $$(-0.31) \quad (47.61) \qquad\qquad (-1.99)$$

   $$R^2 = 0.997 \qquad DW = 2.03$$
   (Estimated on annual data, 1970–81)

B. The above estimated regressions were used to predict values for earnings from 1948 until *NES* data were published.

C. Labour costs were then obtained by adding the employer's NI contribution to the earnings data (part published and part 'predicted').

D. Relative labour costs were then derived as the ratio of labour costs of the under 18s to the 21 and over for males. For females it is a ratio of under 18s to 18 and over.

E. Note that since the age category for females is the same as in Wells the alternative series are similar. However, for males our NES-based series is a ratio of under 18s to 21 and over, while for Wells it is under 21s to 21 and over. In this case the series diverge quite markedly. In the OLS demand equations (Table 4.3) for the latter period (1969–81 for males, 1971–81 for females) predicted values are used for four observations for males and only one observation for females.

Demand equations

Table	11	13	15	12	14	16
Eq. no.	D4	D4	D4	D4	D4	D4
Period	1969–81	1969–81	1969–81	1971–81	1971–81	1971–81
Age	Teenage	<18	18–19	Teenage	<18	18–19
Sex	Male	Male	Male	Female	Female	Female
Constant	−0.01	0.00	−0.02	−0.00	−0.02	0.01
	(0.6)	(0.3)	(0.7)	(0.4)	(0.9)	(0.5)
RLC	−2.30	−4.31	−0.69	−1.44	−2.27	−0.67
	(2.5)	(5.1)	(0.5)	(2.9)	(2.5)	(1.0)
RLC_{t-1}	1.49	1.91	1.60	−0.81	−1.52	−0.23
	(1.8)	(2.4)	(1.1)	(2.9)	(3.0)	(0.7)
CYC	−0.06	−0.07	−0.06	−0.22	−0.34	−0.13
	(1.2)	(1.5)	(0.8)	(2.7)	(2.3)	(1.3)
R^2	0.22	0.70	0.00	0.47	0.45	0.00
DW	2.17	2.82	2.49	1.21	0.90	1.87

Supply equations

Table	11	13	15	12	14	16
Eq. No.	S2	S2	S2	S2	S2	S2
Period	1953–69	1953–69	1953–69	1953–71	1953–71	1953–71
Age	Teenage	<18	18–19	Teenage	<18	18–19
Sex	Male	Male	Male	Female	Female	Female
Constant	−0.01	−0.01	−0.02	−0.01	−0.00	−0.00
	(2.0)	(2.2)	(1.3)	(1.2)	(0.9)	(0.6)
$PPOP$	1.04	0.86	0.97	1.10	0.94	1.05
	(8.9)	(9.3)	(8.1)	(9.8)	(9.6)	(8.9)
$WAGE$	0.45	0.54	0.31	0.35	0.44	1.16
	(2.6)	(3.7)	(1.0)	(3.0)	(3.5)	(0.9)
R^2	0.85	0.86	0.81	0.85	0.84	0.81
DW	2.00	1.67	2.28	1.30	1.14	1.81

Notes

1. The first draft of this chapter was written while the authors were at the Institute for Employment Research, University of Warwick. We are grateful to Ruth Hermitage for competent research assistance. We thank Bill Wells for providing his data set and details of sources can be found in Wells (1983) and in section 4.3 above. This chapter was first presented as a paper at the 'Young Persons' Labour Market Conference' held at the IER, University of Warwick. We thank our ex-colleagues at the IER and Conference participants for helpful comments. We would like to thank Bill Wells for comments on our paper although we did not agree with all of them. Remaining errors are our own responsibility.
2. See Lynch (1985).
3. See Junankar (1984).
4. Of those not remaining in full-time education in 1983, 48 per cent entered the YTS: (*Employment Gazette*, October 1984: 446).
5. See Doeringer and Piore (1971).
6. To the extent that the young are involved in the underground economy this bias is, in part, mitigated.
7. See, for example, Maki and Spindler (1975) and criticisms of that approach in Junankar (1981).
8. However, this is not the way it is usually presented. In general, authors simply estimate equation (4.4) without any justification.
9. In some unpublished work Makeham (1981) reported a significant relative wage effect.
10. Note that a formal model suggests they should use aggregate *output* and not the unemployment rate or vacancies.
11. For a survey of this literature see Hazledine (1981).
12. Layard does not specify whether he tested the imposition of this restriction. As this model is estimated for the whole manufacturing sector, due to aggregation problems we suspect the restriction would be rejected by the data. Hart (1984) elaborates on this point.
13. Note that instability of parameters may reflect a misspecified model in a more general sense than simply a switch in regimes.
14. They estimated their model in first differences of logs and they stated that the implied restrictions 'were generally accepted at the 5 per cent level' (p. 34).
15. Our work on similar lines was carried out before we came across Rice (1986). There are some differences but we shall not deal with them in this paper.
16. This was because the October Earnings Enquiry ended in 1979. Since then, earnings data by age are from the New Earnings Survey which is not a comparable data set. Wells has spliced the two series.
17. There are some minor differences which are of little significance. In chapters 9 and 10, Wells estimates several variants of the demand equation for the latter period. Wells estimates a large number of equations (approximately 100) with slightly different definitions of the dependent variables and alternative sets of independent variables.

Given a very small data set, the tests of significance are pretty meaningless under these circumstances.

18. Note there was conscription (National Service) for males until 1959.

19. Note that the wage (cost) variables are for males (females) less than 21 (18) years and 21 (18) years and over. Although the dependent variables are more finely defined (e.g., males less than 18 years old) the right hand side variables have wage (costs) for less than 21 year olds as a proportion of persons 21 years and over.

20. In Chapter 9 he also estimates unemployment functions, where he finds the cyclical variable is very significant.
    In Chapter 9, Wells estimates alternative versions of the labour demand equation and generally finds that the female equation performs poorly. However, in almost all these *ad hoc* employment demand functions the cyclical variable is insignificant. It is possible that the relative labour cost variable (based on *earnings*, not wage rates) is picking up some cyclical effects.

21. At one stage (p. 71) he argues that in order to concentrate on substitutability or complementarity of different age and sex groups 'the cyclical term was dropped from the equations'. This is an unusual way of doing applied econometrics!

22. Details of these tests are available on request.

23. Note that Garbade (1977) finds that this test has low power and a tendency to produce type II errors under the null hypothesis of stability. However, when we attempted to examine parameter stability via the Kalman filter route the estimates *never* converged; again indicative of poor specification.

24. Results available on request.

25. The precise method is described in the Appendix, p. 104.

26. This is probably because for males the NES data allows us to look at the under 18s, while Wells's data is for under 21s. For females the age separation (under to over 18s) is the same for both series.

27. Although conscription affected only the 18–21 age group, it may have indirect effects on the labour supply of the under 18s because of changing preferences to staying on at school as higher education would be interrupted.

28. This needs further investigation.

29. Similar 'perverse' results were found in Junankar and Price (1984). Note that an increase in supplementary benefit would (according to economic theory) reduce the actual labour supply. It may, however, lead to an increase in the 'apparent' labour supply as individuals 'pretend' to be in the labour market.

5 Relative Wages and the Youth Labour Market: A Reply

William Wells

I think anybody reading Chapter 4 above carefully would conclude that it provides further support for the inferences drawn about the youth labour market in the post-war period by Merrilees and Wilson (1979), Rice (1986) and myself (1983 and Chapter 3 above). In particular, the youth labour market is best characterised as being in disequilibrium, and during periods when young people are in excess supply both their relative labour costs and the general level of demand appear to be important determinates of their employment. Readers would also recognise that the problems with the data require that caution be exercised in interpreting the results for both relative labour costs and the effect of the economic cycle.

This sounds a surprising assertion given the claims in Chapter 4 that it is primarily the level of demand which determines youth employment. But such a conclusion is inescapable given three elements of the chapter by Junankar and Neale (hereafter J–N).

First, J–N agree that the youth labour market is best characterised by disequilibrium. Second, they carry out a detailed scrutiny of one small part of my research and find results that are indistinguishable from mine. (Where they do differ the differences are either inconsequential or based on data which accords neither with commonsense or the evidence.) Third, they estimate a model which finds that for under 18s *both* demand and relative labour costs appear to be important determinates of employment in periods of excess supply of youth labour. The authors, however, choose to disparage the effects of relative labour costs because its coefficient in the male equation is insignificant. This is despite the fact that the equivalent term in the female equation is highly significant and the coefficient in the male equation is significant at the 10 per cent level. What is more, these results emerge from a model which, as I discuss below, I consider to be seriously flawed.

Let me first start with a conclusion with which both J–N and I agree; namely that disequilibrium best characterises the youth labour market with some periods of excess demand for youth labour and some of excess supply. From this, they rightly conclude that previous studies which implicitly assume excess supply of youth labour throughout their estimation period should be viewed with caution. However, it seems that their caution extends only to studies which consider youth *employment*, but does not apply to studies of youth *unemployment*.

Yet, even if the research on unemployment functions is accepted at face value, the results concerning the effect of relative labour costs are reported very oddly. Five studies are considered: Makeham (1980), OECD (1980), Layard (1982), Lynch and Richardson (1982) and Wells (1983). Of these the first two studies are quoted as finding no significant effect. However, it is not surprising that the OECD work did not find any effect of relative wages, given that they did not include them as an explanatory variable. Also, although the earlier work by Makeham finds no effect, in the update of the regression analysis (Makeham, 1981) relative labour costs become almost significant (for young males). Given these facts, it is difficult to consider that 'the relative wages. . . variable has a very mixed outcome'. Of the four studies that considered them, only one (Makeham) found no significant or near-significant effect and even this result was subsequently revised.

Finally, on the studies using unemployment I find it more difficult than J–N to accept that the 'data are. . . (relatively speaking) good'. They point to some of the factors in Chapter 4 which appear to me to affect quite seriously the measurement of unemployment, and there are also a number of additional problems. In particular, the months in which the counts of youth unemployment by age were carried out changed and given the intense seasonality of youth/school leaver unemployment this might drastically affect comparisons over time. Also, the studies that consider unemployment rates not only have to contend with problems in the measurement of the numbers unemployed by age but also require estimates of employment by age for the denominator. They therefore share the data problems of both the employment and unemployment series.

For all these reasons I believe that the caution prescribed by J–N for the consideration of demand or employment functions should also be extended to unemployment functions. The evidence of both demand and relative labour costs effects on unemployment that exists in these studies should thus be viewed in the light of the period of estimation and the quality of the data.

In order to evaluate both the unemployment and the employment studies, it is necessary to obtain some idea of when the market for youth labour was in excess demand and when in excess supply. The contention of J–N is that the method used by Merrilees and Wilson (1979) – and followed in my original paper – leads to an erroneous division of the post-war period between the two states. They also contend that even if this division is accepted the model set out in my original paper is misspecified and lacks robustness.

When testing for robustness J–N considered only one small part of the econometric work in Wells (1983). That is why it is difficult to reconcile the findings of that study as summarised by J–N with those presented in Chapter 3 above (in particular I do conclude that demand is a significant factor in determining youth employment.) There is therefore no mention by J–N of the robustness of the results on relative labour costs and aggregate demand across specifications, because only one specification is considered. Despite this, I would suggest that the evidence presented by J–N – far from indicating misspecification and lack of robustness – actually provide some more support for the approach set out in Chapter 3 above.

The tests for misspecification consider both the dynamic specification and the stability of the model. On the dynamic specification there are two points to make. First, three tests of the validity of the dynamic specification were carried out, but only in one of the 12 cases (females 18–19 year old supply equation) does the same result occur in each of the three tests. It is, therefore, difficult to obtain a consistent evaluation using this evidence. Second, other dynamic specifications (of the demand equations) were estimated, and some are reported in the econometric appendix of Wells (1983). These respecifications continue to yield essentially the same results as in Chapter 3 above.

The results of the stability tests are also rather odd. They do not agree with the results of the Chow test carried out in both my and Merrilees and Wilson's work. Neither do they agree with the switch points found by Rice. Nor, interestingly enough, do they correspond to the results of the model presented by J–N in section 4.4 of Chapter 4. I think this may be due to the fact (acknowledged by J–N) that the test used tends to indicate stability when the opposite is the case. This and the very small number of degrees of freedom might explain the odd results. It seems to me, therefore, that the case for misspecification on the basis of the reported tests of dynamic specification and stability is not proven.

The tests for robustness carried out by J–N, on the other hand, do provide some worrying features. These concern not the effect of the relative labour costs (which are discussed below) but rather the performance of the cyclical variable; in none of the formulations presented by J–N is the variable significant.

I believe that this is not because demand is unimportant, but rather that the variable used is inappropriate. In particular, J–N regard the male unemployment rate as a 'lazy' indicator of aggregate demand: a view with which I have some sympathy. But similarly the variable they use (GDP *less* oil, *MLH* 104) is by the same token an 'overworked' indicator. Not only does it have to pick up the relationship between changes in total employment and changes in youth employment, it also has to pick out the relationship between output and total employment (which almost certainly changed over the period). For this reason, I would suggest that a labour market variable such as unemployment or (perhaps more correctly) total employment is more suitable, as it sidesteps the need to pick out the relationship between output and total employment and allows a concentration on the effects of total employment changes on the employment of young people. It also allows some examination of whether young people are affected more than adults by recessions and upturns. Use of an output measure does not directly allow such consideration. (A more formal description of this approach can be found on p. 22–3 of Merrilees and Wilson, 1979.)

The results on relative labour costs are indistinguishable from those presented in Chapter 3 (with one exception which is discussed below). The fact that the results still emerge even with different specifications of the relationship, could be taken as further indications of their robustness.

Using GDP (excluding *MLH* 104) with either actual or reweighted relative labour costs yields larger and even more significant coefficients on the relative labour costs term in the male under 18s demand equation. Similarly, the results for 18–19 year olds of both sexes suggest that even in the latter period demand factors seem to have had little effect and this is consistent with the findings of Wells (1983) that even in this latter period 'supply functions work better than the demand functions. Thus, it appears that much of the excess supply of young workers is concentrated in the under 18 category and the 18–19 year olds are relatively unaffected'. The findings for under 18 females are also consistent: there is evidence of an effect of relative labour costs, but the result is not as robust as for males under 18 (with respect to either relative labour costs or demand effects). Despite the lack of robustness, I would still argue that given the results of some of the formulations, and the problems of data on female earnings in this latter period, there is sufficient evidence to suggest that both relative labour costs and demand are important factors determining employment of females under 18 in the latter period (see, for example, Rice, 1986).

The one major exception to the overall consistency of results reported by J–N is when a relative labour cost variable for under 18s is used which has been constructed from a method based on NES data. In these equations there are no significant parameters found. Yet, rather than question the data the authors conclude that the model is misspecified and lacks robustness. In fact, the derivation of the relative labour costs estimates from the NES uses a dubious method of calculation, the results that emerge are completely at odds with the available evidence, and some of the implications are close to being nonsensical. I would, therefore, suggest that the results which emerge using these variables should be disregarded.

The method in question considers four groups (males under 18 and 21 and over, and females under 18 and 18 and over). For each group earnings from the NES are regressed on the earnings of the nearest equivalent age group from the October Earnings Survey (males under 21 and 21 and over, females under 18 and 18 and over respectively) together with a *ROSLA* dummy and a constant. These four regressions are carried out over the longest period for which there is equivalent data and then forecasts are extrapolated backwards until 1948. Finally, to get labour costs, estimates of employer NI contributions are added to these estimates of earnings.

It seems to me that there is a major problem with this approach. The period of estimation is extremely short especially for males under 18 where there are only five directly comparable years.[1] To use such estimates as a basis to extrapolate backwards over a period of 25 years would appear to extend the use of extrapolation beyond credibility. (There are also a number of other problems with this method of estimation.[2])

The results of this extrapolation are completely contrary to what is known about youth pay from other sources. For example, relative earnings of young males declined 1948–72 according to J–N's extrapolated data. But evidence on wage rates supports the conventional wisdom (see, for example, Table 3.A4 in Chapter 3). Similarly, the relativities between young people of different ages implicit in these calculations assume almost nonsensical values. For example, in 1952 the estimated earnings of males under 18 using this method were the equivalent of £3.48, which meant that the earnings of 18–20 year old males would have been the equivalent of £3.99 – i.e., less than 15 per cent above the under 18 figure – whereas the equivalent relativity using actual earnings from the NES post-1973 gives the 18–20 year olds earning over 50 per cent more than the under 18s. Yet, there is evidence on wage rates that the very youngest age groups have been gaining ground on their elders.

It would thus seem that these estimates do not accord with reality, and the results of the formulations using these estimates should be discounted. If this is done, the results presented by J–N would appear to provide more support for the robustness of my results (especially on relative labour costs). Even if they did not, I believe that there is sufficient corroborative evidence both from other formulations in Wells (1983) and from other sources (namely, Merrilees and Wilson and Rice) to suggest that the demand and relative labour costs effects emerge in periods of excess supply of youth labour almost whatever the specification. The approach of J–N of picking out one study from a genre and finding fault, succeeds only in discrediting the overall approach if they are able to discredit all the studies, or if the studies differ radically in their results. If they, do not then the differences in method of evaluation add weight to the results.

For example, the method used by Rice (1986) should satisfy most of the criticisms made of my (and Merrilees and Wilson's) work: a disequilibrium estimation technique is used rather than *a priori* sample separation and unemployment rather than employment is used. Yet the results are remarkably similar: excess demand for young males in the 1950s and the 1960s and a transition into excess demand from the turn of the 1970s. Similarly, for females, the 1970s are characterised by excess supply and apart from a period around 1963–65 (when the post-war baby boom was entering the labour force) the period before is characterised by excess demand. Further, during the period of excess supply both relative labour costs and demand appear to be important determinates of youth employment. The dismissal of this work by J–N because 'her data set ends before the sudden increase in unemployment' seems rather feeble unless they can come up with a credible alternative.

This brings me to the final part of my reply. I would suggest that the model put forward by J–N in section 4.4 of Chapter 4 is seriously flawed, and as a result of this flaw the periods of excess supply are incorrectly identified. (I also have some other more detailed problems with their specification,[3] but these are not central to the argument.) This erroneous identification of switch points diminishes the explanatory power of relative labour costs (especially for young males) because it includes periods when young people were in excess demand. The significance of the relative labour costs variable does not, however, disappear (and this may say something about the strength of the effect in periods of excess supply).

The major flaw in the model is that no account is taken of education. This means that the rapid growth in the proportion of the population in education that occurred in the 1960s is implicitly regarded as unregistered unemployment: as the proportion of the population in post-compulsory education rose there was an equivalent fall in the proportion employed, and this is treated in J–N's model as equivalent to a growth in the proportion unemployed. This appears to be the reason why periods which have generally come to be regarded as periods of full employment for young people are classified by J–N as periods of excess supply. It is true that the work of both Merrilees and Wilson and myself can be criticised for a fairly perfunctory examination of the role of education, but at least there is some examination. Also, the results from these two studies as to the timing of the switch points are very similar to those found by Rice who to some extent sidestepped the problem of education by looking at unemployment directly.

I think, therefore, that until a more plausible model is proposed the results J–N report must bow to the consensus on the timing of excess demand and supply.

Notes

1.   For males under 18 the full estimation period is 1973–81. However, ROSLA affects the two earnings series in different years: the October Earnings Series in 1973, and NES in 1974 (as the survey is in April). Therefore, it is 1975 before the figures are comparable. Also (at the other end of the estimation period) the figures in the October Survey for 1980 and 1981 are (for all the age/sex groups) estimates taken from my work which in turn were derived from the NES. This seems a very odd procedure, tantamount to regressing the NES on the NES itself.

2. For example, the effect of ROSLA is found to be negative on under 18 earnings. This result suggests that the fact that ROSLA affects the series in different years is not adequately taken account of, as ROSLA removed the youngest and lowest paid and thus should have boosted the average earnings for compositional reasons.

3. Some of the minor problems I have with the J–N formulation are:

    (i) If output is corrected for employment changes, it may be that this implicitly denies that relative labour costs could affect these changes and transfers all the effect onto the cyclical term.

    (ii) Why should a National Service dummy appear in an equation for under 18s when National Service applied to males aged at least 18? There may be a role, but it needs explanation.

    (iii) Should not some effect for ROSLA be included in at least the supply equations?

6 Relative Wages and the Youth Labour Market: A Rejoinder

P. N. Junankar and Adrian Neale

Wells, in his reply (Chapter 5 above) to our comment's in Chapter 4 above, makes several interesting comments, defending his work and attacking our work with great relish. We are in agreement that a disequilibrium model best represents the youth labour market: in other words, a model where wage rates are sticky (do not adjust completely in the unit period to disequilibrium). In a non-market clearing approach, if the output market does not clear (because of sticky prices), this has repercussions on the factor markets and aggregate demand affects factor demands. Our disagreement centres on *how* this model should be estimated and on the interpretation of some of the econometric results. We also seem to agree on the doubtful quality of the time-series data on employment and earnings, and we are quite happy to be cautious about the quality of unemployment data as well.

Our major criticism of Wells (1983) is based on the view that, when estimating an econometric model, the appropriate procedure is to perform various specification tests, tests of hypotheses and, if data have been created (say the relative labour costs), then sensitivity tests should be carried out for different assumptions in producing the series. We believe that a simple presentation of several tables of results, *without any tests of hypotheses comparing them*, is not an appropriate procedure. Since he chides us for concentrating only on 'one small part of the econometric work', let us look at the rest of his work. With a very small sample (for the labour demand functions he uses 13 observations for males and 11 observations for females), he estimates several equations with six different dependent variables for each age/sex group. These are estimated in logs (with and without a first order autoregressive error structure) and first differences of logs but with no attempt to *test* the implicit restrictions.[1] Several independent variables are introduced (including lagged relative costs, relative costs of male youths to various other age/sex groups, etc.), but no attempt is made to *choose* an equation which performs best in terms of recognised statistical procedures.[2] In particular, in almost all the specifications (except where the first difference of the log of youth unemployment rates is the dependent variable) *the index of aggregate demand used* (defined as the male unemployment rate) *is not significant*. It is, therefore, strange that Wells claims that the aggregate demand is an important variable in explaining youth employment. In our work in Chapter 4 above, we concentrate our attention on the model specified by Wells in his Chapter 7 (1983), which is at least based on economic theory. It is not clear what a 'min' condition means when estimating an equation for *ratios* of youth employment to either total employment or to adult employment. We, therefore, repeat that a proper econometric analysis must carry out hypothesis tests. Our second major criticism of his econometric work is that in estimating a disequilibrium model *a priori* sample separation is inappropriate, and the model should be estimated by maximum likelihood methods making the switch points endogenous.

Wells's main criticism of our model is that no account is taken of education. It is certainly true that we do not explicitly model educational choice (but for that matter nor does Wells or most of the other literature) but, since we are not modelling unemployment, we do not consider it a serious problem. In our model we allow for a time trend in labour supply which can be taken to be a proxy for education (as well as changes in tastes). In other words, our model which is estimated using *all* the data with appropriate econometric techniques gives us sensible parameter estimates in terms of signs, as well as sensible switch points. Overall, we find that aggregate demand is a significant variable in explaining youth employment and that relative labour costs are *not* significant at the 5 per cent level for males, although they are significant for females.

To conclude, we have argued that Wells's study is seriously inadequate because he does not estimate his models appropriately and does *not* carry out any specification tests. In our work we stress the importance of using appropriate econometric methods and discuss the poor quality of the time series data. Overall, we stress the importance of aggregate demand and the relative unimportance of wage costs in explaining (un)employment.

Notes

1. Wells's model, estimated as first differences of logs, have no long run
    solution.
2. When several equations are estimated on a small sample, one would
    expect *by chance* to find some 'significant' parameters. However, these
    statistical tests of significance are no longer valid.

7 Trade Unionism and the Pay of Young Workers[1]

Paul Ryan

7.1 INTRODUCTION

The pay of young workers has become a matter of economic and political interest in a period of high youth unemployment. The current government asserts that young workers have been priced out of jobs and – through youth-related interventions – seeks to counter what it proclaims to be the cause of youth unemployment: high youth pay. The link between the price of youth labour and the employment of young workers has become a major research topic. Recent research suggests a negative relationship between the pay and employment of young workers, although the issue is far from settled (Merrilees and Wilson (1979), Makeham (1980), OECD (1980), Layard (1982), Lynch and Richardson (1982), Hutchinson, Barr and Drobny (1984), Wells (1983), Rice (1986), Marsden (1985), Junankar and Neale (Chapter 4 above) and Marsden and Ryan (1986)).

Despite all the interest, little attention has been paid to the determinants of the pay of young workers. One negative result does, however, stand out. The econometric literature is united in finding the relative price of youth labour to be largely unresponsive to excess supply in the labour market. Another possible determinant of youth pay has featured in political discussion. Asserting that young workers have been priced out of jobs, the present government holds trade unions responsible. Wells has noted that the pay of many young workers is influenced by collective bargaining agreements which embody 'wage for age' schedules—and that the ratio of youth to adult pay rates under such arrangements has risen since 1965 (1983, pp. 22–4). Similar schedules are operated by Wages Council in sectors where collective bargaining is limited in scope, or absent altogether.

As neither market forces nor employer interest favour the inertia of youth pay with respect to excess supplies of labour, attention must focus instead upon the pay policies of trade unions. It may be asked why trade unions would be interested in the pay of young workers in the first place – and, to the extent that they are, what they would want to do about it. This chapter discusses the factors which can be expected to govern the bargaining objectives of trade unions in the context of youth pay. Finally, the empirical relationship between unionism and youth pay is outlined, making use of the variation in pay by industry in Britain during the last decade. The objective is to provide not so much a finished account of the relationship between trade unionism and youth pay as a preliminary exploration of one of the darker recesses of the modern labour market.

7.2 CHARACTERISTICS OF YOUTH LABOUR AND TRADE UNIONISM

Taking young workers in the contemporary context as those aged between 16 and 20 years inclusive, we find important differences between youth and adult labour on both the supply and the demand sides of the market.

The difference between young and adult workers on the supply side involves both the quality and the supply price of their labour power. In terms of labour quality, the typical young worker offers less skill and responsibility than the average adult, consequent on the differences in their work experience, job training and personal maturity. At the same time, young workers are likely to be superior to adults in the level and quality of their education (given the improvements in schooling in recent decades), and in energy, adaptability and willingness to learn (given their lower ages). Such differences are to some extent stereotypical, as well as frequently reversed in comparisons of individual young and adult workers.[2] There is however reason to expect that they characterise to some extent the average young and adult member of the labour force, which is what matters for this analysis.

These differences in labour quality create on the demand side differences between the productivity of youths and adults in particular jobs. The ratio of youth to adult productivity (q_i in Figure 7.1) will be low in jobs which require considerable experience-based skills and responsibility of the worker ($q_i \rightarrow 0$). Indeed, where training is involved, youth productivity may become negative – as in the first year of contemporary apprenticeship ($q_i < 0$: Atkinson, 1982). At the other extreme, jobs which demand neither attribute of adults and which involve no training of youths will show little or no shortfall in youth productivity $(q_i \rightarrow 1)$.[3] We may conceive of the job structure of an industry as a frequency distribution across q, with some sectors (e.g. A in Figure 7.1) exhibiting a substantial share of high q jobs and others (e.g., B) a small share of such jobs.

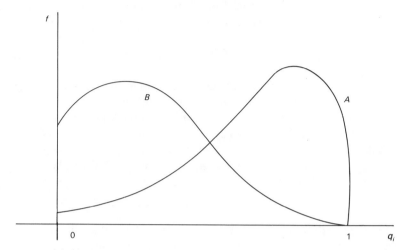

Figure 7.1   Distribution of jobs by relative youth to adult productivity in two industries

Youth and adult labour differ also in their supply prices. Youth is a period of transition – from the low income level provided by pocket money and part-time work to the higher one of adult earnings. Expectations of hourly pay rates will take time to adjust upwards during the transition. Furthermore, even when financially independent of his or her parents, the young worker typically remains in the family home, enjoying therefore lower living costs than does the independent adult. Young people are less likely to be responsible for the support of a spouse and children than are adults.[4] Such factors are reflected in the lower rates of social security benefit payable to young than to adult workers, which in turn provide them with lower levels of alternative income.[5] For all these reasons, young workers are willing to work at lower earnings levels than are adults – and particularly than are male adults, who most often bear primary income responsibility for a family.

Further evidence of low supply prices for many youths is provided by the extent of participation in the Youth Opportunities Programme (YOP) of 1978–83. The £25 allowance paid under YOP amounted in 1981 to less than one-half of the gross weekly earnings of employed 16–17 year olds. The content of most youth activity under YOP was known to be similar to that of mainstream employment – offering, if anything, less rather than more training content. Nevertheless, between 1981 and 1983, roughly one in every two 'out of work' 16–17 year olds chose to enter YOP rather than remain in registered unemployment.[6]

The difference between youth supply price and adult earnings would lead in a competitive market to the substitution of youths for adults in jobs where the cheapness of their labour power more than compensates for any deficiency in its productivity. In a unionised market the incentive to substitution is increased still further according to the success of the union in raising the earnings of adults. Writing s_i as the ratio of youth supply price to adult pay in job i, then if:

$$s_i < q_i$$

employers will want to substitute youth for adult labour. In industries where skill requirements are low and adult earnings high youth labour will be preferred for a wide range of jobs.

The union's reaction to such a situation is of interest. The substitution of youth for adult labour might be thought acceptable, were union objectives to be formulated without reference to the age of affected union members. Even then, however, resistance by the union is to be expected. It is not just the jobs of adults which are being lost to youth, it is also the pay rate attached to them, as adult earnings are competed down by low youth supply prices. Moreover, union policy is unlikely to prove indifferent to the age composition of employment when the councils of most unions are dominated in practice by the adult membership. We therefore examine firstly the ways in which the interests of adults are defended against the competition of youth; and secondly the influence of youth itself within trade unionism.

7.3 'ADULTS ONLY' UNIONISM

We assume initially that the union gives zero weight to the interests of young workers, evaluating situations solely in terms of their implications for the interests of (homogeneous) adult members. The interests of adult unionists straddle two spheres of economic life: the workplace and the family. As workers, adults are seen as interested in two attributes of the labour contract – the rate of pay and the level of employment – with each of significance but with their relative importance conventionally indeterminate. As family members, adults are seen as interested in both total family income and adult power and status within the home. The price of youth labour is a potentially important influence upon each aspect of adult interests. This section concentrates upon the workplace interests of adults, touching only briefly on familial ones at the end.

Turning first to the workplace, as long as relative youth productivity is high in a significant number of jobs, both the rate of pay and the level of adult employment are threatened when youth labour is relatively cheap ($s_i < q_i$). At the same time, there is nothing peculiar to youth about the possibility of substitution for adult union labour. The supply prices of two other categories of secondary workers – immigrants and married females – are generally well below the earnings of adult unionists, particularly males. These groups are also more numerous in contemporary Britain than are young workers.

The competition of immigrants and females is blunted by two methods: 'rate for the job' payment systems and prejudicial discrimination. When a set rate must be paid for the job, the lower supply price of secondary groups proves no advantage to them. To the extent that the quality of their labour power is lower than that of adult males, they will prove unattractive candidates for hire. Should that prove inadequate, there is always the defence of racial and sexual discrimination to fall back upon. The rival group is depicted as inferior. Attempts to employ them are resisted by promoting antagonistic sentiment and insisting on job segregation.

The peculiarity of youth competition is that each of these methods of defence proves either unattractive or ineffective. 'Rate for the job' policies can indeed be pursued rigorously and used to exclude youths from consideration in hiring decisions, as in unionised manufacturing in the US (Osterman, 1980, Ryan, 1984a). The cost is that the reproduction of the adult unionised labour force is hampered, particularly where skill requirements are substantial. At the same time, job opportunities for the teenage children of adult unionists are worsened. Thus British industrial practice follows the 'rate for the job' route in all respects save with regard to youth. 'Wage for age' schedules have traditionally permitted the employment of workers aged less than 21 years at discounts (relative to adult rates) which are highest for the youngest ages. In this way British youth has been able to gain access to employment and training in jobs from which it would be debarred under a strict 'rate for job' regime.[7] Indeed, were it the intention of adult unionists to exclude youths from their job territory, the ascriptive characteristics of youth might lend themselves less readily to prejudicial discrimination than do those of females and foreigners.

The total exclusion of youth constitutes then an unattractive approach for the union of adults threatened by substitution. The presence of 'wage for age' schedules does, however, keep the threat of substitution alive. The danger zone for adult unionists is when under 'wage for age' schedules the pay of young workers exceeds their supply prices but is so low relative to that of adults as to more than cancel the productivity difference between them:

$$s_i \leqslant x_i < q_i$$

where x_i is the relative price of youth labour under 'wage for age' schedules. Then the employer still has the incentive to go beyond simply reproducing the adult labour force and increase profits by substituting youth for adult labour.

The union finding itself in such a position has two defensive options. The first is the traditional one of seeking direct restrictions on the employment of youths. Craft unions in printing and shipbuilding thus imposed formal apprentice–journeyman ratios not only to reduce the supply of qualified labour but also to curtail the usage of apprentices for task substitution at the expense of the craftworkers (Webb and Webb, 1920, Chapter 10). The same objective was sometimes pursued by ancillary restrictions which forbade apprentices from working particular machines (Child, 1967). The second method is indirect: to bargain up the pay of young workers relative to that of adults until the incentive to substitute youth for adult labour has been removed ($x_i \geqslant q_i$ in a sufficient number of jobs).

The respective merits of these two options have gone largely unanalysed. Rottenberg (1961) noted that in the US the practical importance of apprentice–journeyman ratios had dwindled to low levels even in craft markets, a fact which he ascribed to the effects of higher pay ratios on employer interest in taking on apprentices. The observation rings true in the British context as well. Behind it lies a question about union strategy: what determines union preferences between indirect restriction through wage structure and direct restriction through controls on the hiring and usage of youth labour?

Direct controls have clear advantages from the standpoint of the adult-centred union. They permit the scale of the reproduction of the labour force to be influenced explicitly by the union instead of relying on the less certain method of altering the structure of incentives facing employers. They improve the outcomes achieved for adults in the pay/ employment area. When young workers' entry is subject to quota, their pay can be low and their claim upon the payrolls of employers correspondingly limited. Indirect restriction raise the prices of youth labour and (for a given rate of youth entry) reduces the 'payroll potential' available for adults. In this respect, direct restriction may involve unionists as partial beneficiaries in the exploitation of youth labour.[8]

The advantage of indirect rather than direct restriction of youth competition lies simply in its greater attainability. Employer resistance is particularly intense to apprentice – journeyman ratios and related rules, infringing explicitly as they do upon 'managerial prerogative' in the areas of hiring and labour utilisation (Mortimer, 1973, pp. 122; 155). Indirect restriction, which simply alters relative prices, will also be unwelcome to employers, but it is unlikely to generate resistance of such stiffness. The employer is still free to run day-to-day operations without explicit restriction by union rule. Moreover, from the standpoint of union bargaining power, direct restriction suffers from the wedge it drives between the adult unionist and the young worker. Under a system of apprentice – journeyman ratios, the young worker can thank the union neither for a good wage nor for abundant employment opportunities. The union appears responsible for denying jobs to young workers. However, when substitution is regulated by higher youth pay, the young worker in employment has a good wage for which to thank the union; while the limitation of youth access to jobs appears as the decision of firms (not to hire youth) rather than that of the union. The cohesion between youth and adult members of the workforce is therefore greater than under direct restriction, to the benefit of the union's bargaining power in disputes.[9]

For these reasons unions with limited industrial power are expected to favour the indirect control of youth labour by way of 'wage for age' schedules rather than the direct method of quota-type regulation. Only the strongest of craft unions – notably the print compositors – have proved capable of maintaining durable direct controls on the use of youth labour (Child, 1976).[10]

The trade union which acts solely on behalf of its adult members will strive therefore to raise the relative pay of young workers under 'wage for age' schedules so as to neutralise the incentive to substitution. In cases where 'wage for age' rates are job specific this implies for job i in industry j:

$$x_{ij} \geqslant q_{ij}$$

Approximations to such a situation can be seen in wage policy which insists on either 'rate for the job' or small youth discounts in unskilled work (where $q_{ij} \to 1$) but which allows bigger youth discounts for skilled work and trainee status (where $q_{ij} \to 0$). Alternatively, if a single youth discount is applied across the whole spectrum of jobs in a sector ($x_{ij} = x_j$ all $_i$) then the union will seek to reduce the youth discount to low levels ($x_j \to 1$) as long as the share of high q jobs is non-negligible.

Youth pay levels affect the interests of adult workers not solely at the workplace. Even nowadays most teenage workers live with their parents.[11] The interest of the parent in the earning power of the child is potentially important–and distinctly ambivalent. To the extent that incomes are pooled within the family, the adult stands to gain from higher youth pay. Young workers can contribute more to their keep (and indeed towards the overheads of family life) when their earnings are higher. There is, however, more to the family than simply an institution for pooling incomes and living costs (Humphries and Rubery, 1984). In families characterised by paternal dominance, higher earnings for teenage members may be distinctly unwelcome to the family head, encouraging as they do the assertion of juvenile independence, particularly by adolescent sons. Family arrangements are undoubtedly variable but many adult male unionists must have looked unfavourably upon past increases in youth pay. To the extent that they have done so and that their children work in the same industries, the implicit threat to paternal authority may have qualified any adult support for higher youth pay which resulted from substitutability in production. The familial interest of adults in youth pay is therefore ambiguous, as well as more complex, than that associated with the workplace. At this stage, we simply note its potential importance and put it aside for further research.

We have argued in this section that a trade union concerned solely with the workplace interests of its adult members will seek to raise the price at which youth labour is traded when its cheapness more than compensates employers for any shortfall in its productivity relative to that of adults. The only exception arises in the case of unions strong enough to enforce direct restriction on youth employment shares.

7.4 'ALL AGES' UNIONISM: THE ROLE OF YOUTH

Trade unions cannot however be seen as simple vehicles of adult self-interest, in which any concern about youth pay and employment is totally instrumental. The analysis must be broadened to recognise that young people are themselves often members of trade unions, capable both of developing an identity and of articulating a set of interests separate from those of adult members. Moreover adults may actively sympathise with the interests of young workers. The issue is then the influence of youth members and their perceived interests within the union as a whole.

The interests of young workers, like those of adults, may be taken to be a function of current pay rates and access to employment. There is indeed reason to expect differences from the objective function characterising adults, notably: (i) a higher weight to pay than to job security, consistent with the higher quit propensity of youth; and (ii) more concern for access to training, promotion and future pay rates relative to current pay, consistent with the inexperience of youth. For present purposes, however, all that need be postulated is a concern on the part of youth to raise its current earning power.

The cohesion of youth as a separate interest group within the union cannot be taken for granted. The separateness of youth is indeed limited by the lack of clear lines between the work of youths and adults in many contexts. There is also the considerable differentiation of positions and interests within the 'youth' category – notably between those who are and those who are not receiving formal training. Nevertheless, a considerable degree of differentiation between the identities and interests of youths and adults can be seen in the history of some British trade unions, notably in engineering.[12]

Taking youth as a potentially separate group with a distinct set of interests, the prospects for it to exert a significant influence within the union appear at first glance negligible. Young people constitute roughly 5 per cent of total union membership.[13] To the extent that influence over union wage policy increases with the numerical weight of a group (Turner, 1952, Scullion, 1981), the ability of youth to modify the straightforward pursuit of the interests of adults appears very limited indeed – beyond unusual circumstances in which low levels of adult pay result in a large youth share in employment (Ryan, 1980).

The influence of youth is curbed still further by particular attributes of the age group. Young members are of necessity recent recruits to the union, lacking both experience of union affairs and direct representation amongst union officials. In some cases, organs of youth representation have been instituted in order to offset these limitations – such as the (district level) Juvenile Workers Committees and (national) Annual Youth Conferences of the AEU in engineering in the 1940s (Jeffreys, 1946, p. 263, Tuckett, 1974, p. 253). Such institutions have, however, played at most a fitful role in representing youth interests. The rapid turnover of youth membership and the instability of youth opinion prove major sources of weakness. Moreover most unions have avoided the creation of separate organs of youth representation (Wray, 1959).

Under some circumstances, however, the influence of youth interests upon union policy can be considerable. Youth has not always constituted as small a share of both employment and union membership as it does today. In the years up to 1945, with a school leaving age of 14 and low rates of staying on in school, young workers constituted a significant share of the labour forces of several industries (Gollan, 1937). Union membership was by no means universal amongst youth, but AEU records indicate that roughly 12 per cent of its membership was located in the youth sections (IV and IVa) throughout the Second World War (Jeffreys, 1946, Appendix IV).

A strong influence for youth interests could hardly prevail on grounds of membership shares alone, but other characteristics of youth can still promote such a result. There is first the 'volatility' of youth which – while it hampers participation in the regular institutions of the union – nevertheless implies a potential for high levels of industrial activism. Union officials may then be forced to attend to the grievances of youth, whether or not they are so inclined. In particular, the periodic apprentice strikes of 1937–64 in engineering and ship-building (for the most part spontaneous and unofficial) proved directly instrumental in securing increases in the relative pay of young workers.[14]

Not all adult union officials will have to be pushed into support for the claims of youth. Sympathy towards the raising of youth pay may be generated (particularly when fathers and sons are covered by the same collective agreement) by altruistic relationships within the family. Even when a direct family link is absent, the sentiment 'we were young once' may create adult sympathy for youth concerns. In some contexts, the link may be still more direct. To the extent that the youth activists of 1937–64 grew up to become union officials, their pride in their youthful activism may be associated with support for youth interests in their adult years.

The influence of youth interests within trade unions is enhanced still further in the British context as a result of multiunionism. When employees can choose between more than one union within a particular workplace, competition for membership may lead unions to offer immediate benefits to potential recruits. Young workers are particularly well placed to take advantage of competitive recruitment; not only is their rate of unionisation effectively zero at the time of entry into the workforce, but also their allegiances to particular unions will typically be fluid. Much like the approach of clearing banks to students, the union approach to youth will involve provision of particular benefits designed to win what may well prove a member for the longer term. Evidence of such policies can be found in low (and even zero) subscription rates for young workers; in educational and youth-orientated material in union journals; in the offer of strike pay to youths in return for joining the union; as well as in bargaining policies oriented to improving the conditions of youth employment in particular.[15] Such competitive pressures will be weaker (although not wholly absent) when single unionism prevails, and particularly when a closed shop has been attained – in which case the young worker is more likely to be left to approach the union than to be a focus of union attention.[16]

The interests of youth within trade unions are promoted still further by a broader aspect of the allegiance issue. Even in the modern era, with a school leaving age of 16 and a legal age of majority of 18, young entrants to the labour market must undergo further maturation. The balance of loyalties between self, employer and trade union will often be incompletely established. In the struggle for the allegiance of young workers, trade unions have traditionally been placed on the defensive by employer claims to surrogate paternal status.[17] The attempt to wean the loyalty of 'our lads' away from the employer and towards the union has historically been conducive to inproved terms of youth employment. As noted above, the union's bargaining power is undoubtedly strengthened by the resulting growth in youth – adult cohesion. But there is in addition a moral objective for many adult unionists: the winning of young workers to a 'correct' rather than an 'incorrect' view of their own interests and loyalties.

The policy of the union towards youth pay is therefore influenced by the position and activism of young workers themselves. While the influence of youth as an interest group is curtailed by its numerical weakness and inexperience, the propensity of youth towards industrial activism and the interest of adult unionists in securing the adherence and loyalty of the young worker can provide a strategic influence for the interests of youth within union wage policy.

7.5 RELATIVE IMPORTANCE OF THE TWO FACTORS

The trade union may seek therefore to raise the pay of young workers above the supply price of youth labour for two sets of reasons: one concerned with the threat posed by cheap youth labour to the interests of adults and the other with youth as an interest group within the trade union itself. To some extent the two influences are complementary. But cases arise where they are not. In particular, it is possible for the activism of a youth lobby within a union to raise youth relative pay even when rates for young workers are already sufficiently high to cancel incentives to youth-for-adult substitution.

The general importance of the substitution factor may indeed be questioned on several grounds. The possibility of youth-for-adult substitution is constrained in most sectors by the rate of hiring, given the obstacles to firing incumbent workers in favour of cheaper substitutes. It is also curtailed by the limited number of years which a school leaver spends as a young worker. Youths evolve rapidly into adults and unless the ex-youth can be replaced by another youth, substitution will be reversed simply as a result of ageing. In sectors characterised by high pay and low turnover, substitution can therefore proceed only slowly and to a limited extent even when it is desired by employers. In the second place, the job structures of industries such as refining and shipbuilding will contain few jobs in which relative youth productivity (q) is high, reflecting the generally high skill and responsibility requirements of production (e.g., B rather than A in Figure 7.1, p. 121, above). Substitution is unlikely to pose much of a threat to adults in such cases. Third, econometric studies suggest that substitutability between the labour of youths and adults is low or negative, on the male side at least (Layard, 1982, Hutchinson *et al.*, 1984). Finally, although recent youth-related policies have involved substantial reductions in the relative cost of youth labour, youth-for-adult substitution has proved limited even in sectors with a large share of jobs with low skill requirements. In the light of such evidence, can contemporary levels of relative youth pay really reflect the threat of youth-for-adult substitution?

These reasons for doubt carry considerable weight. There are, however, reasons for treating them as less than conclusive. Econometric evidence, in particular, rests largely on aggregate time series, whose value is reduced by problems of limited non-trend variation and structural change. Moreover econometric results typically suggest that the technical substitutability of male for female labour is low – even though it is social rather than technical obstacles which keep women out of some highly paid male preserves (Cockburn, 1983). In the case of youth, similar constraints upon substitution for adults may be imposed by the sentiment of the adult workforce when backed up by a strong workplace organisation. The near absence nowadays of such official and formalised restrictions as apprentice–journeyman ratios by no means establishes that direct restrictions upon youth utilisation are absent. They may be imposed *informally* at the workplace when union organisation is strong – as when national officials have found difficulty in securing grassroots acceptance of YOP trainees.[18]

For this reason the evidence from Special Employment Measures (SEMs) is also less than conclusive. The main form of substitution in response to effectively free (YOP) or cheaper (YWS) youth labour has indeed been simply youth-for-youth, as young workers' jobs are turned into YOP places or YWS subsidies claimed *en masse* for existing youth jobs. Union fears notwithstanding, adult job losses to youths appear to have been small overall and important only in agriculture, distribution and non-professional services (Ryan, 1983; Rajan, Chapter 12 in this volume).

Again, however, the lack of extensive youth-for-adult substitution (in the production industries in particular) may reflect factors other than technical difficulty. Youth programmes come and go, with the duration of the availability of any one subsidy being distinctly uncertain. Unionised employers may not judge it worth their while to incur the hostility of their adult workers by exploiting the temporary profit potential of youth labour under such schemes.

Finally, while in many industries the distribution of relative youth productivity, $f(q)$, undoubtedly looks more like B rather than A in Figure 7.1 above, it must be recognised that the division of labour which lies behind such a distribution is itself a function of the pay of young workers. The share of jobs in which youth productivity (q) is high will rise as the relative price of youth labour (x) falls. When youth labour becomes cheap in ways that are both legitimate and expected to endure, firms have an incentive to invest in a reorganisation of the division of labour so as to use young workers for the less complex and responsible tasks within the jobs of skilled workers. The substitution possibilities created by the redivision of labour may create an instrumental interest for adult unionists in maintaining high levels of youth pay even in sectors which use skill and responsibility intensively.

The relative importance of the two factors which lead a union to bargain up the pay of young workers is therefore difficult to gauge both *a priori* and empirically. Its assessment requires detailed historical research. A preliminary hypothesis states that it was the threat of substitution which fuelled adult interest in raising the price of youth labour in the engineering sector in the 1930s and 1940s, but that by the 1950s the higher relative price of youth labour and the persistence of tight labour markets had reduced adult concern, leaving the activism of the youth lobby as the driving force behind further increases in youth relative pay.

7.6 INDUSTRIAL STRUCTURE OF PAY BY AGE

A full-scale assessment of the issues raised above must await further work. This section takes a first step by examining the broad features of the distribution of youth pay by industry.

Two simple interpretations of the structure of youth pay may be contrasted. In a competitive regime, the prices of youth and adult labour would vary across sectors only as a result of differences in training activities, skill requirements, non-pecuniary benefits and degrees of disequilibrium. We abstract from the two latter influences and assume further that skilled labour is trained solely between the ages of 16 and 20 and wholly within the industry in which it is subsequently employed. On these assumptions, youth and adult pay levels will be inversely related across industries. Industries where the employment share of skilled workers is high will for compositional reasons exhibit adult earnings below average. In the same sectors, the correspondingly large burden of youth training will result in youth earnings below average, as a relatively high proportion of young employees will be trainees – whose pay is predicted to fall below that of other youths according to the costs of training and the transferability of skills (Becker, 1964).

In a world of collective organisation and segmented labour markets, by contrast, youth and adult pay will be positively related across industries. The technological and product market attributes which allow unions to achieve high pay for adult workers independent of skill requirements will do the same for young workers as well, according to the factors discussed above.

A full test of the two contrasting approaches to youth pay would require analysis of data on training levels, skill mixes and product market conditions. A preliminary assessment will be made at this stage by inspecting the associations across industries between: (i) youth and adult pay, and (ii) youth pay, adult pay and degrees of unionisation.

Data are derived from the unpublished results of the annual New Earnings Survey for average hourly earnings of adults and youths between 1974 and 1980 across the 27 sectors of the 1968 Standard Industrial Classification (SIC). Analysis is restricted to manual males. Breakdowns for 16–17 and 18–20 year olds are preserved in order to restrict compositional effects, thereby reducing the discrepancy between average earnings and the underlying price of youth labour.[19] The quality of the data is limited both by fewness of sectors and by small cell sizes in some industries – though weighting by sample size and pooling provide reasonably effective responses to these problems.

The strength of unionism in a sector is proxied by membership density, as developed by Bain and Price (1980) and Price and Bain (1983) and supplemented by unpublished results from Daniel and Millward (1983).[20] Representative data on pay and unionisation in 1979 are provided in Table 7.A1 in the Appendix.

The results indicate that the industrial structure of youth pay in Britain runs largely parallel to that of adult pay. In a regression of youth upon adult earnings across sectors, relationships prove positive and close, particularly for 18–20 year olds (see Table 7.1). During 1974–82 an industry whose adult pay stood 10 per cent above the national adult average would typically exhibit earnings for 18–20 year olds which were nearly 11 per cent above the 18–20 year national average. The corresponding figure for 16–17 year olds exceeds 8 per cent. The associations are statistically significant ($p < 0.01$). The segmentation of the adult labour market by industry is therefore mirrored in its youth counterpart – a finding unfavourable to a competitive interpretation of the youth wage structure. High wage sectors for adults are high wage sectors for youths.

Table 7.1   Pooled regressions of youth upon adult log hourly earnings (manual males 1974–80)

Age group	Intercept	Adult earnings	$\hat{\sigma}^2$	n
16–17 years	0.067 (0.237)	0.814 (0.052)	0.264	161
18–20 years	− 0.593 (0.144)	1.070 (0.033)	0.213	175

Note:
Standard errors in parentheses. Weighted by number of youths in sample. Yearly intercept dummies included for 1975–80. Pooled time series cross-section with autoregressive, heteroscedastic and contemporaneously correlated error matrix. Data missing for four industries for 16–17 year olds and two industries for 18–20 year olds. The model was estimated by the 'Statistical Analysis Systems' package.

Moreover, the association of pay with union organisation is at least as close for young workers as for adults (see Table 7.2). A 10 percentage point difference in membership density between industries was associated during 1974–80 with an earnings difference of roughly 2.5 per cent for both 16–17 year olds and adults. For 18–20 year olds, the point estimate is 2.9 per cent, suggestive of a stronger effect than for adults, but the difference is too small to attain statistical significance.

Table 7.2   Pooled regressions of log absolute hourly earnings on union membership density (manual males 1974–80)

Age group	Intercept	Union density	$\hat{\sigma}^2$	n
16–17 years	3.635 (0.031)	0.247 (0.040)	0.274	161
18–20 years	4.218 (0.018)	0.287 (0.026)	0.240	175
21 + years	4.377 (0.015)	0.258 (0.024)	0.251	175

Notes:
As for Table 7.1. Union density (bounded by zero and unity) refers to all occupations and both sexes. Adult regression unweighted. Time dummy for 1975 dropped for 18–20 year olds in order to maintain full rank.

7.7   CONCLUSIONS

We have argued that reasons for trade union interest in youth pay may be found in the competitive threat to adults posed by cheaper youth labour as well as in the interests, activities and influence of youth itself within trade unions. The importance of each factor is likely to vary across time and place in ways that are not readily determined *a priori*. We have found that the industrial structure of youth pay is (for manual males at least) similar to that of adults – and as closely associated with trade union membership as is that of adults.

The link between unionism and youth pay therefore merits further investigation. The relative importance of the substitution threat to adults (as opposed to the interests of young workers themselves) provides an important topic for historical research. The statistical link between unionism and youth pay needs to be developed further in terms of relative earnings, using a complete specification of union strength, in models incorporating the effects of training activity and demand cyclicality.

Whether or not the link between trade unionism and youth pay stands up to closer examination, there remains in the meanwhile the current policy of reducing relative youth pay. Lower youth pay certainly makes it more attractive for firms to recruit and train young people. But lower youth pay is by itself a potentially damaging response to problems of unemployment and skill shortages. Any gain in youth access to jobs is likely to be offset to a considerable extent by a decline in that of adults, leaving unemployment as a whole largely unaffected. Moreover, while it costs firms less to train youth labour, cheapness alone will not suffice to get the training done. The incentive to employers to use youths for production rather than training stands in the way. Consequently, while a reduction in the price of youth labour may prove a desirable part of a broader policy, without complementary measures to improve job opportunities for adults and to regulate the training of youths within the firm, it is a policy which will do more harm than good.

Table 7.A1 Youth and adult pay and union membership (by sector 1979)

Industry Order (1968 SIC)		(1) W_{y1}	(2) W_{y2}	(3) x_1	(4) x_2	(5) UMD
AFF	1	91.6	127.8	0.611	0.852	0.226
MIN	2	*	237.1	*	0.913	0.893
FDT	3	110.6	148.3	0.551	0.738	0.662
CHM	5	*	165.5	*	0.764	0.588
MET	6	103.9	171.9	0.463	0.766	0.887
MEN	7	94.9	148.7	0.446	0.698	0.772
EEN	9	102.3	153.9	0.505	0.760	0.726
VEH	11	92.5	173.7	0.409	0.768	0.834
OMG	12	*	146.3	*	0.696	0.759
TEX	13	107.2	150.6	0.571	0.801	0.596
BPG	16	*	170.3	*	0.821	0.654
TAF	17	95.6	154.0	0.487	0.785	0.347
PPP	18	*	155.0	*	0.537	0.800
OMF	19	*	152.4	*	0.723	0.433

Table 7.A1 Youth and adult pay and union membership (by sector 1979)

Industry Order (1968 SIC)		(1) W_{y1}	(2) W_{y2}	(3) X_1	(4) X_2	(5) UMD
CON	20	90.8	147.5	0.464	0.754	0.367
GEW	21	*	155.3	*	0.729	0.953
TAC	22	102.8	155.8	0.532	0.807	0.975
DIS	23	95.7	129.6	0.540	0.732	0.149
PSS	25	*	141.3	*	0.842	0.608
MIS	26	80.6	128.1	0.466	0.741	0.118
GOV	27	*	156.0	*	0.893	0.966
ALL	—	97.6	150.0	0.485	0.746	0.536

Notes:

Column

(1) W_{y1}: mean hourly earnings of 16–17 year old manual males in 1979 (pence)

(2) W_{y2}: mean hourly earnings of 18–20 year old manual males in 1979 (pence)

(3) X_1: ratio of (1) to mean hourly earnings of 21+ year old manual males in that industry in 1979.

(4) X_2: ratio of (2) to mean hourly earnings of 21+ year old manual males in that industry in 1979

(5) Union membership density, all workers, 31 December 1978

Sources:

(1) – (4) unpublished results from NES.

(5) Price and Bain. (1983) supplemented by unpublished results from Daniel and Millward (1983).

* indicates data not reported (N.E.S. cell sample size less than 50). Missing Orders have cell sizes below 50 for both youth groups.

Notes

1. A revised version of part of my 1984 conference paper 'Do Trade Unions Raise the Pay of Young Workers?' The empirical research reported in this paper has been made possible by the help of William Wells, Neil Millward and David Blanchflower, and George Bain and Peter Elias in providing access to unpublished data on earnings and unionisation. I would also like to thank Peter Elias, Diego Gambetta, Raja Junankar, Gordon Hughes, Jane Humphries, Edward Lorenz, David Marsden, Lars Osberg, Frank Wilkinson and participants in the Queen's College seminar for helpful comments.

2. Employer characterisations of youth labour (e.g., DE 1977) conform to such generalisations, but also inject an element of potential prejudice along the lines of 'young people aren't what they used to be in my day'. Similarly the descriptions of young workers which have accompanied government policy in recent years have tended to characterise modern youth as insufficiently motivated and lacking in work discipline – partly in order to justify the work-experience focus of youth-related policies (MSC, 1977, Ryan, 1983, Raffe, 1984). An element of scapegoating may be involved in each case.

3. In a few jobs (e.g., pop musician) youth productivity may exceed that of adults. In the broader labour market, however, we assume that adult productivity provides an upper bound to that of youth ($q \leqslant 1$).

4. Amongst 16–19 year olds in the UK during 1979–80, only 5.2 per cent were heads of households while 90.3 per cent lived as children of household heads (CSO, 1982, Table 13.12).

5. The great majority of unemployed young people (85 per cent in November 1983) are ineligible for insurance benefits and receive only the lower supplementary benefit or no benefit at all; while the scale rate for single persons living in another person's household is 62 per cent of the single adult householder rate for 16–17 year olds and 80 per cent for 18–19 year olds (DHSS 1984, Tables 1.36, 34.01; see also Rice, 1986). The current government is moving to reduce the income support available to young workers from social security by temporary suspension of benefit eligibility for those who refuse a place in the YTS; by the proposed removal from 16–17 year olds of the right to set up an independent household; by requiring periodic relocations of town of residence on the part of juvenile claimants; and indirectly by increasing the deductions made to adult housing benefit for 16–20 year old family members in the labour force (Cusack and Roll, 1985).

6. Average gross weekly earnings for 16–17 year olds in April 1981 were £54.90 for males and £50.60 for females; disposable earnings will be lower by the amount of tax and insurance payments – but, at £38 for females, for example, still well above the £25 YOP allowance (Wells, 1983, Tables D2–5). Yet large numbers of youths chose YOP in preference to unemployment. The average number of youths active on YOP proved during 1981–3 roughly equal to registered 16–17 year old unemployment (Ryan, 1983, Table 4).

7. The lack of 'wage for age' schedules in manual employment in the US

(and their presence in Britain) might be seen as reflecting the early demise of the craft tradition in the US (as opposed to its (at most) partial survival in Britain: Lee, 1979). In fact, it has more to do with a lack of concern for youth. Apprentices are still employed (albeit in small numbers) in the US, but under a 'wage for stage of training' rather than a 'wage for age' regime – with the result that median age of apprentices in the US is well above 21 (Ryan, 1984, p. 223). The greater levels of mobility in the US labour market may contribute further by leaving parents less concerned to secure access to their own workplaces for their children.

8. An exploitative element in the relationship of parents to child labour was underlined by Marx in discussing the cotton operatives of the 1830s (1906, p. 432n).

9. Speaking in the aftermath of the 1937 apprentice strike wave and the ensuing concession by the engineering employers of both higher youth pay and the right of trade unions to represent young workers, the president of the AEU remarked that 'apprentices, boys and youths for the first time ... are effectively linked with the workmen inside the factory... this invests the union with a great power indeed' (cited by Jeffreys, 1946, p. 245).

10. In the response of trade unionists to the threat of substitution of youth for adult labour under YOP and YTS one sees calls for adoption of both direct and indirect restriction. Trainees are on occasion informally excluded from the workplace by shopfloor veto while some unions (e.g., GMWU 1982) have adopted national rules about trainee duties which, if enforced, would prevent substitution on the job. Other unions (notably NALGO) have recognised the difficulty of enforcing such rules and have called for the payment to trainees of the rate for the job – which would greatly reduce the benefit to the sponsor of exploiting the labour of 'trainees'. In practice the weakening of union power during the current slump has meant, as in the inter-war years, little ability to enforce either form of restriction in industries where workplace organisation is weak (Ryan, 1983).

11. See note 3 above.

12. Jeffreys (1946, pp. 245–63); Dougan (1975, p. 318); Mortimer (1973, pp. 122, 155); Tuckett (1974, pp. 251–3).

13. The youth share in union membership can be estimated for 1975 (at 5.4 per cent) by matching the share of youth in total employment (7.8 per cent: Wells, 1983, Tables D13–14) with rates of union membership by age. According to the National Training Survey (NTS), 26.9 per cent of employees aged less than 21 years were union members, as compared to 42.2 per cent of adult employees (information kindly supplied by Peter Elias). NTS results indicate that the tendency for union membership density to increase with age is largely confined to males.

14. Details of apprentice strikes in engineering are provided by Jeffreys (1946, pp. 244–5); Croucher (1977, pp. 61–77; 115–122) and (1982, pp. 45–57; 123–31; 230–9), Wigham (1973, pp. 144–5; 241–2) and Frow and Frow (1983, chapter 5). The strikes of 1937, 1941, 1947, 1952, 1960 and 1964 were directly associated with increases in the pay of appren-

tices and youths relative to adults amongst male manual workers (the sole exception being 1947). Methods of youth activism within unions were clearly visible in the 1960 strike. After 3 years of inconsequential efforts by the leadership of the engineering unions (CSEU) to improve the terms of youth employment, a combination of unofficial strikes and lobbying of the CSEU annual conference on the part of apprentices stiffened official union support for the youth claim, resulting in an agreement which increased the relative pay of apprentices and young workers (Tuckett, 1974, pp. 354–7).

15. The Blacksmiths Society, faced with declining demand for its members' skills, decided in the 1950s to insert a regular youth page into its magazine. Urging increased attention to the position of young workers, one leading official stated that 'the big majority of our branch officials are over 50 years of age; and we must get young people into our union to play their part or we will be a back number in the near future' (Tuckett, 1974, p. 312). More recently, the AUEW decided in 1983 to set up a new membership section for YTS trainees – who were to be provided with benefits but who were not expected to contribute to union funds. Sceptical adult members were reassured as follows: 'the key is recruitment. . . many other unions have taken similar steps. . . the long-term benefits to our union will be substantial' (*AUEW Journal*, September 1983, p. 11). See also Croucher (1982, pp. 52; 59).

16. The extent of union competition for membership is difficult to assess empirically. It is most likely to be present in a plant when the number of unions exceeds the number of bargaining units. In 1980 such conditions characterised manual employment in less than one-quarter (22.3 per cent) of all plants where manual unions were recognised. As 44 per cent of manual workers were at that time covered by a closed shop, the scope for membership competition might therefore be considered small in the manual area at least (Daniel and Millward, 1983, Tables II.22, III.1). However, as closed shops may involve more than one union, they do not rule out competition for members. The Donovan Commission (Donovan, 1968, p. 182) noted that competition for membership was 'not uncommon amongst non-craft workers in the engineering industry' – a factor which may help explain the prominence of engineering in post-war activism and youth pay rises.

17. The intensity of employer resistance to union attempts to represent the interests of young workers in engineering in inter-war Britain (as well as to union desires to influence the content of apprentice training in Britain and West Germany in recent decades) reflects in part the importance of youth socialisation in the eyes of employers (Taylor, 1981).

18. As such non-pay attributes as working conditions, redeployment, manning levels and recruitment were found to have been subject to negotiation within the enterprise in 1980 in 75 per cent or more of establishments, the scope for opposition to the use of youth labour (and particularly YOP trainees) may have remained considerable even in the current slump (Daniel and Millward, 1983, Table 8.16).

19. Two compositional factors appear potentially serious, largely in the

16–17 year old group. The decline in apprentice employment – to the extent that it has outstripped that of youth employment in general and to the extent that apprentice pay falls below youth pay (Jones, 1985) – will have raised the average earnings of youth. Secondly, the substitution of YOP trainees for regular 16–17 year old employees affected the distribution of youth pay. Given the concentration of takeup in low paid sectors such as Distribution and Miscellaneous Services, YOP will have involved a compositional increase in youth pay in the economy as a whole, as the lower tail of the 16–17 year old pay distribution was in large part shifted from regular employment to YOP, which lies outside the scope of the NES.

20. Breakdowns of membership density within Metals and Engineering (SIC 7–13) and Services and Government (SIC 25–7) were attained by assuming that either the ratio of densities between Orders within these groups (SIC 25–7) or the absolute difference between the densities (SIC 7–13), as estimated by the 1980 Survey, can be applied to the Bain and Price (1980) estimates for 1979; and that within group ratios or absolute differences remained constant between 1974 and 1980. As the Bain and Price figures reflect end of year counts, while NES earnings data are collected every April, density estimates are lagged one year.

Part II

Characteristics of the Youth Labour Market

8 Earnings, Expected Earnings, and Unemployment Amongst School Leavers

Brian G. M. Main[1]

8.1 INTRODUCTION

The recent recession which has been marked by alarmingly high levels of adult unemployment has brought with it an even more dramatic increase in the level of youth unemployment. This event has sharpened existing concern at what had been seen as an increasing trend to higher levels of unemployment among young persons throughout the 1970s. Two main aspects of youth labour have been singled out as possible contributors to the problem. One is the price, or wage rates, of youth labour and the other is the quality of that labour. This chapter attempts to shed some light on these two issues by discussing the situation of one particular group within the youth labour market, namely school leavers. Data used in the paper come from the 1983 Survey of Scottish School Leavers and pertain to those who left school during the academic year 1981–2.

Wages

In a recent and highly-publicised paper on the youth labour market, Wells (1983) came to the conclusion that:

> The basis of this story is that the relative wages of young people did not appear to adjust rapidly in response to changes in the level of their demand or supply (Wells, 1983, p. 2).

Wells had extended some earlier work by Makeham (1980), who had himself found no significant relationship between youth wages and unemployment. The innovation made by Wells was to introduce a regime-switching methodology that had been suggested earlier by Merrilees and Wilson (1979). The evidence pointed to a shift in the youth labour market from a situation of excess demand to one of excess supply somewhere in the very late 1960s or early 1970s. To some extent the alarm over youth labour costs had already been raised in works by Layard (1982), Lynch and Richardson (1982) and Hutchinson, Barr and Drobny (1984), who all found some significant relationship between youth labour costs and youth employment–unemployment. More recently, Rice (1986) has investigated both equilibrium and disequilibrium models of the youth labour market to find some support for Wells's results.

Rice (1986) also found only a modest role for social security payment. Early work for adults by Maki and Spindler (1975) had found a strong role for social security payments in increasing unemployments. More recent work at the microeconomic level by Atkinson *et al.* (1984) and by Narendranathan, Nickell and Stern (1985) has raised doubts as to the empirical significance of such effects, although the last authors did find that teenagers had the biggest response to variations in benefit levels. Rice found no significant effects for young males, and for young females the effects worked only through increased labour force participation.

This chapter attempts an investigation of the youth wages explanation of youth unemployment, but takes a rather different approach from the work that has preceded it. The test proposed here concentrates on the earnings expectations of unemployed school leavers. It is clearly difficult to talk of the wages of employed school leavers being 'too high'. Given that they have jobs (as distinct from places on any temporary employment schemes), it follows that those wages reflect, in some sense, the school leaver's worth in the market place. It then remains to ask to what extent those who are unemployed are unemployed because they are looking for higher wage rates or earnings than is reasonable.

In terms of partial equilibrium supply and demand analysis, if there is an excess supply of a product (labour services of school leavers, in this case) then it is customary to expect that the price should fall. Even at an excess supply non-equilibrium price, however, some transactions will occur, but it is not reasonable for those who have been unlucky and have not been able to sell their commodity to take the price of those who have been lucky and have sold their commodity as a guide of market worth. The recent work of Okun (1981) and Meade

(1982) among others has forcefully restated the fact that was at the heart of Keynes's analysis of unemployment – the labour market is not like other markets. As Tobin (1972, p. 12) says:

> The market for labor services is not like a market for fresh produce where the entire current supply is auctioned daily.

If the average level of wages for employed persons with a given set of attributes is observed to be £X per hour, then, in a labour market where institutional forces play a large part, the expected wage rate for an unemployed person with the same bundle of attributes might well be £X. As discussed above, in a partial equilibrium analysis of some auctionable commodity this expectation would be too high but in an analysis of a market where custom and practice cannot be ignored, the measure has a certain appeal. Viewed from this perspective, a comparison of the earnings of the employed with the expected earnings of the unemployed (controlling for observed variation in personal characteristics and circumstances) can be viewed as a measure of labour market information. If the two earnings measures are similar, then this would suggest that the information networks in the labour market are functioning. On the other hand, a difference between that two measures that exceeded measurement error in the experiment would suggest some information blockage between the demand and supply sides of the school-leaver labour market.

There are problems inherent in this approach, and these will be discussed below, but for the moment the approach of the chapter can be introduced by saying that the observed earnings and attributes of those school leavers found to be in employment will be used to compute the implied earnings that could be expected by each of the non-employed given his or her attributes, and this will be compared with their stated expected earnings. There is a difficulty of sample selection bias in the sense that the employed and unemployed will differ in many unmeasured characteristics. In addition, these unmeasured characteristics will be correlated with the measured characteristics in a different way for the employed and for the unemployed. A statistical correction suggested by Heckman (1979) will be used to correct for this bias.

Youth Opportunities Programme

The second possible contributor to youth unemployment has been identified as the quality of labour in terms of education and training. There is a feeling that the educational system (although substantially changed by the move to comprehensive education in the 1970s) has failed to adapt to changing demands for labour. Particular attention has been paid to West Germany,[2] where the vast majority of school leavers receive vocational training. A small step in this direction was taken in 1978 when the Youth Opportunities Programme (YOP) was established. The aims of YOP as laid out by the Manpower Services Commission (1979) was to provide young unemployed persons with the chance of training and work experience. First the 'Easter Undertaking' and then the 'Christmas Undertaking' targetted this programme at school leavers. By these undertakings, school leavers who had not found a job by the Easter (later the Christmas) after they left school were guaranteed the offer of a place on a YOP scheme.

As will be seen below, by 1983 – shortly before YOP was replaced by the Youth Training Scheme (YTS) – being on YOP had become as significant a labour market state as being officially unemployed for school leavers. The move to YTS extended the period of experience from approximately 6 months to 12 months, and significantly increased the training dimension. The effectiveness of the YTS scheme has yet to be measured, but evidence of the effectiveness of YOP, presented by Main and Raffe (1983a) and Main (1985) for 1979 and 1981 respectively, suggests that this scheme did little to enhance the 'employability' of its participants. Critics of the scheme have argued that by offering employers essentially free labour it acted more to hold down the wages of young employed persons than to enhance the skills of scheme participants. In this sense, it could be seen as working in conjunction with the Young Workers' Scheme (YWS) which offered a 12-month subsidy of up to £15 per week per employed young person if wages were kept below certain levels.[3]

This chapter makes no attempt to examine the wage-lowering effects of YOP, but does attempt to evaluate the scheme as a manpower policy by measuring whether those school leavers on YOP in October 1982 were any more likely to be employed by the following April than those school leavers who were unemployed. As those school leavers on YOP may be very different from those who are simply unemployed, an attempt is made to control for personal and environmental characteristics. Once again, however, the possibility arises that the host of unmeasured attributes may confound the experimental effect of being on YOP. An attempt is made to highlight this possible bias.

Outline of the Chapter

In section 8.2 the data source used in this study (the 1983 Survey of Scottish School Leavers) is introduced, and the descriptive variables derived from the survey responses are discussed. Section 8.3 offers a theoretical model, drawn from Killingsworth (1983), to assist the explanation of the occurrence of (and possible remedy for) sample-selection bias. Empirical estimates of the wage equation are presented here. In Section 8.4 the estimates derived in section 8.3 are used in a test of the level of earnings expectations among the non-employed compared with the actual earnings of the employed. Section 8.5 switches attention to YOP, and explains a possible source of bias in measuring its effectiveness. Empirical estimates are also presented in this section. Finally, the chapter's conclusions are presented in section 8.6, which also includes a discussion of the policy issues raised by the chapter.

8.2   THE 1983 SURVEY OF SCOTTISH SCHOOL LEAVERS

Approximately 1 in 10 of all those who left school in Scotland in the 1981–2 session received a questionnaire in the 1983 Survey of Scottish School Leavers. A response rate of around 70 per cent was obtained in this postal survey. This surprisingly high response was due, in part, to the long experience of the Centre for Educational Sociology in conducting such surveys and, in part, to the design of the survey whereby each sampled person had been approached while still at school and asked if they would participate in such a survey.[4] The questionnaires were mailed in late March 1983 and returns came in during April.

As well as details about academic performance, the survey solicited information on family background, labour market status (both at the time of the survey and in the previous October – a retrospective question), and current earnings and hours if employed and expected earnings if not employed.[5] Only a 10 per cent random sample of respondents were asked questions about earnings, and it is this sub-sample that is analysed here. By choosing only those who entered and stayed in the labour market – i.e., those who recorded themselves as being either in a job, on YOP or unemployed in both October 1982 and April 1983 – a sample size of 1344 was reduced to 878.[6]

Table 8.1 illustrates the transitions of all the school leavers between

Table 8.1   The status of those who left schools in Scotland during 1981–82 in October 1982 and April 1983

Status in October 1982	Status in April 1983					Proportion by status in October
	Employed	YOP	Unemployed	FT Education	Other	
Employed	0.908	0.032	0.040	0.010	0.010	0.301
YOP	0.235	0.491	0.250	0.015	0.009	0.256
Unemployed	0.189	0.287	0.476	0.006	0.043	0.122
FT Education	0.065	0.016	0.037	0.880	0.003	0.284
Other	0.180	0.010	0.120	0.160	0.440	0.037
Proportion by status in April	0.382	0.179	0.149	0.263	0.028	1.0 $n = 1344$

Source: The 1983 Survey of Scottish School Leavers.

October 1982 and April 1983. Of those in the labour market in October, over 97 per cent were still in the labour force the following April.

The labour market experience of the sub-sample chosen for analysis is illustrated in Table 8.2. Here the importance of YOP as a labour market state is clear. In October less than half of the school leavers have jobs, with almost 2 out of 5 being on YOP. By the following April the situation has improved remarkably little, with a rise in employment by around 10 percentage points and a fall in YOP. Registered unemployment is actually higher in April owing to some of those coming off YOP failing to find jobs. The situation varies somewhat between the sexes, with the main difference being due to the higher propensity of males to be on YOP in October.

The low percentage of school leavers who are in employment in the spring of 1983 can be compared with results from previous surveys. Raffe (1985) reports that this figure had fallen from 83 per cent in

1979 to 66 per cent in 1981, to 53 per cent in 1983 and to 49 per cent in 1984. Raffe's data are restricted to those who left school in the summer term and are therefore not totally consistent with the data in Table 8.1, which covers all school leavers (one-fifth of whom leave at the alternative school-leaving date at Christmas). Nevertheless, the trend is clear and is particularly illuminating when set against the trend in the relative youth to adult average gross weekly earnings as reported by Wells (1985). Measured relative to males aged 21 and over, the weekly earnings of both males and females aged under 18 have fallen over this period. Thus with the number of jobs going to school leavers falling dramatically and their relative earnings also falling, it is difficult to claim that the 1979–84 rise in school leaver unemployment has very much to do with their relative earnings.

The survey response rate shows some variation by level of educational qualification. As the distribution of awards is known at a national level, the sample respondents can be reweighted. Experience shows that reweighting makes very little difference to most measures, and all results presented below represent the raw unweighted data.

It is possible to derive a wide range of personal descriptors from the survey responses. These variables are introduced here as they will be used extensively in the analysis that follows. A dummy variable is used to describe the sex of the respondent, taking value unity for females who comprise 47 per cent of the sample. If the respondent was still aged less than 17 in October 1982, a dummy variable, 'Age 16', takes the value unity. This occurred in 64 per cent of the cases. The educational attainment of the school leaver is described by three dummy variables which captures the hierarchy of school leaving credentials. Achieving one or more Highers[7] (20 per cent) is distinct from achieving four or more 'O' Grades but no Highers (10 per cent), which is distinct from achieving one to three 'O' Grades (24 per cent). A person can be represented by having at most one of these three dummy variables set to unity, and the omitted class (those who passed no school-leaving examination) form 46 per cent of the sample. The implicit assumption is that anyone achieving one Higher will also have at least something of the order of four 'O' Grades. The respondents were also asked to report on their truanting activity while in the fourth form. Those who admitted to playing truant for several days at a time are described by a dummy variable as being serious truants: 8 per cent of the sample fall in this category.

Home background is described in a range of variables. A dummy variable describes whether the respondent has more than three

Table 8.2 Labour market transitions (October 1982–April 1983) for Scottish school leavers who enter the labour market

All Labour market status in October 1982	Labour Market Status in April 1983			Proportion by status in October
	Employed	*YOP*	*Unemployed*	
Employed	0.931	0.031	0.038	0.445
YOP	0.245	0.498	0.257	0.377
Unemployed	0.199	0.301	0.500	0.178
Proportion by status in April	0.542	0.255	0.203	1.0 *n* = 878

Males

	Employed	YOP	Unemployed	
Employed	0.937	0.021	0.042	0.414
YOP	0.245	0.505	0.250	0.414
Unemployed	0.250	0.300	0.450	0.172
	0.532	0.269	0.198	1.0 n = 464

Females

	Employed	YOP	Unemployed	
Employed	0.925	0.040	0.035	0.481
YOP	0.245	0.489	0.266	0.336
Unemployed	0.145	0.303	0.553	0.184
	0.553	0.239	0.208	1.0 n = 414

Source: The 1983 Survey of Scottish School Leavers. Based on those who are observed in the labour market in both October 1982 and April 1983.

brothers and sisters: 17 per cent are defined in this way as coming from large families. A dummy variable also describes the father being unemployed (11 per cent). The social class of the father's job is described in two dummy variables, one capturing whether the father's occupation is professional or intermediate (14 per cent) and the other whether it is skilled non-manual or skilled manual (42 per cent). The remainder (part-skilled, unskilled, etc.) form the omitted category. Parents' education is described by a dummy variable which takes the value unity if either parent had left school after age 17 or later (7 per cent), thus implying post-compulsory education. A small proportion of the sample (9 per cent) had left home by the time of the survey, and this, too, is captured in a dummy variable.

By way of describing the local environment, the travel to work area in which the respondent's school is situated is used to find a local unemployment rate. The figures used are in percentage points, for both males and females, and pertain to April 1983. The sample average figure is 15.5 per cent, with the high of 24.1 per cent being shared by Irvine and Rothesay and the low of 7.1 per cent being in Aberdeen. The official unemployment rate for Scotland in April 1983 was 15.1 per cent.

Of the 476 persons in the sub-sample who were employed in April 1983, a total of 45 gave incomplete answers on their last week's earnings and hours worked. This left 431 usable responses. The distribution of reported (take home) weekly earnings and hours worked is given in Table 8.3. This table shows that over 86 per cent of persons worked between 35 and 44 hours per week. Earnings were less concentrated, but over 82 per cent of persons earned a take home pay of between £30 and £59 per week. Figure 8.1 contrasts the distribution of earnings per week reported by the employed with the distribution of expected earnings which was reported by the 314 non-employed persons.[8] The mean of the expected earnings distribution is significantly higher than the mean of the actual earnings distribution (by £4.55 per week). As measured by the kurtosis (the fourth moment) the expected earnings distribution also has fatter tails[9] than the actual earnings distribution. It seems from Figure 8.1 that the expected earnings although similar to the actual earnings distribution is shifted towards the higher earnings range. This is illustrated in Table 8.4, which compares the percentage of the non-employed who expect to be earning more than a given amount with the percentage of the employed who are actually earning more than that amount. While this is a very crude approach (given that it makes no allowance for the

Table 8.3 Distribution of earnings[a] and hours worked among the employed school leavers (April 1983) (Expressed as a % of employed persons who responded to the questions)

Earnings per week (take home)	Hours worked per week								All by Earnings
	Less than 30	30–34	35–39	40–44	45–49	50–54	55–59	60–64	
£									
<25	0.5		0.2						0.7
25–29	0.5	0.7	2.8	3.7	0.9	0.2			8.8
30–34	0.2	0.5	8.4	4.6	0.2	0.2			14.2
35–39		0.9	11.6	7.4	1.2				21.1
40–44		0.7	10.4	4.9	0.5	0.2		0.2	16.9
45–49		1.4	8.4	2.3	0.5	0.5	0.2		13.2
50–54		0.5	7.4	1.6	0.7				10.2
55–59			3.7	2.1	0.5	0.2			6.5
60–64			2.1	0.9	0.5	0.2			3.7
65–69			1.2	0.5	0.2	0.2		0.2	2.3
70–74			0.7	0.2					0.9
75–79			0.5	0.2					0.7
80 or more		0.5					0.2		0.7
All by hours	1.2	4.6	57.8	28.5	5.1	1.9	0.5	0.5	100[b]

Notes:

[a] Earnings refer to last week's take home pay.

[b] May not sum to 100 due to rounding.

Source: The 1983 Survey of Scottish School Leavers.

variation in personal and environmental characteristics between the employed and the unemployed), it serves to suggest a working hypothesis, namely that the expectations of the non-employed are higher than is indicated by labour market valuations. Taken with Figure 8.1, however, it also suggests that the expected earnings of the non-employed are not totally unrealistic.

A word of caution regarding the data must be added here. It is possible that the non-employed group were unable to differentiate between gross and take-home earnings due to a lack of experience. Such a confusion would certainly explain why the average expected

156

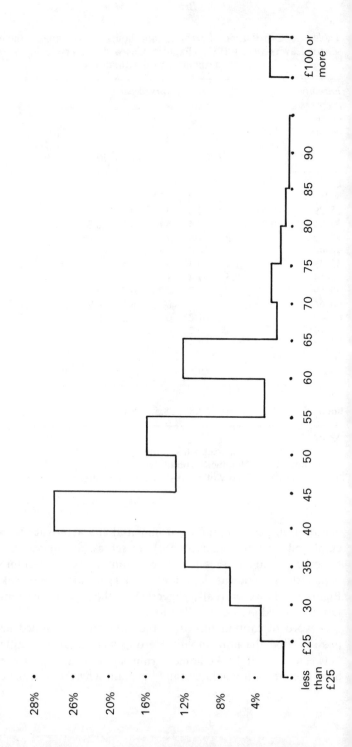

a   *Not employed*

157

b *Employed*

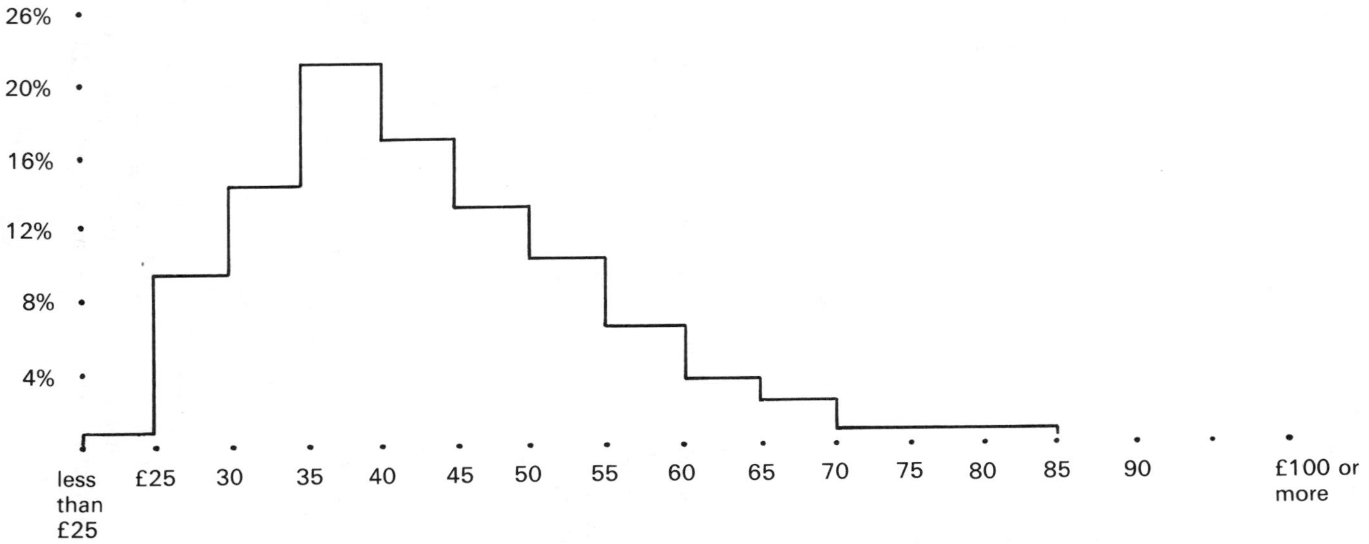

26%
20%
16%
12%
8%
4%

less than £25 · £25 · 30 · 35 · 40 · 45 · 50 · 55 · 60 · 65 · 70 · 75 · 80 · 85 · 90 · · · £100 or more

Figure 8.1 Expected and actual weekly earnings (take home): Scottish School Leavers' Survey 1983
a Not employed. Mean = £46.93, Median = £44.56, Kurtosis = 9.8, $N = 314$.
b Employed. Mean = £42.38, Median = £40.40, Kurtosis = 1.4, $N = 431$.

Table 8.4   Expected and actual earnings compared

Weekly take-home Earnings	% of the non-employed expecting this sum or more	% of the employed receiving this sum or more
£		
100	2.2	0.0
90	2.5	0.2
80	3.5	0.9
70	6.4	2.5
60	19.4	8.5
55	22.3	14.9
50	38.2	24.9
45	51.0	38.2
40	77.1	55.1
35	88.9	76.0
30	95.5	90.2

Source: The 1983 Survey of Scottish School Leavers.

earnings of this group appears higher than the average earnings of the employed group. This possible data flaw should be borne in mind when interpreting all subsequent results, and will be returned to later. However, data from the New Earnings Survey (NES) for April 1983 suggest weekly take home earnings of under 18 year olds to have been around £45.80 for females and £47.90 for males. Although the under 18 year olds in employment and the survey's school leavers in employment are not directly comparable groups, this finding adds some credibility of the reported earnings of those school leavers in employment – the reported average take home weekly earnings for males and females being £42.38.

In Table 8.5, the earnings and hours data are broken down by the level of educational qualifications of the respondents. It is seen that possessing Higher grade qualifications dramatically increases actual (and expected) earnings. Although there is a positive correlation between the number of Highers and wage rates (not reported here) the main difference seems to be between having any Highers and having only 'O' Grades. There may be an element of age entering here, as Highers are a fifth-form qualification and 'O' grades may be taken in the fourth form. But it is also likely that entry to higher-paying jobs is conditional on the possession of some Highers. Table 8.5 also

Table 8.5 Earnings[a] and hours per week for the employed, and expected earnings per week for the non-employed (by education)

School-leaving qualifications	Earnings	Wage rate	Hours worked	(N)	Expected earnings		
					All those not employed	on YOP	Unemployed
	£	£			£	£	£
No credentials	38	0.98	39	(115)	46 (157)	49 (64)	44 (93)
'O' Grades at D and E band only	38	0.97	39	(27)	44 (36)	45 (22)	43 (14)
1–3 'O' Grades at A–C band	40	1.03	39	(117)	47 (71)	49 (48)	45 (23)
4 or more 'O' Grades at A–C band	42	1.08	39	(63)	43 (13)	43 (8)	44 (5)
1 or more H Grade passes	51	1.34	38	(110)	52 (37)	52 (24)	53 (13)
All	42	1.10	39	(431)	47 (314)	49 (166)	45 (148)

Note:
[a] Earnings and expected earnings are in terms of take-home pay.
Source: The 1983 Survey of Scottish School Leavers.

indicates that the average earnings expectations of the non-employed (whether on YOP or unemployed) is closer to actual average earnings of similarly qualified persons at higher levels of education than at the lower or unqualified levels. This last point may be an indication that the better qualified have access to more accurate information about earnings prospects, or are more able to process the available information in an accurate way.

It is now necessary to turn to a multivariate approach to wage rates and hours of work. This will be done by introducing a simple theoretical model.

8.3   A THEORETICAL MODEL OF WAGE RATES AND HOURS OF WORK

The general approach adopted in this paper can be illustrated by working through a model presented in Killingsworth (1983). This expresses an individual's utility in a given period in the form:

$$U = C^a L^b \tag{8.1}$$

where:
L is leisure time expressed as a fraction of the time period.
C is some composite consumer good.

In real terms, the budget constraint can be written as:

$$C = W(1 - L) + V \tag{8.2}$$

where:
W is the real wage rate per period
V is real property income per period.

Representing $(1 - L)$, the fraction of the time period spent in work by H, the utility function (8.1) can be re-expressed to capture the influence of unobservables as:

$$U = [W(H + e) + V]^a [1 - (H + e)]^b \tag{8.3}$$

where:
e is an unobserved term.

Maximising utility results in the familiar first order condition that the marginal rate of substitution (M) between consumption goods and leisure be set equal to the real wage rate.

From equation (8.3):

$$M = [d/(1-d)][W(H+e)+V]/[1-(H+e)] \qquad (8.4)$$

where:
$d = b/(a+b)$.

The reservation wage, M^*, is, of course, evaluated at $L = 1.0$:

$$M^* = [d(1-d)](eW+V)/(1-e)$$

The fact that a school leaver will be observed in paid employment only when the wage rate (W) exceeds the reservation wage (M^*) can be expressed as:

$$-e > dVW - (1-d)$$

Thus in terms of labour supply H:

$$H > 0 \text{ if and only if } e_H > [dV/W - (1-d)] \qquad (8.5)$$

$$H = 0 \text{ if and only if } e_H \leqslant [dV/W - (1-d)] \qquad (8.6)$$

where:
$e_H = -e$

In addition to supply-side considerations that influence a school leaver's decision to take a job, there are also demand-side considerations that determine whether or not that individual will be offered a job. As with the school leaver's tastes, these can be captured by a list of observed personal and environmental characteristics and by unobserved descriptors. The basic approach outlined in equations (8.5) and (8.6) remains unchanged, with unobserved influences being recognised in e_H and observed influences entering on the right hand side as descriptive variables.

Once a job offer is accepted, the exact labour supplied can be determined by equating the real wage with the marginal rate of substitution between consumption goods and leisure. Again this appears to ignore influences from the demand side of the labour market which may constrain choice. Without the complication of such demand imposed constraints, the hours worked (H) can be written as:

$$H = (1 - d) - dV/W + e_H \qquad (8.7)$$

The influence of a school leaver's particular taste for work (crudely captured in the term e_H) can be seen to influence both the participation decision in equations (8.5) and (8.6), and the hours of work decision in equation (8.7). If it is assumed that the distribution of tastes for work e_H in this analysis is normal with mean zero and standard deviation s_H, then the probability of participation for any individual school leaver i can be written from (8.5) as:

$$\text{Prob } (e_{Hi} > dV_i/W_i - (1 - d)) = \text{Prob } (e_{Hi} > -J_i) \qquad (8.8)$$

where:

$$J_i = -dV_i/W_i + (1 - d)$$

Dividing through by the standard deviation (s_H) allows the probability to be stated in terms of the cumulative density function of the standard normal distribution (F):

$$
\begin{aligned}
\text{Prob (school leaver } i \text{ is employed)} & \qquad (8.9) \\
= \text{Prob } (e_{Hi}/s_H > -J_i/s_H) & \\
= 1 - F(-J_i/s_H) &
\end{aligned}
$$

Expression (8.9) leads directly to a probit maximum likelihood analysis of the probability of getting a job. The likelihood function to be maximised uses the probabilities outlined in equation (8.9) to describe the probability of observing all those who have employment in jobs, and of observing all those who do not have employment out of jobs:

$$L = \prod_{i \in E} [1 - F(-J_i/s_H)] \prod_{i \in NE} [F(-J_i/s_H)] \qquad (8.10)$$

where:

E is the set of school leavers observed in employment
NE is the set of school leavers observed without employment.

Equation (8.10) is estimated for the 878 persons in the sub-sample and the results are presented in Table 8.6. Although difficult to interpret in a general sense, if the estimated coefficients are multiplied by 0.40 (in this case), an approximation to the slope of the expected probability of being in employment in April can be obtained at the mean of the regressors.[10] Educational credentials are seen to have a particularly strong and significant effect with the level of 4 or more 'O' Grades being more effective than having Highers. This highlights the different phenomena of finding a job versus the wage rate on that job (which was seen above in a partial analysis to be much greater for those with Highers). Having an unemployed father severely inhibits the probability of a school leaver being in employment.

The approach outlined in equation (8.10) and the results presented

Table 8.6 Maximum likelihood estimates of probit equation for probability of school leaver being employed in April 1983

Descriptive variable	Estimated coefficient (t-statistic)	Descriptive variable	Estimated coefficient (t-statistic)
Father unemployed	−0.645 (4.11)	Large family	−0.119 (0.97)
Female	−0.032 (0.35)	Parents' education	−0.162 (0.85)
Father Prof./Intermed.	0.224 (1.46)	1 or more Highers	0.543 (3.43)
Father skilled	−0.238 (2.43)	4 or more 'O' Grades	1.170 (6.42)
Age 16	−0.170 (1.44)	1–3 'O' Grades	0.517 (4.52)
Left home	−0.033 (0.21)	Unemployment rate	−0.048 (4.09)
Serious truant	−0.199 (1.18)	Constant	0.827 (3.65)

Notes:
$N = 878$
Mean of dependent variable $= 0.542$
$\chi^2_{13} = 156.3$
Log likelihood $= -527.3$

in Table 8.6 represent what has been called the 'characteristics approach' to unemployment. The main criticism of this approach is that it allows very little by way of policy analysis, being an essentially descriptive exercise. Consider the finding that those with four or more 'O' Grade passes have a significantly better chance of being in employment than those with none. This does not, of course, imply that if the Scottish Education Authority were to hire a helicopter and fly over central Scotland distributing 'O' Grade certificates that school-leaver unemployment would be ameliorated. Some insights into the distribution of unemployment are, however, possible from such analysis and in the above exercise the strong relationship between a school leaver's employment chances and the father's unemployment status must surely be a cause for concern. In what follows, the results derived here will be used to allow for the fact that the employed are not a random selection from all school leavers in the labour market.

For those without employment, the wage variable will not be observed. It is possible to use observed wage data for those in employment to estimate some hypothesised wage function:

$$W_i = gX_i + e_{Wi} \qquad (8.11)$$

where:

X_i is a column vector of labour market-pertinent descriptors for the ith school leaver

g is a row vector of parameters to be estimated

e_{Wi} is an error term capturing the unmeasured part of the wage determining process, assumed to be distributed with mean zero.

Estimating (8.11) on the sub-sample of the employed school leavers and using the estimates to compute expected wages for the non-employed school leavers leads to the problem highlighted by Gronau (1974), Heckman (1974), and Lewis (1974) – sample-selection bias. This can be illustrated in terms of the model introduced above. For those in work, equation (8.11) can lead to an expected wage:[11]

$$
\begin{aligned}
E[W_i | H_i > 0] &= E[gX_i + e_{Wi} | e_{Hi} > -J_i] \qquad (8.12)\\
&= gX_i + E[e_{Wi} | e_{Hi}/s_H > (-J_i/s_H)]\\
&= gX_i + (s_{WH}/s_H)1_i
\end{aligned}
$$

where:

s_{WH} = $E(e_{Hi}e_{Wi})$, the covariance between e_{Hi} and e_{Wi}

λ_i = $f(-J_i/s_H)/[1 - F(-J_i/s_H)]$

f, F are the density function and cumulative distribution function respectively of the standard normal distribution function.

If it is true that e_{Hi} and e_{Wi} are uncorrelated, then there is no problem of bias. Unfortunately, there is every reason to expect that particular influences pertaining to school leaver's wage prospects (and, therefore, e_{Wi}) are correlated with those particular influences pertaining to the school leaver's employment prospects (and, hence, e_{Hi}). From Table 8.6 there is clear indication that educational credentials influence employment prospects. If ability is (not unreasonably) assumed to be correlated with educational credentials, and if ability is also correlated with wage rates, it is easy to see how the lack of a measure for ability could produce a bias on the education variables in a wage equation estimated only on those in employment.

The model developed above made the interconnection between wages and labour supply quite clear. The problem arises with every labour market group. A common explanation is that given by Smith (1980) for married women. Smith explains that unmeasured influences causing women to have higher wage rates will make it more likely that that type of woman is observed in the labour market (as the wage exceeds her reservation wage) than women with unmeasured features which tend to depress their market wage rate. If the unmeasured characteristics are correlated with the measured characteristics, then the measured characteristics will act as a proxy for the unmeasured characteristics as well as speaking for themselves. A wage equation estimated on labour market participants will not, therefore, provide unbiased estimates of the expected wage rates of nonparticipants. Sample-selection bias as introduced above is a wide-ranging phenomenon. It indicates that observed market wage rates are essentially endogenous. The problem in terms of equation (8.7) is that W is essentially endogenous and correlated with e_H.

The same point as was made above for wages in equation (8.12) could also have been made for hours of work. These, too, are observed only for workers, and thus from equation (8.7):

$$E[H_i \mid H_i > 0] = E[(1-d) - dV_i/W_i + e_{Hi} \mid e_{Hi} > -J_i] \qquad (8.13)$$
$$= 1 - d - dV_i/W_i + E[e_{Hi} \mid (e_{Hi}/s_H) > -J_i/s_H]$$

Again, using the properties of the truncated normal distribution, equation (8.13) can be rewritten as:

$$E[H_i \mid H_i > 0] = 1 - d - dV_i/W_i + s_H \lambda_i \qquad (8.14)$$

where:

$$\lambda_i = f(-J_i/s_H)/[1 - F(-J_i/s_H)]$$

In both equations (8.12) and (8.14), it can be seen that applying OLS regression to equations (8.11) and (8.7) respectively would be inappropriate, as in the sample of those working the mean of the error term in each equation is not zero. Equations (8.12) and (8.14) indicate that if an estimate of the λ_i term can be obtained, its inclusion on the right hand side as an additional explanatory variable would render each equation susceptible to estimation by OLS. An estimate of λ_i for each person can be obtained from the results of a probit analysis of employment probabilities as outlined in equation (8.10).

Having first estimated the probability of employment function, it is then possible to use the estimates of λ_i so derived in a modified version of equation (8.11) to obtain a bias-corrected wage function:

$$W_i = gX_i + t\hat{\lambda}_i + r_i \qquad \forall i \, \varepsilon \, E \qquad (8.11)^*$$

where:

r_i is a random error term with mean zero.

The resulting estimates of wage rates obtained from the estimated g vector in equation (8.11)* can be used in a linearised form of equation (8.7) to estimate the hours of work function. The linearised form of equation (8.7) contains variables relevant to the hours of work decision (and hence to the marginal rate of substitution between consumption goods and leisure) and can be written:

$$H_i = mW_i + nZ_i + e_{Hi} \qquad (8.15)$$

where:

m is a coefficient to be estimated

Z_i is a column vector of descriptors, including non-wage income, for person i

n is a row vector of coefficients to be estimated

e_{Hi} is an error term capturing the unmeasured part of the hours of work determining process.

Using the results from equations (8.10) and (8.11)*, it is possible to apply OLS to estimate:

$$H_i = mW_i + nZ_i + f\lambda_i + u_i \qquad \forall i \, \varepsilon \, E \qquad (8.15)*$$

where:
u_i is a random error term with mean zero.

It should be emphasised, of course, that the W_i used above has already been corrected for sample-selection bias.

As seen above, supply-side considerations lead to wage rates being entered on the right hand side of the hours equation. It is also possible, however, for demand-side influences to suggest that hours worked should be entered on the right hand side of the wage equation. This would be true where the wage rate was low, but long hours were accepted as the norm thus raising take-home pay. Railway workers, custodians and other such generally low-paid workers often work habitually longer hours than the norm.[12]

Equation (8.11)* could be modified to include hours of work on the right hand side. This would result in equations (8.11)* and (8.15)* forming a pair of simultaneous equations. As the aim of the exercise is to create an estimate of potential market earnings, only the reduced forms for the wage rate equation and the hours equation are presented below.

Results of this approach are shown in Table 8.7. The first column shows a wage equation estimated with no correction for sample-selection bias. As mentioned above, estimated coefficients on education variables would be particularly suspect in such a relationship. The column (2) Table 8.7 uses the results of the probit estimation in Table 8.6 (equation (8.10)) to estimate equation (8.11)*. The coefficient estimated on the λ_i (lambda) term can be seen from equation (8.12) to be an estimate of s_{WH}/s_H. This estimate is not significant, and therefore throws some doubt on the need for (or effectiveness of) the sample-selection bias correction. It will, however, be retained as it does seem sensible on *a priori* reasoning.

Table 8.8 presents the reduced form equations for hours and wage rates respectively. Again, the statistical results are disappointing and offer no support for the two stage procedure.

Table 8.7   Estimates of the wage equation (dependent variable is log (wage))

Descriptive variable	(1) OLS No bias correction Coefficient (t-statistic)		(2) OLS with bias correction Coefficient (t-statistic)	
Female	− 0.013	(0.56)	− 0.014	(0.61)
Age 16	− 0.072	(2.62)	− 0.077	(2.69)
Serious truant	0.074	(1.38)	0.067	(1.21)
One or more Highers	0.266	(7.33)	0.286	(5.99)
Four or more 'O' Grades	0.081	(2.24)	0.112	(1.83)
1–3 'O' Grades	0.040	(1.36)	0.056	(1.44)
Unemployment rate	0.001	(0.20)	− 0.001	(0.30)
Lambda			0.054	(0.64)
Constant	0.006	(0.13)	0.014	(0.24)
N	431		431	
$\overline{R}^2$	0.23		0.23	
F-Statistic	18.95		16.61	
Standard error	0.2295		0.2297	

8.4   WAGE EXPECTATIONS OF THE NON-EMPLOYED

Using the estimated equation (8.11)*, it is possible to produce expected wages, according to the model presented here, for all school leavers in the sample – i.e., whether or not they did have a job in April 1983. Using the reduced form equation, actual hours worked can be

Table 8.8 Reduced form equations for wages and hours

Descriptive variable	Hours equation dependent variable is log (hours)		Wage equation dependent variable is log (wage)	
	Coefficient	(t-statistic)	Coefficient	(t-statistic)
Father unemployed	−0.054	(0.77)	0.017	(0.12)
Female	−0.047	(3.94)	−0.014	(0.59)
Father Prof./Intermed.	0.007	(0.30)	−0.001	(0.02)
Father skilled	−0.009	(0.37)	0.017	(0.37)
Age 16	−0.012	(0.61)	−0.070	(1.80)
Left home	0.022	(1.07)	−0.000	(0.01)
Serious truant	−0.089	(2.60)	0.068	(1.00)
Large family	−0.020	(1.03)	0.041	(1.06)
Parents' education	0.005	(0.19)	−0.019	(0.39)
One or more Highers	0.026	(0.50)	0.267	(2.53)
Four or more 'O' Grades	0.065	(0.69)	0.066	(0.35)
1–3 'O' Grades	0.031	(0.63)	0.034	(0.35)
Unemployment rate	−0.002	(0.41)	0.001	(0.12)
Lambda	0.141	(0.93)	−0.022	(0.07)
Constant	3.60	(59.31)	0.006	(0.05)
N	431		431	
$\bar{R}^2$	0.04		0.22	
F-statistic	2.24		9.53	
Mean of dependent variable	3.65		0.06	

used for those in employment and 40 hours a week can be assumed for those not in employment. From the estimated wage and hours worked (assumed or actual) a level of predicted earnings can be produced for each person in the sub-sample. An alternative (and more direct) route is to take the reduced form equations from Table 8.8 and compute a predicted wage rate and predicted hours of work for each person in the sample. The product of the two gives an alternative estimate of predicted earnings. Both methods are used.

A simple test of whether or not the earnings expectations of the non-employed were realistic would be to measure the expectations held by these individuals against the predictions of the estimated model. As there is a substantial amount of unexplained variation in observed earnings levels, the test can be made simpler and easier to interpret by constructing a left hand side variable for all members of the sample. This has the actual earnings of those who are in employment and the expected earnings of those who are not in employment. This variable is then regressed on the earnings level, as predicted by the above estimates for each individual, plus a dummy variable which describes whether or not the person is employed (it has the value unity if not employed and zero if employed). A significant positive coefficient on the dummy variable could be taken as signifying that the non-employed held unrealistically high earnings expectations.

The results of this exercise are shown in Table 8.9. It can be seen here (in Version 1) that the earnings level expected by the non-employed are £6.46 above that predicted by the wage equation in column two of Table 8.7 and the assumed 40 hours worked per week. In Version 2 in Table 8.9, the expected earnings level of the non-employed is £6.86 above the predicted market earnings computed from the expected wage rate and expected hours worked from the reduced form equations in Table 8.8. Both versions allow for sample-selection bias in the computation of predicted market earnings.

The mean of predicted earnings for the non-employed in Version 1 is £36.58 and in Version 2 is £35.51. Expected earnings would thus appear to be 18 per cent to 19 per cent above predicted market earnings for the non-employed. Although this seems to be a statistically significant result it is necessary to question whether any unaccounted for experimental error could be present. As mentioned above, a major concern with the design of this experiment was whether respondents would accurately distinguish between gross earnings and net earnings. This concern is particularly acute for those who are not in employment and may never have had a job where they were subject

Table 8.9   A regression of actual earnings or expected earnings on predicted earnings and employment status

Descriptive variable	Dependent variable is earnings (if employed) or expected earnings (if not-employed)	
	Version 1[a]	Version 2[b]
Predicted market earnings	0.844 (9.05)	0.803 (8.60)
Not employed	6.462 (6.40)	6.864 (5.67)
Constant	9.583	11.560
N	745	745
$\bar{R}^2$	0.12	0.11
F-Statistic	51.42	47.40
Standard error	13.33	13.39
Mean of dependent variable	44.31	44.31

Notes:

[a] Predicted earnings are computed by the predicted wage in the final column of Table 8.7 times actual hours worked for the employed, or times an assumed 40 hours per week for the non-employed.

[b] Predicted earnings are computed by the predicted wage from Table 8.8 times the predicted hours from Table 8.8.

to deductions. The tax and National Insurance deductions on a gross pay of £45 per week amounted to around £7.31 in 1983. Reporting expected expected weekly earnings in gross terms (£45) rather than take home terms (£37.69) would thus overstate expected earnings by 19 per cent.

It seems impossible, then, to draw any firm conclusions about the information held by non-employed school leavers about their earnings potential on the basis of this experiment. Future work (a 1985 survey) will attempt to allow for the gross/net earnings confusion by asking one-half of a much larger sample about gross earnings and the other other-half about net earnings.

8.5   EFFECTIVENESS OF YOP IN SECURING EMPLOYMENT

As the main government policy instrument targetted on school leaver unemployment, the effectiveness of YOP has come under close scrutiny. Previous investigations – e.g., Main and Raffe (1983a) and Main (1985) – have found that the contribution of participation on a YOP programme to the probability of finding employment is quantitatively small. These studies both took as a measure of YOP's effectiveness the employment status of a sample of school leavers found on YOP in October at a date approximately 6 months later, as measured against the employment status of a sample who were not on YOP in October, again measured 6 months later. The second group could not be viewed as an ideal control group as, owing to institutional considerations such as the 'Christmas Undertaking', those not on YOP in October might enter YOP at a later date and thus be corrupted by the experimental effect.

Table 8.10 describes the transitions made by the non-employed in the 1983 sample between October 1982 and April 1983. The data used here are from the entire 1983 survey (as these questions were asked of everyone) but restricted to individuals who left school in the summer of 1982. Each individual has thus been in the labour market for an approximately identical length of time. Being on YOP in October does seem to increase the probability of a non-employed person being in employment in April. The result is particularly clear for females but far less clear for males. On the other hand, participation in YOP can be seen to be higher among males than females and there may, therefore, be compositional differences in qualifications and other attributes between the two groups. This consideration points to a multivariate analysis which would control for measured differences in attributes between YOP participants and non-participants.

An additional complication arises when one considers that those on YOP in October might not be a randomly selected sample of the non-employed school leavers. A combination of self-selection by school leavers seeking YOP places with varying degrees of aggressiveness, and of assignment effects due to YOP administrators assisting YOP applicants with varying degrees of attention, raises the possibility that those on YOP in October are different from those not on YOP in October in ways that go beyond the measured variation in personal circumstances and characteristics. If these unmeasured factors also influence employment probabilities, then the situation is similar to the sample-selection bias discussed above.

Table 8.10   Labour market transitions (October 1982 – April 1983) for job-seekers in October 1982

All

Labour market status in October 1982	Labour Market Status in April 1983		Proportion by status in October
	Employed	*Not-employed*	
YOP	0.299	0.701	0.694
Unemployed	0.220	0.780	0.306
Proportion by status in April	0.275	0.725	1.0 $n = 1793$

Females

	Employed	*Not-employed*	
YOP	0.347	0.653	0.681
Unemployed	0.227	0.773	0.319
Proportion by status in April	0.309	0.691	1.0 $n = 871$

Males

	Employed	*Not-employed*	
YOP	0.255	0.745	0.706
Unemployed	0.214	0.786	0.294
Proportion by status in April	0.243	0.757	1.0 $n = 922$

Source: The 1983 Survey of Scottish School Leavers.
Based on those who left school in the summer of 1982 and are observed in the labour market in both October 1982 and April 1983.

Considering only those without employment in October 1982, the prospects of any person being in employment approximately 6 months later in April 1983 will depend on a combination of supply and demand factors. It is possible to imagine some sort of indicator variable which measures these employment prospects as a linear combination of each individual's personal and environmental descriptors, thus:

$$I_i = gX_i + u_i \qquad (8.16)$$

where:

g is a row vector of coefficients to be estimated
X_i is a column vector of descriptors for person i
u_i is a normally distributed error term with mean zero and standard deviation s_l.

For all those not employed in October 1982 it is possible to define a variable J_i which takes the value unity if the person i is in employment in April 1983 and is zero otherwise. Used in conjunction with the indicator I_i, this leads to the following specification:

$$I_i > 0 \text{ then } J_i = 1 \qquad (8.17)$$
$$I_i \leqslant 0 \text{ then } J_i = 0$$

The exact level that I_i must reach to indicate employment need not be zero as implied above. The exact level is left undefined but can be accommodated within the constant term in the definition of I_i in equation (8.16). The assumptions made so far allow the probability that a non-employed school leaver in October 1982 be found in employment in April 1983 to be written as:

$$\begin{aligned} \text{Prob } (J_i = 1) &= \text{Prob } (u_i > -gX_i) \qquad (8.18) \\ &= \text{Prob } (u_i/s_l > -gX_i/s_l) \\ &= 1 - F(-gX_i/s_l) \end{aligned}$$

where:

F is the cumulative density function of the standard normal distribution.

This approach leads directly to a probit maximum likelihood estimate of the parameters g. Results of such an exercise (for males and females separately) are presented in Table 8.11. Variables used here are those that were introduced above in the analysis of earnings. The relationship between these descriptive variables and employment success is (in general) much weaker for those who were not employed in October than for the entire sample of school leavers (see Table 8.6). Once again, to ease interpretation in this case the coefficients can be multiplied by 0.34 for females and 0.30 for males to obtain the slope of the expected probability of being in employment in April given not employed in October evaluated at the mean of the regressors. Educational credentials still play an important role, and (for males) having four or more 'O' Grades is of greater assistance in finding employment than having Highers.

The additional variable used to describe individuals here is the variable *YOP* which is a dummy variable taking the value unity if the person is on YOP in October, and is zero otherwise. The results of Table 8.11 seem to indicate that being on YOP in October improves the probability of a person being employed in April. In terms of a school leaver living at home in a family with more than three children, who was aged 17 by October 1982, who has no record of truant but no passes in any school-leaving credentials, whose parents have no further education, whose father is employed in an unskilled job and who lives in an area of 15 per cent unemployment, the YOP factor can change the expected probability of being in a job in April 1983 from 0.20 to 0.38 for females and from 0.14 to 0.18 for males. The effect is statistically significant only for females.

This gender difference in the size of the YOP effect is similar to that found in Main (1985) for 1980 school leavers and in Main and Raffe (1983a) for 1978 school leavers. Quantitatively, being on YOP if unemployed in the October after leaving school has increased the expected probability of being in employment the following spring by around 5 percentage points for male school leavers in each of these studies. Female YOP participants seem to have enjoyed a greater relative advantage over non-participants, estimates of the size of the effect ranging from 14 percentage points (for 1978 school leavers) to 8 percentage points (1980 school leavers) to the 18-percentage point effect found above (for 1982 school leavers). In addition, the effect for females has always been found to be statistically significant.

A problem arises, however, if there is a possibility that the unmeasured variables which influence whether or not a person is on YOP in October also influence whether or not a person is employed in April. It is easy to think of such omitted variables – motivation is an obvious one. More motivated school leavers may be more likely to be on YOP and may also be more likely to secure employment by April 1983. Not all omitted variables will act in the same direction. To formalise the possibility, however, equation (8.16) can be rewritten with the YOP status descriptor formally separated from the other descriptors, X_i:

Table 8.11 Maximum likelihood estimates of probit equations

Descriptive variable	Probability employed in April, given not employed in October			
	Females		Males	
	Coefficient	(t-Statistic)	Coefficient	(t-Statistic)
Father unemployed	−0.148	(0.99)	−0.636	(3.51)
Father professional	0.113	(0.78)	0.220	(1.44)
Father skilled manual	−0.141	(1.39)	0.046	(0.46)
Age 16	−0.236	(1.66)	−0.020	(0.13)
Left home	0.305	(1.60)	0.315	(1.71)
Serious truant	−0.032	(0.15)	−0.140	(0.81)
Large family	−0.090	(0.73)	−0.226	(1.69)

	Model 1		Model 2	
Parents' education	0.028	(0.14)	−0.358	(1.78)
One or more Highers	0.653	(3.71)	0.245	(1.23)
Four or more 'O' Grades	0.358	(1.86)	0.460	(2.28)
1–3 'O' Grades	0.146	(1.22)	0.309	(2.65)
Unemployment rate	−0.031	(2.32)	−0.039	(3.09)
YOP	0.551	(4.98)	0.170	(1.57)
Constant	−0.384	(1.35)	−0.280	(1.03)
N	871		922	
χ^2	93.12		61.43	
Mean of dependent variable	0.309		0.243	

$$I_i = gX_i + bYOP_i + u_i \qquad (8.19)$$

where:

b is a parameter to be estimated

YOP_i takes the value unity if the school leaver is on a YOP scheme in October, and is zero otherwise.

A separate process (and indicator) can be specified as determining whether a person is on a YOP scheme in October, thus:

$$Y_i = cZ_i + e_i \qquad (8.20)$$

where:

c is a row vector of parameters to be estimated

Z_i is a column vector of descriptors for person i that influence whether or not that person is on YOP

e_i is a normally distributed error term with mean zero and standard deviation s_Y

Following from above the YOP indicator variable can then be defined to work as follows:

$$Y_i > 0 \text{ then } YOP_i = 1 \qquad (8.21)$$
$$Y_i \leqslant 0 \text{ then } YOP_i = 0$$

This leads directly to a probit estimation of the probability of being on YOP. Results of such a procedure are presented in Table 8.12. The descriptive variables used here are chosen to be appropriate to a process occurring in October, some 6 months before the survey. The unemployment rate is thus for the appropriate travel to work area in October 1982. Father's employment status and social class descriptors may also have changed, and are therefore omitted. In the same sense, the left-home descriptor is not reliable. Although the relationship is significant (as judged by the Chi-squared test) individual coefficient estimates are disappointingly weak. In the cases of coming from a large family and having Highers passes there is a significant relationship.[13] For males, being relatively young significantly influences the probability of a non-employed school leaver being on YOP in October. On the other hand, truancy behaviour at school reduces the probability of being on YOP for females but plays no significant role for males. In general, it seems possible to say that those on YOP are not a random sample of those without employment

Table 8.12 Maximum likelihood estimates of probit equations

	Probability on YOP in October given not employed in October			
	Females		Males	
Descriptive variable	Coefficient	(t-Statistic)	Coefficient	(t-Statistic)
Age 16	0.037	(0.25)	0.428	(2.84)
Serious truant	−0.374	(1.96)	−0.060	(0.40)
Large family	−0.341	(3.03)	−0.200	(1.73)
Parents' education	−0.104	(0.51)	−0.063	(0.36)
One or more Highers	−0.592	(3.38)	−0.342	(1.81)
Four or more 'O' Grades	0.252	(1.22)	0.161	(0.77)
1–3 'O' Grades	0.112	(0.94)	0.242	(2.04)
Unemployment rate	−0.001	(0.05)	−0.009	(0.80)
Constant	0.636	(2.48)	0.409	(1.68)
N	871		922	
χ^2	51.59		54.06	
Mean of dependent variable	0.681		0.706	

in October. The way that this might bias the measure of the effect of YOP derived above may be seen as follows.

In terms of equation (8.19), the expected value of I_i must now be written:

$$E[I_i] = E[I_i \mid YOP_i = 1] \text{ if } Y_i > 0 \qquad (8.22)$$
$$\text{and} = E[I_i \mid YOP = 0] \text{ if } Y_i \leq 0$$
$$= E[gX_i + bYOP_i + u_i \mid e_i > -cZ_i] \text{ if } YOP_i = 1$$
$$\text{and} = E[gX_i + bYOP_i + U_i \mid e_i \leq -cZ_i] \text{ if } YOP_i = 0$$
$$= gX_i + bYOP_i + E[U_i \mid e_i/s_Y > -cZ_i/s_Y] \text{ if } YOP_i = 1$$
$$\text{and} = gX_i + bYOP_i + E[U_i \mid e_i/s_Y \leq -cZ_i/s_Y] \text{ if } YOP_i = 0$$

Thus:

$$E[I_i] = gX_i + bYOP_i + (s_{IY}/s_Y)\lambda_i \text{ if } YOP_i = 1 \qquad (8.23)$$
$$\text{and} = gX_i + bYOP_i + (s_{IY}/s_Y)\lambda^*_i \text{ if } YOP_i = 0$$

where:

s_{IY} = $E(u_i e_i)$, the covariance between u_i and e_i
λ_i = $f(-cZ_i/s_Y)/[1 - F(-cZ_i/s_Y)]$
λ^*_i = $-f(-cZ_i/s_Y)/F(-cZ_i/s_Y)$
f, F are the density function and cumulative density function respectively of the standard normal distribution function.

As it is possible to estimate λ_i and λ^*_i from the probit equation describing the probability of participation in YOP in October, it is possible to construct an additional variable to add to the right hand side of equation (8.19) that will keep the relationship unbiased. A variable (lambda) which has value λ_i when person i is on YOP and has value λ^*_i when person i is not on YOP will correct for sample-selection bias. The estimated coefficient on this variable will be an estimate of (s_{IY}/s_Y).

No results for this bias-corrected procedure are presented here. This is due to the failure of the approach to yield sensible results. The reason for this may be that many of the factors which influence whether or not a school leaver is on YOP also influence the probability of finding employment. Following the steps outlined above introduces serious multicollinearity. It may well be that a better specified and statistically more significant set of relationships would not be susceptible to this problem.

The fact remains, however, that equations (8.22) and (8.23) above demonstrate the extent to which earlier estimates of the effectiveness of YOP are subject to biases. Those on YOP in October are not a random selection of the non-employed school leavers. If unmeasured factors that influence the probability of a person being on YOP are correlated with unmeasured factors that influence whether a person is in employment 6 months later, then the descriptive variable YOP can act as a proxy for these unmeasured factors, as well as representing its own effect.

8.6   CONCLUSION

Two main findings have been presented. The expected earnings of non-employed school leavers were found to be higher than would be indicated by the earnings of employed leavers with similar characteristics. This finding was statistically significant, and in empirical terms could be said to be of the order of a 18 to 19 per cent difference. Caution must be exercised in interpreting this result, however, as a confusion among the unemployed between gross and net earnings would lead to a difference of around this magnitude. Given the experimental error present, then, it is not possible to conclude that unemployed school leavers have expected earnings that are different from what they might be led to expect by the going market rate for similarly qualified employed school leavers.

The second finding is that – as measured by the probability of being employed 6 months later – YOP gave some advantage to those school leavers who were on the scheme in October 1982 when compared with those non-employed school leavers who were not on the scheme in October 1982. This finding is consistent with results of other investigations of the effectiveness of YOP for 1978–9 and 1980–1. In all three periods, YOP has seemed to impart a 5 percentage point advantage to male participation. The effects for females have been more variable, but always more positive than for males. In this study YOP seems to increase the expected probability of female participants being in employment some 6 months later by around 18 percentage points. The finding above – that those who participate on YOP are not a randomly selected sample of unemployed school leavers – suggests that estimates of YOP's effectiveness are potentially biased.

The policy implications of the finding on expected earnings among non-employed school leavers is difficult to assess. Their high expectations could explain their non-employment. But would a reduction of these expectations – which might be assumed to come about in due course as their search lengthens – bring about their employment? Estimates of the elasticity of demand for youth labour vary. Wells (1983) has suggested a figure in excess of 2.0 for young males, although he is reluctant to treat this as a precise relationship and measures the relative labour costs of young males to adult males.[14] Lynch and Richardson (1982) suggest that a 1 per cent fall in the relative costs of employing young males will lower the share of young male unemployment in male unemployment by 1.3 per cent.[15] Layard (1982) suggests a short-run elasticity of demand for young males of 1.3.[16] Hutchinson *et al.* (1984) suggest a long-run elasticity for young males of 3.6.[17] Due to differences in data sources, time periods and estimating techniques used it is necessary to be particularly cautious when comparing these results. Pike (1984) has illustrated the importance of disaggregating the labour force in the appropriate way, paying particular attention to the distinction between part-time and full-time female employees. What each one indicates, however, is that without any outward shift in the demand for labour, wage levels of the employed youths would have to fall substantially to increase employment opportunities for youths to any significant degree.

By contrast, Main and Raffe (1983b) have demonstrated that between 1977 and 1981 two-thirds of the total decline in the employment of school leavers in Scotland was due to business cycle-induced[18] declines in recruitment of school leavers. Structural change within the economy played a relatively minor part in the lowering of school-leaver recruitment – the effect of the lower level of economic activity on school-leaver recruitment ratios being ten times larger.[19] Had school leaver employment declined in proportion to all employment (i.e., with the ratio of recruited school leavers to adult employees remaining constant), the decline in school-leaver employment would have been only one-quarter of what actually occurred. As mentioned above, the period since 1979 has seen a huge increase in school-leaver unemployment, and yet the relative earnings of young people have not risen over the period but have, in fact, fallen.

From a policy viewpoint an increase in employment through demand management would thus appear to offer a rapid and effective means of lowering school-leaver unemployment. Lowering the expected earnings of school leavers seems to present a more difficult policy option, and offers little certainty of any significant effect.

The evidence presented above also casts doubt on the effectiveness of YOP as a mechanism for improving the employment prospects of young persons. This does not deny YOP its role as a way of reducing the official register of unemployed school leavers (which in the absence of YOP would have shown 55 per cent of school leavers unemployed in October 1982, rather than the recorded 18 per cent). Nor does it say anything about the effect of YOP in holding down school leavers' wage levels in general. It does imply, however, that if YTS is to be judged a success there will have to be jobs for young people to go to on completion of their year of training. The evidence on YOP suggests that it is difficult for such schemes to pull themselves up by their own bootstraps. In a recent review of the New Training Initiative (NTI) Ryan (1984, p. 44) concludes that 'more and better training is of little value to individuals, young or old, without jobs to use it in'. The evidence from the operation of YOP seems to substantiate this conclusion.

Notes

1. The author gratefully acknowledges valuable research support received from the Centre for Educational Sociology, whose activities are financed, in part, by grants from the ESRC. This research project was funded by the Nuffield Foundation's Small Grants Scheme. The paper benefitted from comments received at the IER Conference 'Young Persons' Labour Market' held at the University of Warwick in November 1984. Any remaining errors are my own.
2. For a comparison of the West German and British situations see Prais (1981).
3. Introduced in 1982, a wage rate of less than £40 per week was required to qualify for the maximum subsidy of £15 per week.
4. The 70 per cent response rates includes those who declined to participate when approached while still at school, as well as those who (having been sent a questionnaire) did not reply.
5. The exact questions asked about earnings and hours are as follows:

   If employed:

   > How many hours did you work last week in your job, not counting lunch breaks?

   > Last week, what was your take-home pay for this job, after deductions of tax, etc.?

   If not employed:

   > When you get a job what do you expect your take-home pay to be (each week)?

6. 10 individuals were also eliminated owing to non response on educational attainment, etc.
7. The Higher Grade Scottish Certificate of Education is the main university entrance qualification in Scotland and represents a standard well above 'O' Grade, but somewhat below the English 'A' Level.
8. A total of 88 non-responses were obtained on the expected earnings question from the 402 non-employed persons. Almost exactly two-thirds of these persons were on YOP, and they may have regarded themselves as employed (but it should be stressed that this latter group did not enter into the actual earnings data).
9. The normal distribution would have a kurtosis of zero. A positive value indicates a narrower peak and, therefore, fatter tails.
10. See Maddala (1983, p. 23).
11. This result is a property of the truncated normal distribution. A full discussion is available in Heckman (1979) and in Maddala (1983, pp. 365–8).
12. As will be seen below, a complication arises in interpreting the estimated coefficient on the hours variable in the wage equation. This is due to the wage data being derived from the division of weekly earnings by hours of work. Long hours of work will thus usually include overtime hours which are generally paid at a higher rate.

13.   A simplistic interpretation of the coefficients can be obtained by multiplying each by 0.35 for females and 0.34 for males to obtain the slope of the expected probability of being on YOP evaluated at the mean of the regressors. Again, see Maddala (1983), p. 23).

14.   See Wells (1983, Table 18 and p. 61).

15.   See Lynch and Richardson (1982, pp. 367–8). Their data refers to those aged less than 20 years.

16.   Layard (1982, p. 524), where the data are based on manual workers in manufacturing.

17.   Hutchinson *et al.* (1984, Table 2, p. 200).

18.   Ascribing the effect to the business cycle alone is a strong statement but gains some support from the fact that the relative employment costs of young people showed little or no change throughout this period. See Wells (1983, Figures 10–13 and Wells, 1985, Figure 2).

19.   Raffe (1984) has updated these figures through to 1983 and confirms the finding.

9 Individual Differences in the Youth Labour Market: A Cross-section Analysis of London Youths

Lisa M. Lynch

9.1 INTRODUCTION

The governments of many countries continue to be deeply concerned about the high unemployment rates of young workers, and Great Britain is no exception. Part of this concern has been generated by disturbing trends in unemployment figures for young workers. As Table 9.1 shows, the unemployment rate in Britain for young males under the age of 18 has risen sharply from 12.3 per cent in January 1976 to 23.1 per cent in January 1982, and the rate for young females has increased from 12.0 per cent to 22.0 per cent over the same time period.

While unemployment for the population as a whole has also increased during this period, youths have borne an increasing share of the burden of unemployment. For example, the percentage of young unemployed males (females) of all unemployed males (females) has increased from 8 per cent (15 per cent) in 1950 to 14 per cent (27 per cent) in 1982. It is sometimes argued that policy-makers should not be overly concerned about high youth unemployment rates, for while the incidence of unemployment among young people is high, the duration is quite short. In other words, young people experience spells of unemployment as part of a productive job search process, therefore there is no need for intervention. However, as Table 9.2 shows, young people are now experiencing much longer durations of unemployment, with 35 per cent of young unemployed workers in January 1983 out of work for more than 6 months.

Table 9.1   Unemployment rates, (%), by age and sex (Great Britain)

	Males			Females		
	Under 18	*18–19*	*All*	*Under 18*	*18–19*	*All*
July 1975	13.8	9.6	5.4	10.4	6.1	2.1
January 76	12.3	11.2	6.9	12.0	8.1	2.9
July 76	26.7	10.7	7.2	25.6	9.2	4.0
January 77	12.9	10.8	7.3	14.2	9.8	3.8
July 77	28.6	11.3	7.7	29.6	10.9	4.9
January 78	13.2	11.2	7.6	15.5	10.7	4.4
July 78	26.9	11.2	7.4	27.4	11.1	5.0
January 79	10.8	10.7	7.1	12.0	10.0	4.2
July 79	23.4	10.0	6.7	23.6	10.3	4.7
January 80	10.3	10.7	7.0	11.9	10.3	4.5
July 80	31.1	13.8	8.7	32.1	13.0	6.2
January 81	19.1	18.4	11.9	19.2	15.8	7.1
July 81	30.6	21.6	14.0	31.1	17.6	8.6
January 82	23.1	25.2	15.3	22.0	20.2	8.8
July 82	33.5	26.5	15.6	33.3	21.3	9.6

Source: *Employment Gazette*, various years.

Table 9.2   % unemployed over 25 weeks, by age (Great Britain)

	Aged under 20 *(%)*	*Total unemployed* *(%)*
January 76	14	31
January 77	25	39
January 78	27	41
January 79	25	42
January 80	21	40
January 81	28	39
January 82	35	52
January 83	35	53

Source: *Employment Gazette*, various years.

Although all of these figures indicate both increasing incidence and duration of unemployment among young people in Britain, they do not reveal the entire extent of the youth labour market problem. Studies, such as that by Roberts, Duggan and Noble (1981) have shown that there is a substantial percentage of young people actively looking for work who are not registered as unemployed. Since official statistics refer only to those registered, these numbers may be misleading, especially with non-registration rates among young people as high as 30 or 40 per cent.

Why has the worsening position of young people in the labour market both in absolute and relative terms attracted so much attention? Labour theories such as human capital imply that since substantial investment in human capital should occur in the early years of work, early unemployment is particularly costly. If there is no investment in human capital during periods of non-employment, the entire earnings profile of the worker will be depressed.

Perhaps more importantly, dual labour market theory suggests that early unemployment might lead to poor work habits, weak labour force attachment and general alienation from society. Given the recent riots in Britain and the fear of a rise in crime involving young people, it is this effect in particular that has motivated policy-makers to concentrate on youth unemployment.

There have been a variety of studies which have attempted to determine those factors which influence youth unemployment in Britain. The descriptive study by Casson (1979), and the econometric analyses using time-series data by Layard (1982), Makeham (1980), and Metcalf (1979) stress the importance of demand conditions as a primary determinant of youth unemployment. They argue that young workers are particulary hard hit by cyclical changes in the economy because of their concentration in low skill groups. These studies have also shown that while the increase in the youth population due to the 'baby boom' has had some impact on their current high rates of unemployment, this effect has been minimal. In addition to these factors, recent studies by Lynch and Richardson (1982) and Wells (1983) have pointed out the potential importance of relative employment costs of young workers to adult workers.

Studies such as Daniel and Stilgoe (1977), Jones (1983), and MacLeod, Main and Raffe (1983) have concentrated on analysing the characteristics of unemployed young people using survey data. Some of these studies have found that educational qualifications and part-time work experience prior to leaving school are important determinates of the probability of being unemployed. They also find a high degree of labour market segregation in young male and female employment.

With the exception of the above studies there has been relatively little rigorous analysis of the determinants of youth unemployment in

Britain. There are a variety of ways in which one can analyse the youth labour market experience. One approach is to try to explain changes in youth unemployment using time-series data. Typically, time-series studies have attempted to show how aggregate demand, relative wages and demographic changes have affected both cyclical and secular trends in unemployment. One of the advantages of time-series analysis is that it is possible to assess the impact on aggregate youth employment of those explanatory variables that are under government control.

The disadvantage of time-series analysis is that it is not possible to observe individual differences in the labour market. Using survey data, both cross-section and longitudinal, it is possible to explore a wide range of issues. For example, MacLeod, Main and Raffe (1983) using British data, and Meyer and Wise (1982), using US data show the importance of part-time work experience before leaving school and educational qualifications in determining the probability of being unemployed. At the same time Rees and Gray (1982), with US data, have shown the impact of family characteristics such as occupation of the head of the household and unemployment amongst other family members, on the probability of being unemployed.

In addition to these factors, studies by Leighton and Mincer (1982) and Clark and Summers (1979), using data on US youths, have investigated the impact of job changes or high rates of turnover on unemployment experience. Specifically, Leighton and Mincer (1982) find that the number of job changes is significantly and positively related to the number of unemployment spells. On the other hand, Clark and Summers (1979) point out that over half of all job changes occur without any unemployment at all. Many of the US studies have also analysed white–non-white and sex differentials in the labour market experience and find significantly higher unemployment amongst non-whites and females. Unfortunately, there have been few studies in Britain on racial differentials (one exception is Dex, 1982) or sex differentials in the employment experience of young workers.

In this chapter we attempt to isolate and analyse those characteristics which persistently influence the labour market experience of young people. Using the results of a longitudinal survey of London youths we summarise a portion of their labour market experience by estimating the factors which influence the probability of a young person being unemployed, participating in a government training scheme, returning to school, and finally the determinants of earnings for those actually employed. The results presented in this paper in conjunction with the findings in Lynch (1983) and Lynch (1985) using this same sample should give us a better understanding of the labour market experience of British youths.

The survey that we use for our analysis is based on a sample of 1922 youths from five Greater London boroughs (inner boroughs – Tower Hamlets, Lambeth and Hammersmith; outer boroughs – Bromley and Hounslow) who expected to leave school in the summer of 1979 at the minimum school leaving age of 16. These individuals were first interviewed (by personal interview) in March 1979 (Phase I) before they actually left school. At this stage, a parent or guardian of the respondent was also interviewed. The respondents were then reinterviewed in July–August 1979 (Phase II) after they had finished the school year, November 1979 (Phase III, a postal questionnaire), March–April 1980 (Phase IV), November 1980 (Phase V) and November–December 1981 (Phase VI). This paper presents findings from Phases II, IV and V. We have omitted Phase III from our analysis because this interview had a very low response rate and was limited in the scope of questions. In future work we hope to analyse data from the Phase VI interview and see how labour market experience for these youths alters or remains the same $2\frac{1}{2}$ years after they have left school.[2]

Although the initial sample size in March 1979 was 1922 by November 1980 (Phase V) there were only 1017 economically active young people in the sample. This reflects a 30 per cent dropout rate from the original sample with the remainder of those who were not economically active consisting of those youths who had returned to school, were on a government training scheme, or had dropped out of the labour force (usually due to illness, pregnancy, or prison). In order to have some idea on which respondents were more likely to drop out analysis was conducted on the characteristics of dropouts between Phases II and IV. We found that dropout rates were somewhat higher for those boys employed at Phase II than for those boys looking for work (14 per cent v. 12 per cent). This was not the case for girls for whom the dropout rates for those employed and for those looking for work were 12 per cent and 15 per cent respectively. Dropout rates on average were higher in the inner rather than outer boroughs of London.

This chapter is divided into seven sections. In section 9.2 we discuss some of the relevant variables which may influence the probability of a young person being unemployed. We divide these influences into three categories – individual characteristics, local environmental conditions and work history. In section 9.3 we report results obtained using maximum likelihood estimation for the probability of a young person being unemployed immediately after leaving school. We separate these results from findings obtained using later surveys because we want to isolate the immediate post-school leaving experience from the labour market experience later on. In other words, the dynamics behind the school-to-first-job transition may be quite different than the unemployment–employment transitions experienced later on. In section 9.4 we report results on the probability of being unemployed at Phases IV and V. Until now the analysis has excluded those who went on a government training scheme or went back to school. To see whether or not this omission has biased our estimates in any way, we estimate equations for the probability of being on a government scheme or back in school and these results for Phase IV and V are reported in section 9.5. Section 9.6 presents results on the determinants of earnings for those who are employed at Phase V. This section estimates a standard human capital earnings equation with the addition of race, sex and borough of residence as explanatory variables. Finally, section 9.7 summarises the cross-section results, discusses policy implications, and points out possible limitations of the results presented.

9.2 DETERMINANTS OF THE PROBABILITY OF BEING UNEMPLOYED

The probability of observing an unemployed respondent at an interview date will be affected by the factors which influence both the incidence and the duration of a young worker's unemployment. There is a wide range of variables which may influence the probability of a young person being unemployed. We have grouped these variables into three broad categories – individual characteristics, local environmental conditions, and work history.

Individual Characteristics

There are six variables which fall into this category – ethnicity, appearance, extent of education (whether or not any exams such as CSE or GCE have been taken), comprehension, ability to express oneself and health. If there is discrimination in the labour market non-whites may experience both higher incidence and longer duration of unemployment; they are therefore more likely to be found in the stock of the unemployed. Those young people who do not take any exams before leaving school may have greater difficulty in obtaining their first and subsequent employment, especially if employers use exams as a signal of potential productivity. This type of 'statistical discrimination' could also be relevant for the interpretation of the appearance, expression and comprehension variables. Finally, poor health could have an influence on the probability of being unemployed for at least two reasons. First, illness after leaving school will mean that the young person has not accumulated as much valuable work experience. Second, employers may be concerned about hiring and training an individual with a poor health record since this could imply a high absentee rate and consequently lower productivity.

Environment

This category contains three variables – the borough of residence, the occupation of the head of the household and unemployment amongst other members of the respondent's household. The borough of residence may affect the ability to find a job for several reasons. If an individual is living in a borough which has a depressed local labour market and high transport costs to those areas with more opportunities, he or she may be unwilling (or unable) to look for employment in other areas. Also, it may be more difficult to obtain information about potential employment possibilities outside the local labour market. One problem with this argument is that it is difficult to define the local labour market for the individuals in the survey. We have used as a proxy for the local labour market the borough that the individual lives in, but clearly this is inadequate. We might have preferred to define a local labour market for an individual as the area within a given distance from his or her home. But even this would have been an inadequate definition since the availability of transport could decrease or increase the geographical size of the potential labour market for each individual. Those young people living in areas within a borough with limited transport are much more constrained in their employment opportunities than those living in areas with excellent transport. Another reason why the borough of residence may be significant is that it proxies for poor quality education, poor housing, or lack of community services, all of which contribute to a general alienation from society and the world of work. Evidence of this alienation may be found in the recent riots of youths in Britain.

A second variable which may affect the motivation of the young person is the presence of unemployment amongst other members of the household. This may make the young person feel more discouraged about his or her own chances of finding employment. It may also limit the amount of information that working members of the household can provide to the respondent about potential jobs.

Finally, the socioeconomic status of the family, which we proxy with the occupation of the head of the household,[3] may influence the probability of a young person being unemployed. Those young people from middle class families may have greater access to information about potential jobs and resources to help find jobs. On the other hand, as Rees and Gray (1982) discuss, youths with the head of the household working in an occupation similar to the type of job they want – such as junior non-manual or semi-/unskilled manual job – may have more information about potential jobs. It is therefore difficult to determine *a priori* which effect will dominate.

Work History

This category contains three variables – part-time work experience prior to leaving school, lagged employment status and turnover. The first of these variables should be especially important in finding the first job after leaving school. Those who have worked part-time while in school will have more contacts in the labour market and employers will probably prefer those who have already worked to those with no previous experience.

The lagged employment status variable could be significant for two reasons. The first is that past unemployment experience can influence the behaviour of the individual. For example, an individual who experiences a long unemployment spell early in his or her work experience may become discouraged and not look as hard for other employment. Past unemployment also implies a loss of work experience and employers may use employment records as a sorting device and label those applicants who have been unemployed as potentially unreliable, less productive, or undesirable. The second reason why this variable may be significant is that lagged unemployment status is simply a proxy for unobserved variables such as motivation. If this is the case, we have the problem of 'uncontrolled heterogeneity' (see Heckman and Borjas, 1980 or Flinn and Heckman, 1982).

The final variable is whether or not the individual has changed jobs. Again this variable could act as a signal to the employer if the employer believes that those who have changed jobs in the past may not be very reliable and may leave the firm after a short period of time. This would mean that any investment that the firm makes in the individual would be lost, and therefore they would be reluctant to hire those who have changed jobs frequently.

9.3 IMMEDIATE POST-SCHOOL LEAVING EXPERIENCES

We separate this part of the analysis from the study of the labour market experience at Phases IV and V because of the nature of the sample at Phase II. Our analysis at Phase II is basically of the outcomes of the transition from school-to-first-job while the analysis at Phases IV and V is related to subsequent employment-unemployment-employment transitions. The sample at Phase II contains two types of young people – those leaving school temporarily and those leaving permanently. For those planning to return to school in the autumn, employment is a temporary state. This may imply that these young people are more willing to take any job since it will last only a short period of time. On the other hand, those young people leaving school permanently are presumably searching for a permanent job. Consequently, they may turn down offers of temporary work in the hope of finding a more satisfactory permanent position. For these reasons we anticipate different results at Phase II than at Phases IV and V, even though we include the same explanatory variables in all equations estimated.

We estimate the equations for boys and girls separately because the two groups appear to differ a great deal in their labour market experience. For example, the girls are concentrated into three occupations – shop assistants, clerks, and typists – while the boys are spread over a much wider range of jobs – motor mechanics, construction workers, assembly workers, general labourers, etc. The girls also earn more than the boys on average, perhaps because they are not receiving the same amount of training as boys.

We also estimate three equations at each phase: the first equation includes all the variables except borough of residence, lagged unemployment status, and turnover; the second equation omits only lagged unemployment status and turnover; and the third equation includes all of the variables. One reason why we estimate these three equations is that we were concerned about the correlation between the boroughs and other explanatory variables such as ethnicity, household unemployment, and occupation of the head of the household. The inner city boroughs in our survey have a high concentration of non-whites and unskilled workers, and this multicollinearity could render imprecise the estimate of the impact of particular variables on the probability of being unemployed. Another reason is that those youths who are unemployed in the current period have experienced a job status change, and as a result the turnover variable automatically becomes spuriously significant. Finally, if an individual was unemployed in the past because he or she was non-white, or did not have any exams, this is reflected in the current period in the lagged employment status variable. This may imply that even though variables such as ethnicity or exams do not appear to be significant in the current period, their effect is shown in the significance of the lagged employment status variable.

Table 9.3 shows the percentage of young people who have not found a job immediately after leaving school. The numbers in parentheses represent the number of valid cases used for estimation.

Since we are estimating a model in which the individual is either employed or not employed we describe his or her state in probabilistic terms and use Logit maximum likelihood estimation. We have defined as 'unemployed' all those who are out of the labour force and all those who are not working but have looked for a job in the past month. We have not included in this analysis individuals who returned to school,

Table 9.3 Unemployment rates and sample size of those economically active

	Unemployment rate	
Date	*Boys (%)*	*Girls (%)*
Phase II July/August 1979 (summer holidays)	51	49
Sample size of those economically active	(701)	(642)

Table 9.4   The determinants of the probability of being unemployed, Phase II (Boys)

Variable	Equation (1)	Equation (2)	Equation (3)
Constant	0.94[a]	1.00	1.01
	(2.29)	(2.00)	(1.84)
OCC1	−0.24	−0.15	−0.25
	(−0.96)	(−0.60)	(−0.81)
OCC2	−0.66	−0.63	−0.85
	(−2.13)	(−2.03)	(−2.30)
OCC3	0.11	0.12	−0.35
	(0.32)	(0.35)	(−0.85)
OCC5	−0.50	−0.46	−0.98
	(−1.67)	(−1.53)	(−2.65)
Appearance	0.13	0.13	0.20
	(0.72)	(0.72)	(0.95)
Comprehension	−0.19	−0.16	0.16
	(−0.86)	(−0.89)	(0.59)
Expression	0.02	−0.03	0.23
	(0.09)	(−0.13)	(0.82)
Ethnicity (white)	−0.50	−0.43	0.01
	(−2.38)	(−1.95)	(0.04)
Health	−0.38	−0.42	−0.26
	(−1.41)	(−1.83)	(−0.96)
Part-time work	−0.29	−0.27	−0.43
	(−1.71)	(−1.59)	(−2.05)
Exams	0.31	0.38	0.69
	(1.35)	(1.65)	(2.46)
Household unemployment	0.32	0.27	0.16
	(1.78)	(1.50)	(0.73)
Lambeth	—	−0.19	−0.07
		(−0.70)	(−0.21)
Tower Hamlets		−0.06	−0.13
		(−0.21)	(−0.39)
Hounslow	—	−0.18	−0.42
	—	(−0.69)	(−1.35)
Bromley		−0.63	−0.61
		(−2.10)	(−1.69)
Job status (t-1)	—	—	2.58
			(8.32)
Turnover	—	—	2.10
			(6.77)
Log L =	−469.53	−466.44	−357.02

Notes:

[a]Asymptotic *t*-test in brackets.

OCC4 and Hammersmith have been retained in all equations.

Table 9.5   The determinants of the probability of being unemployed, Phase
II (Girls)

Variable	Equation (1)	Equation (2)	Equation (3)
Constant	1.32	1.57	1.27
	(2.93)	(3.14)	(2.35)
OCC1	−0.11	−0.70	−0.04
	(−0.48)	(−2.69)	(−0.14)
OCC2	−0.06	−0.57	−0.34
	(−0.18)	(−1.68)	(−0.92)
OCC3	0.17	0.08	−0.09
	(0.53)	(0.24)	(−0.25)
OCC5	−0.59	−0.40	−0.19
	(−1.90)	(−1.29)	(−0.56)
Appearance	−0.16	−0.24	−0.02
	(−0.89)	(−1.33)	(−0.10)
Comprehension	0.27	0.27	0.12
	(1.13)	(1.08)	(0.44)
Ethnicity	−0.88	−0.82	−0.64
(white)	(−3.14)	(−2.83)	(−2.00)
Health	−0.21	−0.26	−0.18
	(−1.05)	(−1.24)	(−0.78)
Part-time work	−0.33	−0.32	−0.32
	(−1.83)	(−1.78)	(−1.60)
Exams	−0.34	−0.25	0.09
	(−1.42)	(−1.00)	(0.32)
Household	0.43	0.38	0.34
unemployment	(2.39)	(2.11)	(1.70)
Lambeth	—	−0.25	−0.06
		(−0.86)	(−0.19)
Tower Hamlets	—	−0.07	−0.00
		(−0.26)	(0.00)
Hounslow	—	−0.50	−0.35
		(−1.85)	(−1.21)
Bromley	—	−0.70	−0.72
		(−2.41)	(−2.25)
Job status	—	—	2.08
(t-1)			(9.04)
Turnover	—	—	1.20
			(3.87)
Log L =	−426.57	−422.14	−364.54

went on a government training scheme or are out of the labour force due to ill health, pregnancy, or in prison.

The results for Phase II are presented in Tables 9.4 and 9.5. A description of the variables can be found in Appendix A. The variables that appear to be significant determinants of the probability of being unemployed at Phase II include ethnicity, exams, the presence of other unemployed household members, part-time work experience prior to leaving school, living in the outer borough of Bromley, lagged employment status and turnover. There are several differences between the results presented for the girls and those presented for the boys. For the boys exams is an important variable in explaining the probability of being unemployed whereas this variable is insignificant for the girls. Another variable which is significant for the boys but not for the girls is the occupation of the head of the household. Those boys with a junior non-manual or semi/unskilled worker as the head of the household are more likely to be employed at Phase II. This may suggest that having a parent or guardian working in a skilled category similar to the area a young person is looking for work in may provide the youth with more information about potential employment opportunities.

Although most of the variables that are significant have the expected sign there is one perplexing finding which is the sign on the exams variable in the boys' equation. We had expected that those who took any exams would be less likely to be unemployed; however, the results seem to suggest just the opposite. This is not as surprising as it might first appear if those individuals who had already arranged a job before leaving school did not see the necessity of taking any exams and those who took exams did not have as much time to search for employment.

9.4 LABOUR MARKET EXPERIENCE 1 YEAR AND $1\frac{1}{2}$ YEARS AFTER LEAVING SCHOOL

In this section we present the results of the determinants of the probability of being employed at Phases IV and V. Recall that at Phase IV the school leavers have been out of school for approximately 1 year and at Phase V they have been out of school for almost $1\frac{1}{2}$ years. Table 9.6 shows the unemployment rates at Phases IV and V and the number of valid cases at each phase. (Results for Phase IV are reported in Appendix B.)

Table 9.6   Unemployment rates and sample size for those economically active

Date	Unemployment rate	
	Boys (%)	Girls (%)
Phase *IV* March/April 1980	8	8
Sample size of those economically active	(588)	(541)
Phase *V* November 1980	7	10
Sample size of those economically active	(529)	(488)

The variables at Phase IV and V that explain the probability of being unemployed include ethnicity, exams, comprehension, part-time work experience prior to leaving school, unemployment of other household members, the outer boroughs of Hounslow and Bromley (boys Phase IV), having a manual worker as the head of household (boys Phase IV), lagged employment status and turnover. It is interesting to see how the inclusion of borough of residence, lagged employment status, and turnover seem to dampen the significance of the ethnicity and household unemployment variables.

Let us examine our results in terms of the original three categories of variables. There are three individual characteristics that seem to determine the probability of being unemployed. These include ethnicity, comprehension and exams. The inclusion of the borough of residence does not seem to dampen the significance of the ethnicity variable for the girls as much as the boys. Since girls are more likely to be in 'high visibility' jobs than boys, and discriminating employers may regard ethnicity as a component of appearance, ethnicity may be an even stronger determination of unemployment for the girls than for the boys. The exam variable is significant for girls at Phase V but not for the boys, while at Phase IV just the opposite is true. Overall the exam variable does seem to play some role in the labour market experience of both boys and the girls.

Two of the three environment variables are occasionally significant, and these are the borough of residence and the occupation of the head of the household. However, the third variable in this category – the presence of other unemployed household members – is almost always significant. The significance of this variable may indicate greater discouragement among those young workers living in households where other members of the family are unemployed. The fact that other workers in the household cannot find employment may make the young person more discouraged about his or her own chances of finding a job and, perhaps, less motivated in seeking employment. A similar result has been found by Main (see Chapter 8 in this volume) for Scottish youths, with their probability of not working increasing if their father was unemployed.

All three of the work history variables are usually significant. These variables predict that those people who have changed jobs or were unemployed in the past are more likely to be unemployed in the present. The part-time work variable suggests that those individuals who worked while in school are more likely to be employed. This seems to give weight to the argument that employers use employment records as a signal of reliability and work attitude.

Since we have discrete data, it is not clear how to interpret what the coefficients on our explanatory variables imply about the marginal effect of a particular variable. However, there is a way to examine how particular variables affect the probability of an individual being unemployed. In the equations estimated the probability of an individual being unemployed can be expressed as:

$$P = \frac{1}{1 - e^{-X'B}}$$

Where X' is the vector of explanatory variables and B their coefficients. Using equation (3) in Tables 9.7 and 9.8 we can calculate the probability of a 'privileged' individual being unemployed and compare that result with the probability of a 'disadvantaged' youth being unemployed. At Phase V we define a 'privileged' youth as being: white; head of household is a manager; excellent appearance, comprehension, expression, and health; no household unemployment; exams taken; part-time work experience before leaving school; lives in Bromley; obtained a job immediately after leaving school; and is still working for the same employer. A 'disadvantaged youth' is: non-white; head of household is a semi/unskilled manual worker; poor appearance, comprehension, expression, and health; household

Table 9.7   The determinants of the probability of being unemployed, Phase V (Boys)

Variable	Equation (1)	Equation (2)	Equation (3)
Constant	− 0.71	− 0.74	− 0.65
	(− 0.95)	(− 0.88)	(− 0.60)
OCC1	− 0.33	− 0.34	− 0.34
	(− 0.66)	(− 0.67)	(− 0.60)
OCC2	− 0.49	− 0.49	− 0.70
	(− 0.72)	(− 0.72)	(− 0.89)
OCC3	− 0.89	− 0.88	− 0.71
	(− 1.20)	(− 1.17)	(− 0.88)
OCC5	− 0.74	− 0.70	− 1.04
	(− 1.10)	(− 1.03)	(− 1.35)
Appearance	− 0.14	− 0.19	− 0.27
	(− 0.35)	(− 0.46)	(− 0.61)
Comprehension	0.14	0.16	0.62
	(0.27)	(0.31)	(1.13)
Ethnicity	− 0.83	− 0.96	− 0.78
(white)	(− 2.02)	(− 2.18)	(− 1.66)
Health	− 0.22	− 0.23	− 0.23
	(− 0.49)	(− 0.51)	(− 0.48)
Part-time work	− 0.42	− 0.44	− 0.36
	(− 1.17)	(− 1.19)	(− 0.88)
Exams	− 0.72	− 0.60	− 0.33
	(− 1.60)	(− 1.28)	(− 0.63)
Household	0.90	0.94	0.91
unemployment	(2.43)	(2.54)	(2.28)
Lambeth	—	− 0.37	− 0.12
		(− 0.60)	(− 0.18)
Tower Hamlets	—	0.55	0.30
		(0.92)	(0.44)
Hounslow	—	0.42	0.98
		(0.75)	(1.53)
Bromley	—	− 0.08	0.41
		(− 0.11)	(0.51)
Job status	—	—	1.76
(Phase IV)			(3.38)
Job status	—	—	0.42
(Phase II)			(0.98)
			1.25
Turnover	—	—	(3.57)
Log L =	− 121.23	− 120.05	− 101.68

Table 9.8   The determinants of the probability of being unemployed, Phase V (Girls)

Variable	Equation (1)	Equation (2)	Equation (3)
Constant	−0.58	−0.71	0.45
	(−0.70)	(−0.76)	(0.39)
OCC1	0.49	0.51	0.47
	(0.89)	(0.93)	(0.80)
OCC2	−0.50	−0.52	−0.77
	(−0.61)	(−0.63)	(−0.87)
OCC3	0.44	0.34	−0.16
	(0.68)	(0.52)	(−0.22)
OCC5	0.46	0.35	−0.09
	(0.73)	(0.55)	(−0.13)
Appearance	−0.35	−0.39	−0.33
	(−1.00)	(−1.08)	(−0.80)
Comprehension	−1.07	−1.08	−1.11
	(−1.91)	(−1.93)	(−1.71)
Expression	0.82	0.77	1.00
	(1.44)	(1.35)	(1.54)
Ethnicity	−0.96	−0.95	−0.43
(white)	(−2.29)	(−2.16)	(−0.83)
Part-time work	−0.89	−0.86	−1.00
	(−2.78)	(−2.53)	(−2.56)
Exams	−0.80	−0.83	−0.83
	(−1.95)	(−1.98)	(−1.77)
Household	0.88	0.83	0.59
unemployment	(2.67)	(2.52)	(1.51)
Lambeth	—	−0.04	0.26
		(−0.06)	(0.37)
Tower Hamlets	—	0.66	0.93
		(1.22)	(1.50)
Hounslow	—	0.03	0.41
		(0.05)	(0.60)
Bromley	—	0.19	0.42
		(0.30)	(0.58)
Job status	—	—	2.61
(Phase IV)			(5.44)
Job status	—	—	0.29
(Phase II)			(0.76)
Turnover	—	—	0.68
			(2.19)
Log $L =$	−140.59	−138.92	−113.99

unemployment; no exams; no part-time work experience; lives in Lambeth; has been unemployed in the past; and has changed jobs. Another way to examine the marginal effects of particular variables is to calculate the probability of being unemployed of a 'typical' respondent in our survey and then alter one characteristic at a time. Our 'typical' boy at Phase V is: white, head of household a manager, average appearance; excellent comprehension, and health; average expression; no household unemployment; exams taken; part-time work experience before leaving school; lives in Hounslow; and is working for the same employer. Our 'typical girl' is similar except that she has excellent appearance and expression. Table 9.9 presents the probability of being unemployed at Phase V of these different types of individuals.

The results in Table 9.9 show a dramatic difference between the most 'privileged' and 'disadvantaged' youths in terms of the probability of being unemployed. A 'typical' individual's probability of being unemployed increases sharply if he or she is: non-white; has not taken any exams; has other members of the household unemployed; was unemployed at Phase IV; or changed jobs. The impact of past unemployment on current status is particularly strong for the girls.

Table 9.9   The probability of being unemployed $1\frac{1}{2}$ years after leaving school

	Probability of being unemployed	
Characteristics	*Boys* (%)	*Girls* (%)
'Privileged'	9.0	30.0
'Disadvantaged'	93.0	99.0
'Typical':	25.2	30.0
but non-white	42.4	40.0
but no exams	31.8	49.3
but household unemployment	45.5	43.5
but unemployed at Phase IV	66.2	85.5
but no job change	54.1	45.5

9.5   PROBABILITY OF BEING IN SCHOOL OR ON A GOVERNMENT TRAINING SCHEME

Although the discussion until now has focused on the probability of a school leaver being employed or not, there are other options available to the young person. Some of these options include returning to school, or going on a government training scheme. Since we have excluded those young people who were in school or on a government scheme in our previous analysis, we decided to analyse the factors determining the decision to be on a government scheme or to be in school. The analysis is particularly important in order correctly to interpret the parameter estimates presented in Tables 9.4, 9.5, 9.7 and 9.8. If the decision to return to school or go on a government training scheme is not independent of the labour market experience, we may be underestimating the impact of certain variables in our equations on the probability of being unemployed. For example, if non-whites are more likely to return to school due to an unsatisfactory labour market experience the coefficient on ethnicity in the equation on the probability of unemployment will be biased downwards due to this sample-solution bias.

We therefore estimated eight separate equations for boys and girls at Phases IV and V to determine the probability of being in school and the probability of being on a goverment scheme. The independent variables remained identical to those reported earlier for the equations for the probability of being unemployed. The results for the probability of being on a government training scheme at Phase V for the girls have not been reported because there were only three girls on a scheme. Consequently, the following discussion centres on the results of the seven other equations.

Clearly, the most significant variable in Tables 9.10 and 9.11 for both the probability of being in school or on a government scheme is ethnicity. Non-whites are much more likely to stay on or return to school or be on a government scheme. This is not a surprising result since we know from our unemployment equations that non-whites have a more difficult time in finding a job than their white counterparts. This may have influenced their decision to return to school since the cost of foregone earnings is minimal given their greater probability of being unemployed. Similarly, these non-whites who did decide to enter the labour force are more likely to be unemployed for a longer period of time and, therefore, to become eligible for a place on a government training scheme.

The only other variable that is frequently significant is lagged unemployment status. This is a more difficult variable to interpret since the sign on the variable changes with the length of the lag in the equations for the probability of returning to school. We had expected

Table 9.10   The determinants of the probability of being in school, Phases IV and V

	Phase IV		Phase V	
Variable	Boys	Girls	Boys	Girls
Constant	−0.86	−3.60	0.16	−13.27
	(−0.91)	(−2.21)	(0.12)	(0.00)
OCC1	−0.05	1.48	−1.18	11.21
	(−0.09)	(1.36)	(−1.48)	(0.00)
OCC2	−0.60	0.86	−1.50	10.76
	(−0.78)	(0.66)	(−1.22)	(0.00)
OCC3	0.31	0.28	−0.68	11.28
	(0.44)	(0.19)	(−0.67)	(0.00)
OCC5	−2.13	1.08	−10.53	10.66
	(−1.85)	(0.90)	(0.00)	(0.00)
Appearance	−0.38	−0.26	−1.66	0.32
	(−0.86)	(−0.50)	(−1.80)	(0.39)
Comprehension	0.15	−0.26	−0.22	2.49
	(0.27)	(−0.39)	(−0.24)	(2.28)
Expression	0.22	−0.32	0.39	−2.01
	(0.39)	(−0.46)	(0.41)	(−2.09)
Ethnicity	−1.84	−2.26	−0.65	−2.44
	(−4.28)	(−3.48)	(−0.88)	(−2.71)
Health	−0.68	0.05	−0.68	0.34
	(−1.51)	(0.07)	(−0.89)	(0.30)
Part-time work	−0.43	0.81	−1.63	−0.77
	(−1.10)	(1.33)	(−2.40)	(−0.95)
Exams	−0.33	0.59	0.59	1.11
	(−0.31)	(0.66)	(0.50)	(0.82)
Household	0.09	0.26	0.76	0.19
Unemployment	(0.20)	(0.46)	(1.17)	(0.22)
Lambeth	0.27	1.02	−0.68	−0.30
	(0.46)	(1.32)	(−0.67)	(−0.28)
Tower Hamlets	−0.45	0.33	−0.92	−1.71
	(−0.62)	(0.40)	(−0.82)	(−1.21)
Hounslow	0.19	0.00	−0.14	−0.35
	(0.32)	(0.00)	(−0.15)	(−0.33)
Bromley	0.63	−0.99	−0.90	−11.36
	(0.88)	(−0.82)	(−0.68)	(0.00)
Status (t-1)	−1.61	−2.34	−8.47	−10.86
	(−3.35)	(−3.12)	(0.00)	(0.00)
Status (t-2)	1.10	1.77	−1.10	0.07
	(2.29)	(2.46)	(−1.51)	(0.08)
Turnover	−1.74	−11.93	−1.59	−11.12
	(−3.05)	(0.00)	(−1.45)	(0.00)
Log L =	−117.00	−67.92	−47.16	−30.82
% in school	5	3.5	1.7	1.5

Table 9.11   The determinants of the probability of being on a government training scheme, Phases IV and V

| Variable | Phase IV | | Phase V |
	Boys	Girls	Boys
Constant	− 14.84	− 23.12	− 4.96
	(0.00)	(0.00)	(2.25)
OCC1	0.23	11.28	0.13
	(0.24)	(0.00)	(0.11)
OCC2	0.40	9.97	0.18
	(0.35)	(0.00)	(0.12)
OCC3	− 0.89	10.80	− 10.53
	(− 0.65)	(0.00)	(0.00)
OCC5	− 0.91	10.10	0.30
	(− 0.69)	(0.00)	(0.00)
Appearance	0.21	− 0.29	1.21
	(0.28)	(− 0.38)	(1.46)
Comprehension	0.08	− 0.19	− 1.55
	(0.08)	(− 0.20)	(− 0.97)
Expression	− 1.43	− 0.15	1.85
	(− 1.30)	(− 0.15)	(1.15)
Ethnicity	− 0.90	− 1.89	− 3.03
	(− 1.32)	(− 2.33)	(− 2.91)
Health	1.17	0.48	0.01
	(1.04)	(0.41)	(0.01)
Part-time work	0.18	− 0.92	0.03
	(0.26)	(− 1.30)	(0.04)
Exams	0.62	− 1.17	1.63
	(0.49)	(− 0.93)	(1.05)
Household	1.69	0.76	0.98
unemployment	(2.49)	(1.03)	(1.24)
Lambeth	− 0.39	0.59	1.74
	(− 0.49)	(0.60)	(1.37)
Tower Hamlets	− 1.06	− 0.81	1.12
	(− 1.08)	(− 0.72)	(0.81)
Hounslow	− 11.17	− 10.60	− 8.05
	(0.00)	(0.00)	(0.00)
Bromley	− 0.34	− 0.81	2.39
	(− 0.27)	(− 0.60)	(1.34)
Status (t-1)	− 0.32	0.02	2.17
	(0.49)	(0.02)	(1.87)
Status (t-2)	11.14	10.90	− 0.27
	(0.00)	(0.00)	(− 0.35)
Turnover	− 0.71	− 1.69	− 1.67
	(− 0.93)	(− 1.90)	(− 1.46)
Log $L =$	− 43.47	− 37.53	− 33.15
% on scheme	1.6	1.9	1.4

that those who suffered unemployment would be more likely to go back to school or go on a government scheme, and therefore the anticipated sign on the status variables was positive. However, at Phase IV, in the school equation, this variable is significant with a negative sign at time $(t-1)$ and significant with a positive sign at time $(t-2)$. Perhaps a reason why we have this peculiar sign on the Phase II status variable is that at that time our sample included individuals who had originally planned to leave school permanently but changed their minds by July. Therefore, it was more probable that they would be employed over the summer since they were only interested in finding temporary employment.

The implication of the above discussion on the results of our unemployment equations is that we have probably underestimated the importance of the ethnicity variable on the probability of being unemployed. However, since the ethnicity variable is usually significant, these results simply reinforce the conclusion that ethnicity is an important determinant of the probability of not being employed.

9.6 EARNINGS

So far, we have concentrated on the determinants of the probability of a young person being unemployed, in school or on a government training scheme. In this section we examine the determinants of earnings for those individuals who have been able to find employment using a human capital type earnings equation. We include as explanatory variables whether or not any exams were taken, and whether or not the individual has had any additional training since leaving school. While we expect those who have taken exams to obtain higher earnings, it is not clear what effect training has on earnings at this stage. Most of the youths who have had some training are still receiving that training, and this is usually being currently financed by the firm they are working for. This implies that in the short run these youths may actually earn less, while in the long run they will probably earn more than their untrained counterparts. More boys than girls in our survey are receiving some type of on-the-job training, and this may explain why the average earnings of the girls is higher than the average earnings of the boys at this stage.

We have also included variables such as length of initial employment duration, percentage of total weeks unemployed, total weeks employed, total number of weeks in current job, and total number of weeks in current job squared. All of these variables attempt to capture the increasing returns associated with being employed in a single job and the loss of valuable work experience associated with unemployment. Although it appears that the total number of weeks employed and the percentage of total weeks unemployed should measure the same thing, we have not included as time 'unemployed' those weeks spent out of the labour force.

We have included three personal characteristics – health, sex and ethnicity. We expect that those who suffer from poor health are more likely to have lost valuable work experience through illness, and therefore have lower earnings. We also expected that since there is substantial labour market segmentation there may be some difference in earnings on the basis of sex. In addition, both sexual and racial discrimination may depress the earnings of the girls and non-whites.

Finally, the borough of residence is included in our earnings equation as a proxy for local labour market conditions. If the local labour market is depressed there should be downward pressure on the wage rate for individuals working there. However, as we discussed earlier, the borough of residence is probably an inadequate representation of the 'local' labour market for the young worker.

Table 9.12 presents the results of our earnings equation at Phase V. There is no significant difference between the coefficients in the boys' and girls' equation so we have estimated a final equation for boys and girls together.

These results suggest that whites, and those who have taken exams, will earn more, and those individuals who have experienced a long period of initial unemployment, have just started a new job, or live in the outer borough of Bromley will earn less. The only result that is surprising is the sign on the Bromley variable. In our previous analysis on the determinants of the probability of being unemployed we found that those youths who lived in Bromley were more likely to be employed, yet here we observe that they are also more likely to be earning less. A possible explanation of this may be that those who live in Bromley do not have as high transport costs to work as those who live in other boroughs and therefore accept jobs with lower gross wages.

The R squared and F statistics are very small for this equation and this must be a result of the homogeneity of the sample. It is more likely that the reason why one school leaver earns £53.50 per week and another earns £53.25 is going to be explained by chance or unobserved variables rather than by any variables we can observe.

Table 9.12   Dependent variable, log of gross weekly earnings (Phase V)

Variables	Coefficients	t-test
Total weeks employed	− 0.001	− 1.11
% of time unemployed	− 0.138	− 1.19
Weeks in current job	− 0.005	− 1.69
Weeks in current job squared	0.001	1.55
Exams	0.062	2.50
Training	0.011	0.67
Sex	− 0.004	− 0.25
Ethnicity	0.056	2.29
Health	0.011	0.66
Initial unemployment duration	− 0.003	− 2.96
Tower Hamlets	0.018	0.71
Lambeth	− 0.015	− 0.55
Hounslow	− 0.037	− 1.48
Bromley	− 0.051	− 1.85
Constant	4.063	56.58

Notes:
$\overline{R}^2 = 0.03$
$F = 3.42$
No. of cases = 1180

Nevertheless, it is interesting to see the significance once again of ethnicity, work experience, and educational qualifications.

9.7   CONCLUSIONS

To summarise the results we shall use the three categories of variables that we introduced in section 9.1 – individual characteristics, local environmental conditions and work history. The individual characteristics that are persistently significant are ethnicity, exams (educational qualifications), and comprehension. The significance of educational qualifications for young workers reaffirms similar findings for Scottish school leavers as presented by MacLeod, Main and Raffe (1983), and for US youths as discussed by Meyer and Wise (1982). The Meyer and Wise study shows that not only are educational qualifications important for determining the number of weeks worked in a year but also for determining the earnings of young people. Therefore, given the importance of exams as a determinant of being unemployed and earnings one should consider the abolition of disincentives to taking exams (such as the loss of supplementary benefit over the summer months) for those young people who stay on in school until July to sit CSE or GCE exams.

Perhaps one of the most robust results is the significance of ethnicity for many aspects of the labour market experience – the probability of being unemployed, in school or on a government training scheme, and earnings. Nine per cent of the girls are non-white yet they represent 17 per cent of the unemployed girls. A similar result holds for the boys, with 20 per cent of the respondents non-white, while 26 per cent of the unemployed are non-white. Our results suggest that non-whites bear a disproportionate share of unemployment, all other things being equal. Unfortunately, we are not able to compare these results with other studies on Britain since there has been relatively little rigorous analysis of the impact of ethnicity on the youth labour market experience. However, there have been a substantial number of studies on this issue in the US. Studies by Leighton and Mincer (1982), Meyer and Wise (1982), and Rees and Gray (1982) find significantly worse employment experience for blacks than for whites. Rees and Gray find that being black, *ceteris paribus*, lowers the probability of being employed by 17 to 25 per cent. Meyer and Wise find, as we did, that the probability of non-whites being in school is significantly higher than for whites. The difficulty in interpreting the significance of the ethnicity variable for policy purposes is that it is not easy to distinguish between difficulties in the labour market caused by discrimination, perception of potential productivity differences by employers, or informational inefficiency in the job search process. Nevertheless, the government should consider ways in which to redress this racial imbalance in the labour market.

The most important variable in our environment category is the presence of household unemployment. Rees and Gray suggest that the significance of household employment may be due to either a weaker family work ethic or fewer job contacts. However, our analysis does not allow us to identify which (if either) of these two possibilities is important.

While the borough of residence is never significant except for those who live in Bromley, this does imply that the government should not allocate more resources to the inner cities. The boroughs themselves may not be a significant determinant of unemployment but the inner city boroughs have a higher concentration of those most likely to be unemployed – non-whites, youths with other members of the family unemployed, youths who have not taken any exams, and youths who have experienced many and/or long spells of unemployment. For example, at Phase IV, approximately half of the survey sample came from inner city boroughs, yet 80 per cent of the unemployed were from inner city boroughs.

Finally, our results suggest that of all the variables in the work experience category (part-time work, lagged employment status and turnover) are significant determinants of the probability of being unemployed and of earnings. There appears, therefore, to be evidence that early unemployment experience 'scars' the young worker in both future earnings and employment. However, this 'scarring' may be more apparent than real if work experience is simply a proxy for some other unobserved variable. In other work, Lynch (1985), we examine in greater detail this issue of scarring or state dependency in unemployment in an analysis of the determinants of reemployment probabilities for young workers. We attempt to control for unobserved heterogeneity but still find that increasing durations of unemployment lead to lower reemployment probabilities. Keeping this in mind, any programmes which help those young people who have experienced frequent and/or long spells of unemployment should be encouraged, especially those programmes which provide valuable work experience.

APPENDIX A   VARIABLES USED IN THE ANALYSIS

Variables in Unemployment Equations

OCC1 – managerial and professional workers
OCC2 – junior non-manual workers
OCC3 – skilled manual workers
OCC4 – semi/unskilled non-manual (retained)
OCC5 – semi/unskilled workers
Appearance – Smart = 1; Adequate or poor = 0
Comprehension – Excellent = 1; Else = 0
Expression – Excellent = 1; Else = 0
Ethnicity – White = 1; Else = 0
Health – Healthy = 1; Else = 0
Exams – Taken = 1; Not taken = 0
Household unemployment – Presence of = 1; Else = 0
Part-time work experience – Yes = 1; No = 0
Lambeth
Tower Hamlets

Hounslow
Hammersmith (retained)
Lambeth
Job status $(t+i)$ – Unemployed = 1; Else = 0; i = 1, 2
Turnover – Yes = 1; Else = 0

Variables for Earnings Equation

Exams – Taken = 1; Not taken = 0
Training – Yes = 1; No training = 0
Sex – Boys = 1; Girls = 0
Health – Ill = 1; Else = 0

APPENDIX B PROBABILITY OF BEING UNEMPLOYED

Table 9.A1 The determinants of the probability of being unemployed, Phase IV (Boys)

Variable	Equation (1)	Equation(2)	Equation (3)
Constant	−1.62	1.32	−3.11
	(−2.08)	(1.53)	(3.31)
OCC1	0.05	0.19	0.51
	(0.10)	(0.37)	(0.88)
OCC2	0.29	0.37	0.74
	(0.47)	(0.59)	(1.06)
OCC3	−0.09	−0.16	0.44
	(−0.13)	(−0.23)	(0.56)
OCC5	0.97	1.09	1.29
	(1.73)	(1.95)	(1.98)
Appearance	0.24	0.26	0.35
	(0.65)	(0.68)	(0.83)
Comprehension	−1.50	−1.70	−1.79
	(−2.46)	(−2.58)	(−2.59)
Expression	0.43	0.54	0.69
	(0.68)	(0.81)	(1.03)
Ethnicity	−0.82	0.48	−0.30
(white)	(−2.41)	(1.26)	(−0.70)
Health	0.85	0.81	0.92
	(1.63)	(1.53)	(1.61)
Part-time work	−0.71	−0.63	−0.70
	(−2.22)	(−1.91)	(−1.84)
Exams	−0.86	−0.90	−0.55
	(−2.21)	(−2.25)	(−1.22)
Household	0.89	0.77	0.55
unemployment	(2.70)	(2.26)	(1.45)
Lambeth	—	0.00	0.18
		(0.00)	(0.34)
Tower Hamlets	—	0.61	−0.71
		(1.24)	(−1.31)
Hounslow	—	−1.48	−1.58
		(−2.47)	(−2.39)
Bromley	—	−1.22	−1.53
		(−1.69)	(−1.91)
Job status	—	—	0.26
$(t-1)$			(0.63)
Job status	—	—	0.72
$(t-2)$			(1.50)
Turnover	—	—	2.55
			(6.07)
Log $L =$	−140.58	−135.23	−108.15

Table 9.A2   The determinants of the probability of being unemployed,
Phase IV (Girls)

Variable	Equation (1)	Equation (2)	Equation (3)
Constant	1.11	−0.81	−1.36
	(1.35)	(−0.90)	(−1.37)
OCC1	0.41	0.44	0.29
	(0.67)	(0.72)	(0.46)
OCC2	0.73	0.74	0.59
	(1.20)	(1.21)	(0.94)
OCC3	1.27	1.13	0.89
	(1.95)	(1.71)	(1.31)
OCC5	0.75	0.63	0.44
	(1.09)	(0.91)	(0.61)
Appearance	−0.31	−0.36	−0.65
	(−0.84)	(−0.97)	(−1.59)
Comprehension	−0.45	−0.47	−0.07
	(−0.85)	(−0.89)	(−0.13)
Ethnicity	−1.18	−1.22	−1.29
(white)	(−2.88)	(−2.84)	(−2.74)
Health	−0.12	−0.11	0.21
	(−0.29)	(−0.26)	(0.45)
Part-time work	−0.63	−0.59	−0.71
	(−1.85)	(−1.64)	(−1.82)
Exams	−0.62	−0.51	−0.19
	(−1.44)	(−1.16)	(−0.41)
Household	0.69	0.61	0.20
unemployment	(2.03)	(1.74)	(0.51)
Lambeth	—	−0.61	−0.86
		(−1.00)	(−1.30)
Tower Hamlets	—	−0.16	−0.22
		(−0.33)	(−0.42)
Hounslow	—	−0.58	−0.84
		(−1.05)	(−1.32)
Bromley	—	−0.72	−0.96
		(−1.07)	(−1.35)
Job status	—	—	1.22
(t-1)			(2.77)
Job status	—	—	0.61
(t-2)			(1.27)
Turnover	—	—	1.98
			(4.95)
Log L =	−134.19	−131.65	−113.28

Notes

1. This chapter was originally prepared for the IER Young Persons' Labour Market Conference, University of Warwick, November 1984. I would like to thank Richard Disney, Steve Nickell, David Piachaud, and Ray Richardson for comments on an earlier draft of this paper. I would also like to thank Ben Knox for the use of his SPSS Logit program.
2. See R. Richardson, 'Unemployment and the Inner City–A Study of School Leavers', LSE (mimeo) June 1982 for a thorough descriptive analysis of this data set. This data is available for public use through the University of London Computer Service on the Amdahl 470/V8 on magnetic tape in SPSS archive format. Contact Anne McGlone, London School of Economics Computer Advisory for further details.
3. The categories have been developed along the lines of a study by J. Stern (1981).

Part III

Policies for the Youth Labour Market

10 YTS: Training or a Placebo?

Patricia Dutton[1]

10.1 INTRODUCTION

The main purpose of this chapter is to establish the facts, as far as they are available, on the Youth Training Scheme (YTS) and use them in an attempt to consider its success with regard to a limited number of objectives. In addition, it will attempt to highlight what statistics should be collected and what pitfalls should be avoided when interpreting them.

YTS was introduced by a 'strictly non-interventionist' government in 1983, with the first trainees entering in April–May but with the bulk entering in late summer–autumn of the same year. Despite its pledges to reduce government intervention in the economy (and in the labour market in particular) it found itself backing a new scheme aimed at the school leaving population at the cost of approximately £1.1bn over two years. The main features of the new scheme were its longer duration (1 year) and the obligatory element of a minimum of 13 weeks off-the-job training or education not present in the earlier schemes.

Despite the fact that the majority of school leavers in the UK traditionally entered jobs with which there was little or no off-the-job training associated (and consequently minimal training costs for employers), throughout the 1970s a smaller and smaller percentage were able to find jobs (compare Department of Employment (hereafter DE), 1982 and 1984b). For those who usually went into jobs that had associated training costs, things were relatively worse. The recession of 1981–2 saw the collapse of the traditional route into skilled occupations via apprenticeship in many manufacturing industries. In answer to a parliamentary question, Mr Peter Morrison indicated that by 1983 apprenticeships in manufacturing had fallen by 37 per cent between 1979 and 1983.[2]

Without wishing to enter the debate about the role of increased relative earnings and increased costs of training in determining the employment of young people, it seems that the recession played a major role in reducing prospects for young people which the former causes, had they been rectified, could not have put right. A reduction in recruitment is an employer's first step in adjusting the labour force to a desired lower level in the face of decreased demand for the firm's output. When natural wastage then fails to bring the numbers down sufficiently far (and/or sufficiently fast), the employer resorts to redundancy. Within engineering, at least, the fall in the recruitment of craft and technician apprentices preceded the increases in redundancies. During the recession the principle of last-in–first-out (LIFO) operated, adding further to the problems which faced the 16–24 year olds.

From the mid–1970s, what provision there was for the young unemployed was mainly aimed at the disadvantaged groups, and initially the numbers involved were quite small. However, in response to the increase in youth unemployment, the existing provision was stretched far beyond its original size and scope. The major programme, the Youth Opportunities Programme (YOP), was in fact due to disappear in 1983 and had begun to lose credibility with the youngsters, the trade unions and to some degree with the employers.

Youth unemployment, and particularly school leaver unemployment, is an emotive subject and the government, aware of the political, social and economic implications, issued its first White Paper in 1981 setting out the aims of the New Training Initiative (NTI) (DE, 1981). The most important element in terms of resources and the numbers involved was the Youth Training Scheme. The government's initial proposals for YTS seemed to suggest that its main objective was that of removing 350 000 young people from the unemployment register. It did, however, introduce for the first time a training element, which had been missing from all but a few of the measures aimed at unemployed 16 year olds.

The immediate reasoning behind the decision to adopt a 'training' scheme for school leavers (as opposed to a job-creation scheme) may have been entirely cosmetic – an attempt to identify the scheme as something different from YOP. It may have been influenced by political and social considerations as well as economic ones, but there is no room here to trace the development of all the thinking in this area. Instead this chapter concentrates on the two main economic arguments for the introduction of such a training scheme. One approaches training from a macroeconomic point of view and the other can be thought of as a micro or individual approach.

Those looking at our training effort from an international perspective have long commented on the paucity of the British training effort. Examining the economic performance of rival countries has led commentators to conclude that one of the reasons for the poor performance of the British economy is its lack of training; hence more training will improve the performance of the British economy through improved productivity (and hopefully lower costs). This view is expressed by such bodies as the National Economic Development Office (see NEDC, 1984) and the MSC (see MSC, 1981b) but has been most consistently put by the National Institute for Economic and Social Research (see Daly *et al.*, 1985 for the latest NIESR findings). In addition, British industrial training has proved to be very cyclical. This has contributed to skill shortages in upturns. The Industrial Training Boards initially introduced in an attempt to remedy this problem were being dismantled at the time of the Government's White Paper on the NTI (DE, 1981), as a result of the Employment and Training Act passed earlier in 1981. As this mechanism was now not available, the intervention had to be organised nationally through the MSC, although the emphasis was to be placed on local labour needs rather than industry level needs. (Only in the construction industry which retained its training board was the scheme operated as an industry-wide scheme.)

On a more micro level, there was a great deal of concern expressed (particularly in the 1970s) about school leavers not having the 'right' qualities, qualifications and skills, and that this was preventing them getting jobs (one of the arguments used to justify the education debate of the 1970s). There was also a faction who believed that 16 was too young to enter the labour market directly, and that the ideal solution would be to create a 'bridge from school to work' rather like the traditional apprenticeship (or German traineeship) but available to all youngsters.[3] Others noted that studies of employment probabilities (and earnings functions) showed that the better qualified did better than the unqualified.[4] A solution for youth unemployment could therefore be found not simply in taking them out of the labour force but by providing training to increase their employability by raising their productivity. This argument for training has a weakness, however. The estimated probabilities can measure the impact of training for an individual relative to others with no training, but it does not imply that if everyone received that training all would increase their chances of a job (or their earnings) by that amount.

Belief in the market mechanism might have led the government to believe that firms had got it right in reducing training dramatically in the recession, but the government could not accept the unemployment implications. No doubt their motives in introducing YTS were a mix of political imperative and economic reasoning; in the event, an attempt has been made to judge the scheme by its stated aims and objectives, and those that might reasonably be expected of it.

10.2 THE SCHEME

The scheme that was eventually adopted was a compromise between the wishes of the government and the consensus that emerged, rather surprisingly, among the members of the Youth Task Group (YTG). To its surprise, the government found its usual ally, the Confederation of British Industry (CBI), aligning itself alongside the Trades Union Congress (TUC) over the issues of training allowances and compulsion. (An insight into how this position emerged within the CBI can be gained from Keep, 1984). The scheme that eventually emerged showed the influence of the trains of thought mentioned above, including the need to make people more attractive to employers in terms of their attributes and their costs, and the desire to increase the quality and quantity of training in an attempt to restore UK competitiveness as well as the political imperative of being seen to be doing something particularly in the wake of the summer riots of 1981 (see Dutton, 1981).

The YTG were given the task of coming up with a viable scheme in a very short time, and initially much of that time was taken up with finding an acceptable alternative to the government's proposals within the budget that had been allocated. The government was finally persuaded by the YTG's arguments, and backtracked on its initial proposals for a £15 a week allowance and the loss of social security payments for refusal to accept a YTS place. Although they retained the right to review both of these elements, they in fact raised the allowances to £26.25 as from September 1984.[5]

Another innovation of the YTG was the extension of the original scheme to all school leavers, not just the unemployed; MSC officials managed to persuade the YTG members (and through them the government) that the scheme should apply to all 16 year old school leavers, unemployed 17 year old school leavers and any disabled school leavers up to the age of 21.

Once the government accepted the YTG's recommendations, it was committed to the scheme for 2 years. However, it made it perfectly plain from the outset that the delivery of the places was the responsibility of industry, and that validation of the scheme had to be sorted out between employers, the MSC and the validation bodies. The MSC was to act as co-ordinator, but responsibility for getting the scheme off the ground rested with industry. Although the trade unions (through the TUC) had been involved in the negotiations on the form of YTS through their membership of the YTG and MSC, there was no role for them in the delivery of YTS, especially as the vast majority of YTS trainees were not to have employee status. In the past, trade unions were not only directly involved in determining trainee pay and conditions, some of them determined trainee numbers and the content and form of training (see Ryan, Chapter 7 in this volume). They are now involved only indirectly, where their members fear that a particular YTS scheme is jeopardising the jobs of their membership. This tends to mean that – apart from their participation through the MSC and the remaining statutory training boards – their involvement in YTS appears to be a very negative one of criticism and potential opposition.

10.3   ARE THE OBJECTIVES BEING MET?

Measuring the success of YTS at this stage is virtually impossible for we do not have the full information. In fact, it will be a number of years before we are in a position to observe the longer-term effects of the introduction of the scheme. It is fair to say that the very fact that YTS got off the ground at all in such a short time is some measure of its success. That was due to the work of MSC officials, the TUC, the CBI, the individual employers, validation bodies, training organisations and colleges of further education. However, this very hectic timetable did mean that places had first priority and the composition, quality and relevance of the places offered took a much lower priority in the discussions.

Although the government claims there is little it can do to reduce unemployment, YTS has been successful in reducing unemployment among 16–17 year old school leavers. The scheme is aimed almost exclusively at this age group and is of a year's duration, whereas YOP applied to a wider age band and was usually of 6 months' duration. Unemployment among the under 24 year olds has seen no dramatic reduction. This finding seems to imply that unemployment has simply been switched to those in the age group not qualifying for the scheme.[6]

In terms of meeting targets on YTS itself, the evidence is mixed. The expansion of the scheme to all 16 year olds, etc. expanded the target group from the government's original estimate of 350 000 to nearer 461 000. By November 1983, the MSC had already exchanged contracts with managing agents and sponsors to provide some 434 000 places. The question of take-up is, however, much more complex – not least because of data problems arising out of the need to set up the scheme so quickly. In its White Paper, *Training for Jobs* (DE, 1984a), the Department of Employment reviews progress on the NTI and admits to a shortfall of 20 per cent on YTS – that is, there were fewer youngsters than anticipated on the scheme. The major reason for this is that the scheme has not managed to encompass 16 year old employees. YTS remains a scheme for the unemployed, and in that sense it has failed in one of its prime objectives: that of being comprehensive.

The figures quoted in the 1984 White Paper (DE, 1984a) were 300 000 YTS registrations as at January 1984. Subsequently, MSC figures showed totals of around 350 000. Interpretation of the figures is difficult as a number of reregistrations occured. Consequently, some youngsters are double counted. The 'in-training' totals at spot dates throughout the year record smaller numbers of trainees in YTS places at any point in time. The 'leavers' surveys conducted by the MSC show a varying proportion of YTS trainees leaving their original schemes and rejoining YTS on different ones. The earlier surveys show a higher proportion than the later surveys, which is only to be expected for in the later surveys a greater proportion would be nearing completion of their YTS placement (see MSC, 1984e).

Partly as a result of the lower demand, the government was able to fulfil the additional objective it had grafted on to YTS, that of being able to offer all unemployed 16 year olds a YTS place by Christmas 1983 (the 'Christmas Undertaking'). Undoubtedly, the shortfall has also meant a substantial saving out of the budget allocated for 1983–4 which may have contributed to the more generous allowances for 1984–5.

The official statistics reveal that employers did indeed fulfil their side of the bargain in making places available and there is no evidence to support the claim made by Baxter and McCormick (1984) that the shortfall was a result of a shortage of places under Mode A. In fact, the number of Mode B places on offer were fewer than anticipated (see Dutton, 1984). Anecdotal evidence suggests that some employers' schemes were closed or reduced due to lack of YTS recruits (see Rainbird and Grant, 1985). The reason propounded for the shortfall by the White Paper is that more young people than anticipated found jobs outside the scheme. While it is true that the proportion of 16 year olds staying on at school rose between 1979 and 1982, the evidence suggests that 1983 saw no increase over 1982.[7] In addition, acknowledging that the number of youngsters going straight into jobs was higher than anticipated is no real excuse for the shortfall of YTS numbers – the scheme was meant to encompass employed as well as unemployed youngsters. In fact if – as is mooted in the YTS Review – the Young Worker Subsidy (YWS) was a major contributing factor to the shortfall on YTS, this clearly demonstrates not only a lack of consistent policy but a higher priority for employment over training, for those on YWS were not guarenteed training. The government has now acknowledged this anomaly and made 16 year old school leavers ineligible for YWS.[8]

The YTS Review itself is much more forthright than the White Paper on the alternative explanation of the shortfall – the higher than expected level of unemployment among school leavers. It stresses that the the scheme is voluntary in nature, and is concerned that the government's proposed action of abolishing individual social security entitlement for 16 year olds will jeopardise the goodwill of potential trainees.[9] It goes on to state that 'members of the Review Group are concerned that officers charged with implementing benefit rules do so sensitively and use the advice of the Careers Service on the merits of individual cases' (MSC, 1984d, p. 13). In saying this, they are arguing only for a continuation of what has apparently already been happening (see the *Times Educational Supplement*, 13 January 1984). It is a mark of failure that a significant number of young people preferred unemployment and the possible loss of 6 weeks' social security benefit to accepting the offer of a place on YTS.[10] Quite what will happen when 16 year olds are no longer eligible for social security in their own right is difficult to anticipate.

One of the things that the government is already claiming is that YTS raises the chances of young people getting jobs. Although there is some evidence to this effect from the surveys of YTS leavers, interpretations must be made cautiously. One of the main reasons is the problem of deadweight loss – it is difficult to assess how many would have got jobs anyway. Additionally, there is the problem of substitution – how many have got jobs at the expense of another group? Ministers had already begun to make such claims as 60 to 70 per cent of all those leaving YTS went straight into jobs (*Hansard*, 30 October 1984 and the *Times Educational Supplement*, 26 October 1984). Even if the figures were correct, the net effect of YTS on employment is bound to be very much smaller.

The first sample survey of early leavers was conducted between February and March 1984 and investigated those who left YTS before the expected completion date – that was between 1 April 1983 and 17 November 1983 (MSC, 1984c). Only about 2000 questionaires were sent out and the response rate was just over 50 per cent. The sample is therefore very small. In response to the question 'Why did you leave your YTS scheme?' over 20 per cent had indicated they had simply transferred to another scheme, while 35 per cent left for a full-time job.[11] Respondents were also asked what they were currently doing – i.e., in February–March 1984. By then the percentage who had joined another scheme had risen to 27 per cent, the percentage in full-time work was the same, 8 per cent were back in full-time education, while 24 per cent were unemployed (MSC, 1984c). One of the major problems with surveys with such low response rates is that we do not know how representative the respondents are of the total population. It may be that the non-respondents are more likely than the respondents to be unemployed, for example. If this were the case, then the survey results would be biased.

The MSC have followed this survey with two more surveys – one of 3000 trainees who left YTS between April 1983 and March 1984 (conducted in April–May 1984), and one of 3500 young people who left YTS between April 1984 and July 1984 (conducted in September–October 1984) (see MSC, 1984e). Of those leaving between April 1983 and March 1984 ('first stage') the percentage who were in employment at the time of the survey had risen to 49 per cent. However, the proportion who were unemployed had also risen – to 34 per cent. Included in this sample would have been a higher proportion of YTS trainees who had completed (or nearly completed) a full YTS year. The third survey ('second stage') conducted in the Autumn of 1984 included those who left between April and July 1984. Very few YTS trainees began their year in April 1984 (approximately 7000), so that the majority of those surveyed were therefore likely to have joined YTS between summer and Christmas 1983. This implies the bulk of those leaving would have in fact finished their YTS training rather than being early leavers (36 per cent of the sample claimed to have completed YTS). Of this group, as many as 56 per cent were in employment at the time of the survey; however, 35 per cent were unemployed.

Various problems remain in quoting this figure of 56 per cent. The data really need to be analysed to separate out early leavers from completers to get some information on whether or not there are statistically significant differences between the two groups. The data also need a geographical dimension; many of the trainees in heavily depressed regions of the UK will complete YTS with little or no improvement in their probability of getting permanent employment, while in other areas success rates may look very good, In fact, if job prospects are better in one region than another this may be reflected in a higher proportion of early leavers in the better regions moving into jobs than in the poorer regions. The impact of seasonality on the chances of moving into employment on leaving YTS should also be taken into account. By autumn 1984 the response rate to the questionnaires had risen to 70 per cent, lessening somewhat the problems of representativeness. Even so, it still remains confusing that the analysis is not extended to enable one to differentiate adequately between early leavers and completers. (This, of course, leads to problems of defining 'completion', and what constitutes 'successful completion'.)[12]

It is debatable, too, what role YTS has played in getting youngsters into these jobs (and it is even more debatable how important the training element is compared with the work experience element), given that the majority of early leavers have not completed the YTS experience. The very size of the numbers leaving YTS could be taken as a criticism of the scheme, but it must be borne in mind that the youth labour market always has a high turnover. In addition, the haste with which the scheme was delivered meant that the time and trouble taken in Germany to match school leavers to traineeships could not be done in the UK in the case of YTS, at least not in its first year: undoubtedly, there was a great deal of mismatching. In the first 6 months, 83 000 youngsters left YTS – approximately 27 per cent of the total registrations (including reentrants) – but in the earlier period 30 per cent of these were transferring to other programmes (see the *Guardian*, 4th April 1984).

There are of course many other measures of success which are outside the scope of this chapter. Such issues as the administration of funding, the selection and monitoring of managing agents and sponsors, quality control, equal opportunities' objectives, health and safety issues and the usefulness of the 2:3 trainee ratio originally stipulated for Mode A schemes are all outside our scope. The *YTS Review* tackles some of these issues, but even in these areas the full facts are still not available.

10.4   FURTHER ISSUES

Not being able to answer such issues does not mean that it is not proper to ask a question not posed by the Review team. That is: 'Given that YTS is supposed to provide a foundation for working life, to make the workforce more flexible and in some sense more skilled, was there some national policy towards achieving a particular occupational or industrial distribution of trainees?' The short answer to that question appears to be: 'no'. Not only did the MSC not have a policy in this area, they were not – and to some degree still are not – sure what the distributions are. This is undoubtedly one aspect of a national training policy that was initially sacrificed in order to get the number of places required within a certain time limit. There was very little time for policy discussion on the content of YTS, let alone the occupational and industrial distribution to be achieved. The research that the MSC had commissioned on Occupational Training Families (OTFs) was not finalised at the time YTS was launched and many schemes were accepted that would not fit easily into the classification (Keep, 1984).

In Dutton (1984) it was possible to analyse only the data from survey of YTS schemes. Since then, data has become available from a sample survey of YTS start certificates (or registrations) (MSC, 1984b). The survey was conducted in November 1983 and comprised a 10 per cent sample of start certificates. It is simply an analysis of the information from an administrative document supplemented by data on the industrial classification of the managing agent or sponsor; if the trainee had left YTS, it also included the date of leaving. There are many caveats one should mention when using such data in an attempt to get industrial and occupational information on YTS trainees. In the case of OTFs, as mentioned above, many schemes could not be classified (or were classified to more than one OTF). This was not due to the MSC's lack of familiarity with OTFs (although they were undoubtedly a new concept to those administering YTS) but due to the fact that some schemes were different and did not fit into the classification. Fitting into the classification was obviously not a criterion for judging the acceptability of an offer of YTS places. In addition, the only industrial information is on managing agents rather than on the firms providing work experience. A large number of managing agencies which were set up to operate YTS would have automatically been classified to the service sector. However, the industrial experience they arranged for their trainees could have been more widely spread. At the time of writing, however, this is the only information of this kind to hand and, bearing in mind the above comments, an attempt is made to get some flavour of the occupational and industrial distribution of YTS trainees in comparison with those youngsters who found jobs outside YTS.

Information is now available from the 'first employment of young people' survey conducted by the Department of Employment in 1983 (DE, 1984c). Before we can compare the information from the two sources, it is necessary to say something about how the recession was affecting the kind of jobs for which young people were being recruited. In an earlier survey of young entrants conducted in 1980 there was already evidence that the recession was having some impact not only on the numbers getting jobs but on the pattern of entry into employment, particularly the industrial pattern (see DE, 1984b). In 1980 approximately 33 per cent of those who left school were not in employment, in 1979 the unemployed had constituted only 10 per cent. By 1983, 62 per cent were not in employment but the difference was that (compared with 1980) only 14 per cent were unemployed, the remainder were on YTS. Consequently, the numbers in the 1983 sample were very much smaller than in previous years.

Table 10.1 compares the industrial distribution of 16 year old entrants into new jobs in 1980 with those entering in 1983. In terms of shares, 1983 saw something of a reversal of the trend of the late 1970s and early 1980s – that is, the proportion of 16 year olds getting jobs in manufacturing rose in 1983, while the proportion in insurance, banking and finance and public administration fell. No doubt the distribution of YTS places has had some impact on the distribution of jobs with employee status.

Bearing in mind the earlier caveat regarding the industrial distribution of YTS trainees, Table 10.2 compares the distribution of young entrants with that of the YTS trainees (or more strictly, their managing agents). One striking factor of Table 10.2 is the heavy concentration of trainees in the service sector – in particular in distribution and other services. The need to make the two industrial classifications as compatible as possible does result in a loss of information through aggregation. Despite the bias in the distribution

Table 10.1   Comparison of the distribution of 16 year old school leavers'
first employment by industry 1980 and 1983

1980 SIC	Industry	1980 (%)	1983 (%)
I	Agriculture	3.7	3.8
II	Mining and quarrying	1.3	0.5
III–XIX	Manufacturing	29.7	33.2
XX	Construction	9.7	10.7
XXI	Gas, water and electricity	1.1	0.5
XXII	Transport and communication	3.7	2.9
XXIII	Distribution	20.1	21.6
XXIV	Insurance, banking and finance	6.3	4.4
XXV	Professional and scientific services	3.1	3.5
XXVI	Miscellaneous services	14.0	14.4
XXVII	Public administration	7.3	4.6
	Sample size (100% =)	24 578	13 338

Note: SIC = Standard Industrial Classification.
Sources: DE(1984b), Table 3 and DE(1984c), Table 3.

(caused by the classification of some managing agents to the service
sector irrespective of the training received by trainees), the drop in the
proportion of 16 year olds finding jobs in banking and public
administration might well be explained by the number of competing
YTS schemes being offered in this sector. Associated with this is the
rise in the proportion of 16 year old school leavers finding full-time
jobs in manufacturing.

As mentioned in an earlier study (Dutton, 1984), we would not
expect the first employment of young people to fit well into the
pattern of employment of the total population, but there seems at first
sight to be something of a mismatch between the industrial experience
of YTS trainees and that of young people getting jobs outside YTS.
Better information on the industrial experience of YTS trainees would
help to clarify the situation. In addition, it may be important to know
what kind of experience is important in a young person's career; a first
job may be more important in itself than where the job is located.

On the occupational front, the classification used by the MSC is not
strictly an occupational classification. An attempt has been made in
Table 10.3 to tie together the occupational information on the first
employment of 16 year olds with OTF information from the YTS

Table 10.2   The industrial distribution of young entrants to employment and YTS trainees (1983)

1968 SIC	1980 SIC	Industry group	16 year old school leavers in employment (%)	YTS trainees[a] (%)
I	0	Agriculture	4	1
II, XXI	1	Energy	1	1
IV–VI, XVI	2	Ore extraction	3	2
VII–XII	3	Engineering	12	8
III, XIII–XV, XVII–XIX	4	Other manufacturing	18	3
XX	5	Construction	11	7
XXIII, XXV–	6	Distribution		
XXVII	9	Other services	44	68
XXII	7	Transport	3	2
XXIV	8	Finance	4	5
		Undefined	—	4
		Total (100% =)	13 338	24 740[b]

Notes: SIC = Standard Industrial Classification.

[a] All YTS trainees including some employees, some 17 year olds, etc. Strictly speaking the industrial classification is that of their managing agent or sponsor.

[b] Notes to the table explain that 10 per cent of the sample could not be classified by SIC and are excluded, the actual sample is therefore approximately 22 000.

Sources: DE(1984c), Table 3 and MSC(1984b), Table 3.

start certificates. At least 30 per cent of start certificates did not have OTFs recorded, while a further 7 per cent showed two or more OTFs; the distribution given refers only to those certificates that could be classified. The data is available by sex, which enables us to look for differences between boys and girls, as well as the differences between employees and YTS trainees. Once again, matching up the classifications leads to aggregation and a loss of information, particularly in the manufacturing occupations.

Table 10.3   The occupational distribution of 16 year old school leavers in employment and YTS trainees (1983)

Occupational training family classification	Males		Females		(%) Total	
	Young entrants to employ-ment	*YTS trainees*	*Young entrants to employ-ment*	*YTS trainees*	*Young entrants to employ-ment*	*YTS trainees*
Administration and clerical	7	9	26	36	15	21
Agriculture	6	8	2	2	5	6
Craft Maintenance and repair Manufacturing Processing	50	52	27	10	40	32
Technical and scientific	6	4	1	1	4	3
Sales	9	7	20	29	14	17
Transport	7	3	1	—	4	2
Food preparation Community and health services	10	5	20	14	15	9
Miscellaneous	5	—	3	—	4	—
Multiple	—	10	—	8	—	9
Total (100% =)	7 558	n.a.	5 780	n.a.	13 338	24 740[a]

Note:
[a]   The note to the table indicates that 30 per cent of YTS start certificates did not contain information on the relevant OTF. The appropriate number is therefore likely to be 17 000.

Sources: DE(1984c), Table 4 and MSC(1984b), Table 4.

In total, it would seem that a higher proportion of YTS trainees are receiving training in the area of administrative and clerical work than those who found jobs straight from school. Looking across the row, the reason for this is mainly the large proportion of girls receiving such training – 36 per cent of all girls' start certificates had this OTF classification. Another notable difference is the proportion of YTS trainees receiving training in the area of manufacturing and repair (including craft occupations of all kinds), compared with the proportion of school leavers directly employed by firms. Once again, it would appear that the main problem lies with YTS places for girls. Only 10 per cent of the girls obtained YTS places in these occupational areas in comparison with 27 per cent of employees. Finally, the other notable difference between employees and YTS trainees is in the area of food preparation and community and health services (this includes catering, cleaning, hairdressing, security and other personal services). It would seem that proportionally fewer places in these occupations are available for both boys and girls on YTS schemes than are available for those finding jobs.

It has already been mentioned that to some extent employment opportunities and YTS training places may be competitive in some sectors. In Dutton (1984) a remarkable similarity was found between YTS places on offer and the distribution of employment by occupation among 16 year old school leavers for 1980. The biggest impact of YTS may therefore have been to distort the distribution of *employment* for those actually securing jobs in 1983. Certainly on the occupational front, the opportunities appear more limited than in the labour market, especially for girls. However, it has to be borne in mind that the actual *number* of jobs was severely restricted in 1983. The Department of Employment (1984c) estimate that approximately 166 000 young people in England and Wales who left school at 16 in 1983 were in employment at the end of 1983. In comparison, by this time, there had been approximately 290 000 registrations on YTS throughout Great Britain.

One aspect of the occupational distribution of YTS trainees which may give cause for concern – if you believe that Britain needs to keep up with technological developments (see NEDC, 1984) – is that only 3 per cent of all identifiable YTS places were in science and technology (and a further 4 per cent in craft and design). Information on YTS places for September 1983 indicated that only 9000 YTS places were of a scientific or a technical nature (MSC, 1984a). Although at least 5000 of these places were in ITECs and the proportion of youngsters in scientific and technical training is higher on Mode B2, it is difficult to tell from this sample survey (MSC, 1984a) how many places industry was actually offering in this area.

What should really be of concern is not so much the degree to which YTS fits in with the historic pattern of young people's employment but the degree to which it facilitates future economic growth. The latest forecasts of future employment trends (at the time of writing) produced within the Institute for Employment Research (IER, 1983) suggest that in terms of sectoral employment, growth is most likely to occur in the service sector, particularly in professional services and miscellaneous services and in public administration. However, growth in the last of those areas now seems less likely, given the present government's stance on public expenditure. For the manufacturing sector, the picture is one of decreasing employment in the main. On the occupational front, growth is expected in most of the non-manual occupations (apart from the education professions and sales occupations which are expected to decline). Where does that leave YTS and its trainees? What might at first sight seem to be a top-heavy distribution towards the service sector (see Table 10.2) may, in fact, be reflecting future job opportunities quite well. Despite the recommendations of the NEDC report, there are very few places in science and technology, craft and design.

In the growth areas – non-manual jobs – the main occupations into which 16 year olds enter directly are clerical and sales jobs. The former is expected to grow only slightly over the medium term, while the latter is actually expected to decline. The type of non-manual jobs most likely to show growth in the medium term are usually entered at a later age, and frequently require qualifications that the 16 year old school leaver would not possess. Of course, simply because an occupation is likely to decline does not mean that recruitment to it will stop. However, job opportunities for the average 16 year old school leaver look more limited than they did at the beginning of the 1970s.

Of course, there is also the supply of places to be considered. The apparent concentration of training places in the sector might also have something to do with the greater potential for profit-taking due to the low cost of providing such training in comparison, say, with craft training, and with the greater possibility of substituting YTS trainees for other workers in these less unionised sectors. Part of the reason for the very few places in science and technology and craft and design must be the higher cost of providing such places, and the fact that such training is normally of a longer duration than 1 year.

One thing that these comparisons reveal is the need for individual data on YTS trainees, and an accurate coding of the industry in which they are receiving their work experience. It is to be hoped that this kind of information on YTS will eventually become available.

Even this, however, will not make it easier to assess the impact of YTS on the probability of getting a job. Although YTS was initially introduced as a pilot, no comparative analysis was undertaken by selecting a sample of similar youngsters who did not receive YTS and comparing the subsequent employment probabilities of the two groups. It is almost impossible to judge the impact of YTS on finding a job if virtually everyone who has not found a job by the Christmas of the year they leave school enters YTS. What proportion of such youngsters would have found a job by the following summer in the absence of YTS? The quoted figure of approximately 60 per cent of all YTS participants getting jobs needs to be compared with a comparable figure in the absence of such a programme. One of the things YTS is doing is redistributing job opportunities in favour of school leavers and at the expense of 'older' youngsters (in the main). Thus even a straightforward comparison of the probabilities of YTS and non-YTS school leavers finding jobs would not be valid without some analysis of the knock-on effects of YTS on other age groups.

10.5 IMPACT ON TRAINING

In conclusion, it is necessary to say something about the impact of YTS, a publically-financed scheme, on the initial training provided by industry. In the past – apart from the small proportion of youngsters who got apprenticeships (mainly boys) – the vast majority received no training of a general transferable nature. What most youngsters got was work experience and socialisation plus specific training through learning-by-doing. What little training industry did of its own accord is likely to be replaced by YTS. The employers are unlikely to pay for such training themselves if they can get the government to fund it for them. For the group as a whole, however, it will probably mean more exposure to training and further education than had they gone straight into employment at 16. With regard to skill training, YTS funds can make only a contribution towards the cost. Where no barriers to implementing YTS apprenticeships exist – e.g., in construction – it is not likely to expand greatly the number, but it certainly will not discourage such training.[13] In industries such as engineering, the industrial relations aspect of YTS make it unlikely that it will have a substantial impact on the numbers recruited for apprentice training, at least not initially. However, where these problems can be overcome it may lead to a marginal increase. The most important factors in the supply of apprenticeship places are the state of demand in the industry at the moment and the prospects for the future, neither of which are particularly favourable.[14]

One thing that YTS might be doing is breaking down the traditional pattern of skill training in some industries by making training more flexible. The acceptance of a relevant YTS off-the-job training as a contribution towards craft status could mean that employers could recruit 17 year olds (or above) to complete their apprenticeship, so long as they had completed their YTS component. YTS might also have the side effect of reducing union power by removing trainees and initial training from the province of the unions.

Overall, therefore, YTS should increase the amount of initial training given to school leavers – at least to those on YTS (who are mainly the unemployed). Quite how this will assist the individual in getting a job is difficult to say for – although the individual's chances of getting a job are raised relative to others when he/she acquires attributes preferred by employers – raising the quality of all youngsters may have no great impact on the overall demand for youngsters, unless it is at the expense of some other group. To the extent that better trained young people will be an asset to the UK, then this initiative will be beneficial, but unless the other investment required for growth occurs this effort on its own can do little to improve the UK's productivity performance.

10.6 CONCLUSION

This chapter has attempted to present what information is available on YTS, particularly with respect to where the training is being given – in what industries and in what skills – as well as the data on what happens to YTS leavers. In doing so, it has shown that the haste for places prevented any long-term planning for the needs of individuals and the needs of the economy. It has also highlighted some shortcomings in the collection of relevant statistics and their interpretation, some of which the MSC are in the process of rectifying.

Despite the fact that in some cases it is not possible to measure the success of YTS because data has not been collected (or is still in the process of being collected), it is possible to form some kind of judgement on YTS. For instance, for too long an individual's chances of access to training and qualifications have been tied to obtaining the right job; YTS has introduced greater equity in this respect. The economic cycle has made life difficult both for firms and for individuals; the prolonged recession may well have disadvantaged a whole generation. Adopting YTS as a permanent feature of the labour market could mean that such disasters are avoided in the future. It is therefore very important to find some way of making YTS a comprehensive scheme. If not, it will soon be viewed as a scheme for the unemployed and suffer the fate of similar schemes, eventually disappearing from view.

Initially the first White Paper (DE, 1981) gave YTS only a 2 year horizon. Since then, in the hands of MSC and all the parties involved, it is slowly being transformed into a permanent feature of the labour market. The direction it takes could have important implications both for the young people, and for the economy. However, in the short run, their job prospects at the end of their training will be determined more by the level of aggregate demand within the economy than by the merits or demerits of YTS.

Notes

1. The author is grateful to the Manpower Services Commission for access to the reports on the various surveys mentioned in this chapter. The interpretation placed on this information is, however, that of the author and not that of the MSC. The author would like to thank colleagues from the Institute for Employment Research, particularly Robert Lindley, and Raja Junankar, University of Essex, and participants in the Young Persons' Labour Market Conference held at Warwick in November 1984 and Mrs Christine Jones for her clerical assistance. The opinions expressed and the remaining errors are the sole responsibility of the author.

2. In answer to a parliamentary question in November 1983, Mr Peter Morrison said: 'The number of people undertaking apprenticeships in manufacturing in each of the years 1979–1983 are estimated to be as follows:

1979	155 800
1980	149 500
1981	147 600
1982	123 700
1983	99 000

   (*Hansard*, Vol. 47, 24 October–4 November 1983, col. 317).
   Figures for the engineering industry show a drop in registrations for the first year apprentices of 61 per cent between 1979–83. *Engineering Industry Training Board Report and Accounts* 1983–4.

3. For further references on this point see Dutton (1981).

4. Evidence is not totally conclusive on this issue, but in his analysis of the inflow rates to unemployment for autumn 1978, Stern (1982) shows that those with 'relevant' qualifications were less likely to enter

unemployment than those with no qualifications. (However, it showed a much higher than average inflow for those with 'A' Levels.) In a later paper Stern (1984) shows that the likelihood of a repeat spell of unemployment within 12 months is lower for men with educational qualifications than without, but that those with vocational training were actually more likely to experience a repeat spell than those without. Earlier multiple regression results, however, on the probability of *leaving* unemployment was unaffected by qualification (see Nickell, 1977).

5. See *Employment Gazette* 1984, 92 (August): 339.

6. The impact of YTS can be seen in the fall in the numbers of under 18 year olds who are unemployed now compared with the period before the introduction of YTS. In April 1983, before the start of the scheme, 207 476 people in this group were unemployed but by April 1985 this figure had reduced to 160 501. However, this has been more than compensated for by the rise in unemployment for the 19–24 year old men and the 20–24 year old women. (Department of Employment *Employment Gazette* (various issues), Labour Market Data, Tables 2.5 and 2.6).

7. Sample survey data for 1978 from the Department of Employment's first employment survey (DE, 1982) found that 40 per cent of 16 year olds stayed on at school. This rose to 50 per cent in 1979 and 1980 (DE, 1982 and 1984b), while in 1983 the proportion appears to have fallen back to around 43 per cent (DE, 1984c).

8. The March 1985 Budget announced the phasing out of the YWS altogether.

9. So far the government appears to have heeded their warning.

10. The survey of the first employment of young people (DE, 1984c) conducted in December 1983 found that 13.7 per cent of those who had left school during the academic year 1982–3 had not yet found employment.

    The survey of Scottish school leavers records as many as 16.5 per cent of those who were 16 on leaving school in 1983 were unemployed in spring 1984; however, some had had jobs and some had been on YTS and left (see Raffe, Chapter 11 this volume).

11. In the most recent analysis of YTS leavers, the questions have been analysed by duration in YTS. This demonstrates that on average the shorter the time on YTS the higher the percentage transferring to another scheme. Interestingly, the percentage who are unemployed (at 28 per cent) is lower for those who leave before 14 weeks than it is for those who leave after 14 and before 39 weeks (where the unemployment rate was 39 per cent).

    In answer to a parliamentary question Mr Peter Morrison gave the following information on those leaving YTS between July and September 1984:

Destination of YTS leavers

	Duration in weeks					
	0–13	*14–26*	*27–39*	*40–47*	*48–52*	*All*
In full-time work (same employer)	5	11	20	25	40	31
In full-time work (different employer)	30	31	30	38	26	28
Full-time college or training	8	6	5	4	3	4
Back at school	3	1	—	—	—	1
On another YTS	23	10	2	1	1	5
Something else	3	3	3	3	3	3
Unemployed	28	39	39	29	26	28
% of all respondents	15	5	6	8	67	100

Source: *Weekly Hansard* 80, 1350, 3–7 June 1985, col. 58.

12. See note 11 above; the MSC now seem to have rectified this to some extent.
13. That is, so long as the MSC are not sucessful in getting the CITB to broaden the nature of the apprentice training given under the auspices of YTS. The emphasis on obtaining vocational qualifications may assist the CITB's cause.
14. Compare IER (1983), chapter 3.

11 Small Expectations: the First Year of the Youth Training Scheme

David Raffe

11.1 INTRODUCTION: YTS: UNEMPLOYMENT SAFETY NET OR TRAINING SCHEME?

The Youth Training Scheme (YTS) attempts to supplant – or at least to supplement – the market forces which determine the quality and quantity of youth training. It represents the latest stage in a recurring policy debate whose main theme has been the distorting effects of externalities and imperfections in the market for industrial training (Anderson and Fairley, 1983; Lindley, 1983). Hitherto this debate has focussed mainly on the delivery (or non-delivery) of training. This chapter's underlying theme is that the focus should now shift, towards those market imperfections and externalities which affect the quality and quantity of young people's demand for training (and education) and of employers' demand for its products. Its perspective is drawn from one of the main traditions in the sociology of education, which emphasises the centrality of the selective function to the analysis of systems of education – and, by extension, of training.[1]

Debates about YTS have focussed largely on questions of content, quality and control. They have touched on the level of funding, the allowance, the future of Mode B, the privatisation of off-the-job training, the adequacy of monitoring, the status of political education and, more generally, the balance between training and education and between foundation and specific occupational training.[2] However, important as these matters are, the long-run success of the scheme may depend on another issue: on whether it functions as as unemployment-based measure, or else fulfils the second New Training Initiative (NTI) objective of enabling all young people under 16 either to continue in full-time education or to enter 'training or a period of planned work experience combining work-related training and education' (MSC, 1981a, p.4).

From the conception of YTS its objectives have been ambivalent. Both of its parent documents – the Youth Task Group Report of April 1982 and the earlier (December 1981) White Paper – made clear that the scheme was 'not about youth unemployment' (MSC, 1982, p. 1); it was 'first and last a training scheme' (DE, 1981, p. 9). However the political impetus for YTS undoubtedly derived from the problem of youth unemployment and from the goverment's need to be seen not only to be doing something about it, but also to be doing something recognisably different from the Youth Opportunities Programme (YOP). An informal alliance of youth education and training interests, embracing the Manpower Services Commission (MSC) itself, exploited this political opportunity by redefining the problem as one not of youth unemployment but of the quality and quantity of youth training. Capitalising on public disillusion with YOP, and with its failure to solve the problem of youth unemployment, this 'pro-training' alliance managed to define the political task as one not of finding new measures to cure youth unemployment, but of converting the existing measures to pursue a new objective, a universal system of foundation training for all young workers.

The government fell in with this strategy, partly because there was in any case no available method for curing youth unemployment that was likely to be both politically acceptable and effective.[3] However differences of emphasis remained between the government and the pro-training alliance, visible in the difference between the December 1981 White Paper and the MSC's *Agenda for Action*, published simultaneously. The White Paper proposed to restrict the new training scheme to unemployed 16 year olds (in addition to its more widely publicised proposals to withhold benefits from 16 year olds who did not participate, and to set a low trainee allowance of £14.42). By contrast, the MSC document, summarising the consensus of responses to its earlier Consultative Document (MSC, 1981a), stressed once again that new provision should not be restricted to the unemployed: 'for the first time there is agreement amongst employers, unions, the education and training services and other interests that *all* young people entering employment need good quality basic training as a foundation for work and for further training or retraining' (MSC, 1981b, p. 7) (emphasis in original). This principle, conceded by the government after the publication of the Youth Task Group Report (MSC, 1982), remains central to the objectives of the pro-training alliance. YTS should not be just another unemployment-based scheme.

However the history, the politics and the situational logic of YTS combine to make its unemployment function dominant. Among 16 year olds, the unemployed are guaranteed places on the scheme; among 17 year olds, only the unemployed may enter. The need to provide a safety net for the young unemployed may conflict with YTS's other role as the harbinger of universal foundation training. Moreover, the new scheme has developed incrementally out of YOP, an unemployment-based measure; it may therefore inherit YOP's position in the labour market, its aura as a low-status quasi-remedial intervention and, above all, the set of expectations that was associated with YOP. Perhaps the main initial handicap of YTS is that people expect it to be similar to YOP, and they did not expect much of YOP.

If YTS is to reform youth training on a universal basis it must attract a much broader clientele than YOP. It must be seen by young people as preferable to jobs which do not offer training to YTS standards. Otherwise, it would be regarded as a scheme for the unemployed and the unemployable, its trainees would be stigmatised, and it would fail to attract the support of employers. Student motivation would be low and dropout rates high. The scale of the scheme would be determined, not by the need for foundation training, but by the level of youth unemployment. With a return to full employment, it would collapse.

In particular, YTS must attract recruits from the whole range of educational attainment, unlike YOP whose trainees were disproportionately less qualified on leaving school. This is important for two reasons. First, in the recent recession most of the available jobs have been taken by relatively well qualified young people (Jones, 1984; Payne, 1984; Raffe, 1984b). If more of these young people entered YTS instead this would be the best indication that YTS was seen (by at least some youngsters) as preferable to ordinary (non-YTS) jobs and not merely as preferable to unemployment. Second, if this did not happen, and YTS became established as a scheme for the less able or the less motivated, it – and, more importantly, the education and training philosophy it represents – would lack credibility both with employers and with young people. Employers would not use it as a main source of recruitment, and, seen from within the education system, it would lack status and fail to attract abler, more motivated young people who did not wish to lose their place in the educational (and consequently occupational) hierarchy. In those parts of the education system where its selective function is dominant, change has usually been a process of diffusion from the top downwards. This is exemplified by the post-war history of the secondary school curriculum. Innovations that affect the whole age group have rarely if ever been successfully introduced from the bottom upwards.

11.2   DATA: THE 1984 SURVEY

This chapter offers a tentative assessment of the first impact of YTS on the youth labour market in Scotland; in particular, it asks to what extent has YTS functioned, like YOP, as an unemployment-based scheme. It reports early analyses of data from a postal survey of young people in Scotland, conducted in the spring of 1984.[4] The survey's main aims were methodological, to explore how to adapt the Scottish School Leavers' Surveys to collect valid information on YTS, and to pilot new survey techniques; but since the survey covered a representative sample of young people in Scotland, it also provides useful data on patterns of participation in YTS. Questionnaires were sent in March 1984 to a target sample of 3726 young people, of whom 2929 responded.[5]

The full sample covered young people who left school at any time during the 1982–3 school session, as well as 16 year olds who stayed on at school in autumn 1983. In this chapter the analysis is restricted to the 1421 sample members who left school in summer 1983. Among other things this standardises the length of time between leaving school and the time of the survey, and it avoids confusion of YTS with YOP (which was still available to people who left school earlier in the session). Focussing on school leavers also permits direct comparisons with earlier Scottish School Leavers' Surveys.

11.3   TRENDS IN SCHOOL LEAVERS' DESTINATIONS

Table 11.1 sets the 1984 survey in its historical context by comparing the destinations of the summer 1983 school leavers with summer term school leavers in earlier years. Destinations are shown for the October after leaving school and for the following spring (all the surveys were despatched in March or April); they are reported for all school leavers (of all ages) and for fourth-year leavers. The fourth year (equivalent to the English fifth form) is the last compulsory year for a majority of pupils; most fourth-year leavers are 16 year old leavers, the main target group for YTS.

Table 11.1 Destinations of summer term school leavers, Scotland, 1978–1983 (%)

	All leavers				Fourth year leavers			
	1978	80	82	83	1978	80	82	83
(a) In October after leaving school								
Full-time course	—	27.0	31.1	31.9	—	10.2	11.9	11.6
Full-time job	—	42.4	27.9	26.5	—	48.7	31.3	30.1
YOP/YTS	—	14.3	25.2	24.2	—	21.4	38.5	38.4
Unemployment	—	13.5	11.4	13.0	—	17.8	14.6	17.1
Others/Not Known	—	2.8	4.3	4.4	—	2.0	3.7	2.8
Total	—	100.0	99.9	100.0	—	100.0	100.0	100.0
n		(4758)	(6015)	(1421)		(2449)	(2849)	(620)
(b) In following spring								
Full-time course	23.1	25.8	29.3	30.5	8.4	8.1	10.2	9.7
Full-time job	61.1	48.4	35.7	32.7	72.2	55.0	40.2	33.7
YOP/YTS	5.7	12.8	17.5	21.8	8.3	18.9	27.1	37.0
Unemployment	6.8	11.9	13.8	12.0	9.6	16.9	19.6	16.5
Others/Not Known	3.4	1.1	3.6	3.0	1.4	1.1	2.8	3.1
Total	100.0	100.0	99.9	100.0	99.9	100.0	99.9	100.0
n	(6475)	(4758)	(6015)	(1421)	(4239)	(2449)	(2849)	(620)

Notes: Data for October 1978 are available only for less qualified leavers and are not shown here. The 1978 leavers' sample did not cover unqualified leavers from grant aided and independent schools, but the effect of this ommision is negligible. A majority of Scottish pupils are first eligible to leave school in or at the end of the fourth year.

Source: Scottish School Leavers' Surveys (various).

Analyses reported elsewhere show that the destinations of 1978 school leavers were very similar to those of 1976 leavers (Raffe, 1984b). Since 1978, however, the youth labour market has collapsed; the lower half of Table 11.1 shows that between spring 1979 and spring 1984 the proportion of the previous summer's school leavers in employment fell by nearly a half, and by more than a half among fourth-year leavers.[6] The gap this created was partly filled by a rise in participation in full-time education and by the growth of special programmes, although the table underestimates the scale of the latter since it records participation only at given points in time.

The seasonal character of school leaver recruitment makes it difficult to infer underlying trends in youth employment. The top half of Table 11.1 (the October destinations) suggests that the decline in school leaver employment almost levelled off between 1982 and 1983. The bottom half of the table (the spring destinations) shows the decline continuing, especially among fourth-year leavers, but this probably reflects the fact that YTS kept its trainees off the labour market (in the sense of reducing job search) for a year rather than for 6 months as with most YOP schemes. The October date is probably the better guide to the most recent trends.[7] The levelling off of employment between October 1982 and October 1983 is the more remarkable in view of the specific intention that YTS should embrace jobs that young people would normally have entered. With respect to the aggregate impact of YTS, therefore, the main conclusion of Table 11.1 is that it does not seem to have displaced many jobs through decisions either on the demand side of the labour market (through jobs being incorporated into YTS under the additionality rule) or on the supply side (through young people entering YTS in preference to 'ordinary' jobs). Its main impact may have been to defer the job search of some unemployed young people for a year rather than for 6 months.

This conclusion is qualified by Table 11.2 which presents the October destinations for males and females separately. Among females, employment not only levelled off but increased slightly between 1982 and 1983, and participation on YTS fell compared with YOP. These changes may reflect an underlying increase in demand – possibly encouraged by Young Workers' Scheme (YWS) – but they may also reflect the return to the ordinary labour market of jobs formerly substituted by YOP. Among males, however, the opposite trends can be seen, with a continuing fall in employment and an expansion of YTS relative to YOP. To the extent that these trends

Table 11.2 Destinations of summer term school leavers in October after leaving school, by sex, Scotland, 1980–3 (%)

	All Leavers			Fourth-Year Leavers		
	1980	82	83	1980	82	83
Males						
Full-time course	22.4	26.2	26.3	3.4	5.5	4.9
Full-time job	45.9	32.1	28.5	55.2	37.4	33.4
YOP/YTS	15.1	26.5	28.3	21.5	40.0	44.5
Unemployment	13.9	11.1	12.9	17.8	13.5	15.6
Others/Not Known	2.7	4.1	3.9	2.0	3.6	1.6
Total	100.0	100.0	99.9	99.9	100.0	99.9
n	(2266)	(3053)	(687)	(1234)	(1541)	(335)
Females						
Full-time course	31.8	36.2	37.2	18.0	19.5	19.2
Full-time job	38.8	23.5	24.6	41.1	24.1	26.4
YOP/YTS	13.5	23.8	20.3	21.3	36.7	31.2
Unemployment	13.0	11.7	13.1	17.8	15.9	18.9
Others/Not Known	2.9	4.8	4.8	1.8	3.7	4.3
Total	100.0	100.0	0	100.0	99.9	100.0
n	(2492)	(2962)	(734)	(1215)	(1308)	(285)

Source: Scottish School Leavers' Surveys (various).

reflect the impact of YTS they suggest that any success in displacing or incorporating ordinary jobs was largely restricted to the male labour market.

11.4 EXPERIENCES IN THE LABOUR MARKET

Table 11.3 adds a longitudinal dimension to the cross-sectional 'snapshots' of Tables 11.1 and 11.2. It is restricted to labour market entrants – a term used to describe young people who were in employment, on YTS, or unemployed, both in the October after leaving school and in the following spring. Most of the remainder were in full-time further or higher education. Labour market entrants included more males than females (since more females entered full-time education) and had lower average qualifications than school leavers as a whole.[8]

Table 11.3   Typology of 'careers' of labour-market entrants (%)

	Males	Females	Males and females
In full-time job in spring 1984			
no previous job or YTS	33.8	34.9	34.3
previous job(s), no YTS	4.7	5.9	5.3
formerly on YTS, no previous job	6.8	10.2	8.4
previous job(s) and YTS	1.3	1.4	1.3
total in full-time job	(46.6)	(52.4)	(49.3)
On YTS in spring 1984			
no job since school	36.6	24.8	31.1
formerly in job	1.9	4.3	3.0
total on YTS	(38.5)	(29.1)	(34.1)
Unemployed in spring 1984			
no job or YTS since school	6.4	9.5	7.8
formerly in a job, no YTS	3.6	2.9	3.3
formerly on YTS, no job	4.4	5.7	5.0
formerly in a job and on YTS	0.5	0.5	0.5
total unemployed	(14.9)	(18.6)	(16.6)
Total	100.0	100.1	100.0
n	(475)	(404)	(879)

Source: 1984 Scottish School Leavers' Surveys.

Table 11.3 summarises the experiences of the labour market entrants in the 10 or so months since they had left school. Nearly a half were in jobs in spring 1984 (49.3 per cent) but only a third had moved directly from school to employment, without going on YTS, and had remained in their first jobs. 1 in 10 labour market entrants had already entered a YTS scheme and left it for a job (8.4 + 1.3 = 9.7 per cent); the proportion was higher among females than among males. About a third of labour market entrants were on YTS, and less than 1 in 10 of these had previously been in a job. 1 in 6 labour market entrants were unemployed in spring 1984;[9] a third of these had previously been on YTS, and others had been in jobs, but 7.8 per cent of labour market entrants – 9.5 per cent of females – had been, as far as the survey data can tell, continuously unemployed since school.

11.5   PATTERNS OF ENTRY TO YTS

Nearly half of the labour market entrants (49.3 per cent), and nearly one-third of all summer term leavers (32.2 per cent), had entered YTS by spring 1984. More male than female school leavers joined the scheme (36.5 per cent compared with 28.2 per cent).[10] Young people were asked to give their reasons for entering the scheme (Table 11.4). Although answers to fixed-choice questions of this kind need to be viewed with caution, they are consistent with the interpretation that most young people who entered YTS did so for reasons that were predominantly unemployment-related. The reason offered by the greatest number of trainees, especially females, was that they 'thought it would help them get a job', with the implication that jobs were not available by a more direct route. The next most frequent reason, offered by the greatest number of males, was simply that they 'couldn't find a job'. Both reasons were offered by slightly more of the fourth-year leavers than of the older entrants to the scheme, despite the fact that only among the latter was the scheme meant to be solely unemployment-based. Nearly half the trainees said they entered because they 'wanted to be trained', but only 11.9 per cent said this was their 'most important' reason. Similar proportions joined because they simply 'wanted something to do' or 'wanted more money'.

The survey did not collect reliable data on the mode of YTS schemes, but it obtained nearly complete information on the type of work performed (Table 11.5). The 'occupations' of YTS trainees were similar to those of young people in ordinary jobs, with three main

Table 11.4 'Why did you join the scheme? Was it because you...'

	% giving item as 'reason'	% giving item as 'most important reason'
...couldn't find a job	64.8	18.1
...wanted to be trained	46.4	11.9
...liked the idea of the scheme	24.2	2.7
...wanted more money	38.2	8.4
...wanted something to do	53.7	9.7
...thought it would help you get a job	69.4	35.7
no 'most important' reason identified	–	13.5
n	(221)	100.0

Note: Based on random sub-sample of summer-term leavers who had entered YTS.

Source: 1984 Scottish School Leavers' Surveys.

exceptions. YTS trainees were less likely to be engaged in the more sought-after types of white-collar work; among males, many more YTS trainees did 'construction, mining and related' work; and among females, many more YTS trainees worked in 'selling' occupations. An important similarity between YTS and ordinary jobs was that the occupational differentiation of males and females was at least as strong on YTS as in ordinary employment.

Figure 11.1 is restricted (like Table 11.3) to labour market entrants. Figure 11.1a shows (broken line) the percentage of YTS entrants from each of four school qualification groups: those with Highers (the nearest equivalent to English 'A' Levels, taken at 17 or 18), those with four or more 'O' Grades in bands A–C, those with 1–3 'O' Grades in bands A–C and those with no A–C awards. ('O' Grades are roughly equivalent to the English 'O' Level; more than three-quarters of the age group attempt 'O' Grades at 16.) Figure 11.1b shows the

Table 11.5 'Occupations' of summer leavers currently on YTS or in jobs, by sex (%)

	YTS		Jobs	
	Males	Females	Males	Females
Professional and related supporting management	0.4	0	2.0	0.4
Professional and related in education, welfare and health	0	0.9	0.9	10.5
Literary, artistic and sports	1.2	0	0.7	1.3
Professional and related in science, engineering, technology	0.9	0	4.0	0.9
Managerial	0.6	0	1.4	0
Clerical and related	6.6	43.8	11.0	49.1
Selling	1.8	27.6	1.7	8.6
Security and protective services	0	0	7.4	0
Catering, cleaning, hairdressing and other personal services	2.2	18.9	2.7	12.1
Farming, fishing and related	8.0	0.9	6.6	0.5
Materials processing, making and repairing (excluding metal and electrical)	18.4	7.1	18.0	12.7
Processing, making, repairing and related (metal and electrical)	26.0	0	26.9	1.4
Painting, repetitive assembling, product inspecting, packaging and related	7.4	0	5.3	2.0
Construction, mining and related nes	22.7	0	6.3	0
Transport operating, materials moving and storing and related	2.8	0.9	4.8	0.5
Miscellaneous	1.1	0	0.4	0
Total	100.1	100.1	100.1	100.0
n	(172)	(114)	(226)	(219)

Note: Inadequate or blank answers (about 6 per cent of the total) are omitted.
Source: 1984 Scottish School Leavers' Surveys.

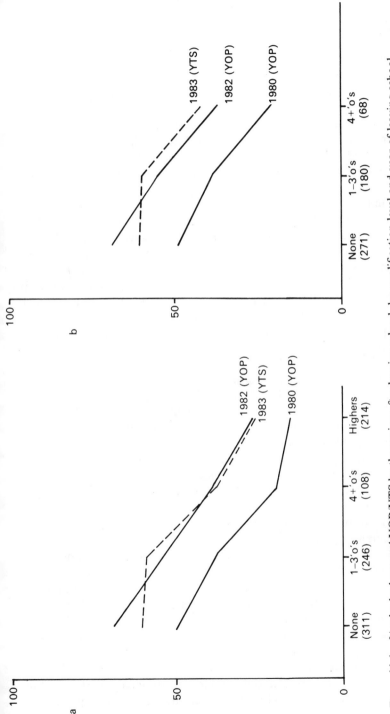

Figure 11.1   % who had entered YOP/YTS by the spring after leaving school, by qualification level and year of leaving school

a   % of all summer term leavers who entered the labour market

b   % of fourth-year summer term leavers who entered the labour market

Bracketed figures are numbers for 1983 leavers: the previous surveys were based on considerably larger samples

corresponding percentages among fourth-year leavers, the main target group for YTS.

Figure 11.1 also presents the equivalent data for YOP entrants among school leavers in 1980 and 1982 (unbroken lines).

For all three leaver groups the lines slope downwards from left to right, indicating that both YOP and YTS tended to attract the less qualified labour market entrants, even though labour market entrants were themselves a selected group which excluded many of the better qualified school leavers. At the higher (right hand) end of the qualification range the slopes for YOP and YTS run parallel; at the lower (left hand) end of the qualification range, however, a levelling off appears; fewer of the least qualified 1983 leavers entered YTS than would be expected on the basis of the expenditure of YOP in earlier years. As measured by the difference in slopes between the two lowest qualification groups in 1982 and 1983, this levelling off is statistically significant ($p < 0.01$).[11] It admits of at least three possible explanations: (i) that employers recruiting for ordinary jobs reduced their emphasis on qualifications in 1983, recruiting more unqualified school leavers of whom fewer were available for YTS; (ii) that less qualified school leavers in 1983 were, if unemployed, less likely to enter YTS than their equivalents of earlier years were likely to enter YOP; (iii) that some better qualified school leavers entered YTS in preference to ordinary jobs, making more jobs available to the less qualified.

Of the three explanations, the first seems unlikely and is not considered here. The second is consistent with anecdotal evidence – supported by pilot work for the survey – that some unqualified young people, alienated by (school) education, were put off YTS by the requirement (absent from YOP) that they spend 3 months off-the-job, often at college. The third is the most optimistic explanation; it suggests that some young people (if only a few) entered YTS in preference to ordinary jobs.

Figure 11.2 suggests that both the second and third explanations may be partly correct. The top line shows (for each year's leavers) the proportion of labour market entrants in each attainment group who had entered either a job or YOP/YTS by the spring after leaving school (the remainder are assumed to have been continuously unemployed). The bottom line shows the proportion who had entered jobs *without* going on YOP/YTS. The distance between the two lines shows, for each year, the proportions entering YOP/YTS, as shown in Figure 11.1; Figure 11.2 thus presents recruitment to YOP/YTS as something determined after direct recruitment to ordinary jobs.

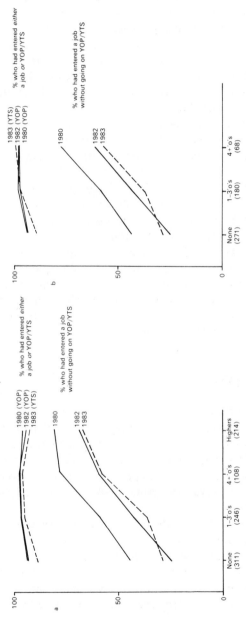

Figure 11.2 % who had entered either a job or YOP/YTS, and % who had entered a job without going on YOP/YTS, by the spring after leaving school, by qualification level and year of leaving school

a % of all summer term leavers who entered the labour market
b % of fourth-year summer term leavers who entered the labour market
Bracketed figures are numbers for 1983 leavers: the previous surveys were based on considerably larger samples

In all 3 years employment was strongly correlated with qualifications, and most labour market entrants were accounted for by either jobs or YOP/YTS. However, there are two modest but statistically significant ($0.01 < p < 0.05$) differences between 1982 and 1983 leavers. First, the least qualified 1983 leavers were more likely to remain continuously unemployed, entering neither employment nor YTS. Second, at the bottom end of the qualification range the association between qualifications and employment was weaker among the 1983 leavers. These changes correspond respectively to the second and third explanations above.

Figures 11.3 and 11.4 show, further, that the second explanation applies only to females. A much higher proportion of females with low qualifications remained continuously unemployed in 1983–4 than had done in the previous year. Since most of these young women had been offered YTS places (MSC, 1984b, p. 16; Bryant, Burnhill and Raffe, 1985, chapter 13) it follows that among poorly qualified females the YTS refusal rate was substantially higher than the YOP refusal rate in earlier years. The third explanation applies most clearly to males (Figure 11.3) particularly fourth-year leavers; among this group the link between qualifications and employment outside YTS weakened, probably because some apprenticeships were incorporated into YTS. However, small sample numbers make this conclusion tentative,[12] and may account for the more erratic employment patterns among females in Figure 11.4.

11.6   LEAVING YTS

More than a third of the 1983 leavers who had started a YTS scheme had left it, prematurely, by spring 1984. Only 1 in 10 of these had joined another scheme; 32.3 per cent of YTS trainees had left YTS outright. This proportion was much higher among females (39.5 per cent) than among males (26.5 per cent). Of those who had left YTS 6 in 10 were employed in spring 1984, and most of the others were unemployed.

More than a third of those who had left expressed dissatisfaction with YTS, although most were dissatisfied with their particular schemes rather than with YTS in general. The main reasons given were that the training did not come up to expectations, or that the work was pointless or boring. A few respondents mentioned health reasons for leaving. However, most of those who left YTS for

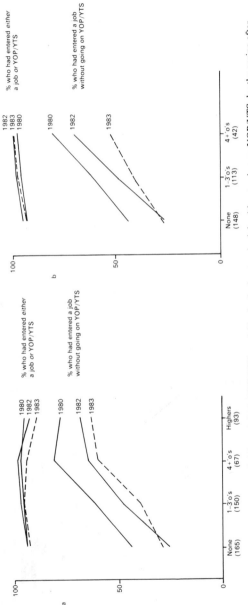

Figure 11.3 % who had entered either a job or YOP/YTS, and % who had entered a job without going on YOP/YTS, by the spring after leaving school, by qualification level and year of leaving school: males

a % of all summer term leavers who entered the labour market
b % of fourth-year summer term leavers who entered the labour market
Bracketed figures are numbers for 1983 leavers: the previous surveys were based on considerably larger samples

254

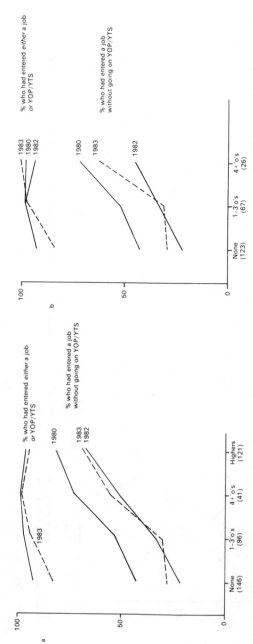

Figure 11.4 · % who had entered either a job or YTS/YOP, and % who had entered a job without going on YOP/YTS, by the spring after leaving school, by qualification level and year of leaving school: females
a % of all summer term leavers who entered the labour market.
b % of all fourth-year summer term leavers who entered the labour market.
(Figures in parentheses are numbers for 1983 leavers: the previous surveys were based on considerably larger samples.)

permanent employment gave this as the reason for leaving – the unstated assumption being that ordinary jobs, when they could be found, were naturally to be preferred to YTS. Precise comparisons with YOP are not possible but it appears that many young people in 1983–4, and especially females, regarded YTS much as earlier cohorts had regarded YOP – as a temporary refuge from unemployment, to be used only as long as was necessary in order to find a permanent job.

Data are not available on the eventual destinations of the young people who completed their YTS schemes. In spring 1984, when most YTS trainees were at least half way through their schemes, 21.6 per cent of males, but only 13.4 per cent of females, thought they would be kept on by their YTS employer or sponsor.

11.7 ATTITUDES TO YTS

Finally, Table 11.6 compares the attitudes (in 1984) of the 1983 leavers to YTS, with the attitudes (in 1981) of 1980 leavers to YOP.[13] The table contains both bad and good news for YTS.

The bad news is shown in the two right hand columns. By 1981 criticism of YOP was widespread, and many 1981 sample members expressed their dissatisfaction strongly (Raffe, 1984c, chapter 10). YTS was to be a fresh start, with a new name, new objectives and a new image. Despite this, the profiles of attitudes to YOP and YTS respectively are uncannily alike. YTS attracted slightly fewer positive replies with respect to job finding and slightly more with respect to training, but the differences were slight. Moreover, two additional items, introduced in 1984, showed that nearly two-thirds of summer term leavers agreed that YTS was 'just to keep unemployment figures down', and more than three-quarters agreed that it was 'a source of cheap labour' (with only 7 per cent disagreeing). Both attitudes were expressed open endedly about YOP by many of the 1981 leavers. Whatever the differences between YOP and YTS, they appear not to have been perceived as such by the first group of young people to be affected by the change.

The good news is that whereas in 1981 there was little difference between YOP trainees and others in their attitudes to YOP (the main difference was that the trainees were less likely to believe that they had interesting things to do), in 1984 YTS trainees were significantly more positive than others in their evaluations of YTS.

Females were slightly more positive than males in their attitudes to

256

Table 11.6 Attitudes to YOP/YTS; previous session's summer term leavers who entered the labour market, 1981 and 1984 (% responding 'yes')

Do you think that YOP/YTS...	YOP/YTS trainees		Others		All	
	1981	84	1981	84	1981	84
...helps unemployed people to find jobs?	47.9	55.2	47.8	34.8	47.8	44.9
...gives people interesting things to do?	54.4	59.9	61.0	54.1	58.5	57.0
...is a useful way to get training?	69.8	77.8	69.1	66.9	69.4	72.3
n	(988)	(213)	(1137)	(226)	(2125)	(439)

Notes: Based on random sub-samples. In 1981, the questions referred to 'special schemes of work experience or training' for unemployed young people. Item non-respondents are included in the 100 per cent base; item non-response ranged from 10 per cent to 17 per cent, but does not affect the comparison between years.

Source: Scottish School Leavers' Surveys (various).

YTS, especially with respect to the item on training. This may reflect the relative scarcity of other training opportunities for young women.

11.8 YTS: YOP IN SHEEP'S CLOTHING?

The question posed at the beginning of the paper was whether YTS has functioned, like YOP, as an unemployment-based scheme.

With respect to females, the answer appears to be: 'Yes'. YTS in 1983 did not displace or incorporate a significant number of ordinary jobs for young women. Like YOP, it attracted mainly less qualified young recruits, who entered for reasons that were largely unemployment-related. There is little evidence of young women preferring YTS to ordinary jobs; on aggregate, at least, their attitudes to YTS were very similar to previous school leavers' attitudes to YOP. Many young women appeared to regard the scheme as a temporary refuge from unemployment only, and took for granted that they should leave it on finding a permanent job; 4 in 10 of young women who entered the scheme had left it by spring 1984. In sum, YTS appears to have functioned (and been regarded) very much like YOP before it – as an unemployment-based scheme. The main differences were that it kept unemployed young people – at least, those who remained on the scheme – off the market for a longer period than YOP, and it appears to have been rejected by a larger proportion of the less qualified unemployed.

With respect to males, however, the survey data are more equivocal. YTS appears to have displaced, or incorporated, a number of male jobs. Although small sample numbers make definite conclusions impossible, YTS appears to have weakened the link between qualifications and (non-YTS) employment, especially among 16 year olds; this suggests that at least some young men entered YTS in preference to ordinary jobs, or at least to those jobs that were available to them. Males were less likely than females to leave their YTS schemes early; they were more likely to expect to be kept on afterwards. However, the differences between males and females were only a matter of degree. Among males, too, a majority of YTS trainees gave unemployment-linked reasons for joining the scheme, and the attitudes of young men were rather less favourable to YTS than those of young women. YTS still appeared as a predominantly unemployment-based scheme.

One way to interpret these data involves relaxing the assumption, implicit in much of the preceding discussion, of the internal homogeneity of YTS. It is possible that those young men who did enter YTS in preference to ordinary jobs were opting not for YTS as such, but for particular schemes which gave them access to the jobs and apprenticeships they wished to enter. The survey results are consistent with earlier speculation about internal stratification within the scheme (Main and Raffe, 1983c); a two-tier YTS may be emerging. In the primary tier are YTS schemes which either provide the principal or only port of entry to particular occupations, or offer their trainees a guarantee or a good chance of subsequent employment. These schemes attract the same kinds of young people as would ordinarily have sought entry to the relevant occupations. On the evidence of this study, most of these trainees are male,[14] perhaps on schemes related to predominantly male jobs such as construction and engineering. Schemes in the secondary tier function as schemes for the unemployed, whose main selling points are an allowance somewhat higher than supplementary benefit, the perception that future employers might regard YTS participation as more indicative of motivation than continuous unemployment, and a small but uncertain chance of being kept on by managing agent or work experience provider. Most female trainees, and a good proportion of the males, enter schemes in the secondary tier.

This interpretation is speculative and cannot be tested directly against the survey data. Moreover, just as the concept of labour market dualism has been rejected in favour of more elaborate theories of differentiation, so is the notion of a two-tier YTS likely to prove inadequate to describe the complex differentiation within the scheme. The simpler and more confident conclusion from this study is that for most people (including 16 year olds), and especially for females, YTS has functioned mainly as an unemployment-based scheme. Any improvement on YOP in this respect has been modest.

This conclusion is necessarily provisional; it relates only to the first year of YTS. Moreover, it is based on data which refer, at least directly, only to the supply side of the labour market. Yet in the long run it is the demand side which will principally determine the success of the scheme. If YTS provides reasonably secure routes to good jobs, young people will follow those routes. Whether it succeeds in this remains to be seen. One of the many paradoxes of YOP was that it aimed to influence the youth labour market by intervening on the supply side, but its actual effects (beyond the immediate register effect) came about mainly through unintended consequences on the demand side.[15] YTS may likewise have unintended and unforeseen effects on the demand for youth labour. However, to become the preferred option of young people it may need not only to provide jobs for its graduates, but also to restrict the job opportunities for the young people who do not enter YTS. Otherwise, few young people would prefer a year on YTS – with a low allowance and no guarantee of a job at the end – to a 'real' job elsewhere. YTS must therefore bring all employment opportunities for young school leavers within the scheme. Yet, while many employers prefer to recruit young people outside the framework of YTS, and especially while the boundaries between the youth and adult labour markets remain flexible, it is unlikely that YTS can monopolise youth employment opportunities in this way.[16]

In summer 1983 young people were in no position to judge the effects of YTS on their prospects of employment. They were ignorant and uncertain about the new scheme, and many of their teachers and advisers were scarcely more knowledgeable. It is hardly surprising that young people – and others – should have framed their expectations of YTS in terms of YOP, the programme it replaced; and it is encouraging that the attitudes of young people who had direct experience of YTS were distinctly more positive than the attitudes of those who had not.

However, social institutions, sustained by the reciprocity of mutual expectations, are typically slow to change. The great danger for YTS is that it may be constrained to continue in the way it began, that a vicious circle may be created in which the mutual expectations of employers and young people became mutually reinforcing. On the one hand, young people would continue to enter YTS schemes (in the secondary tier) only if they could not find a job. On the other hand, employers would regard the schemes as quasi-remedial, unemployment-based measures; their graduates would be stigmatised as the unemployable, the less able and the poorly motivated; employers would be reluctant to recruit former trainees; the schemes would offer poor employment prospects; only the unemployed would want to enter them; and so on.

This vicious circle would not apply to schemes in the primary tier of YTS. Some of these schemes might overcome the problem of stigmatisation by providing trainees with highly marketable credentials in specific skills, or through high reputations gained from the employers running the scheme. But in most primary-tier schemes, trainees would be selected as potential future employees by the employers running the schemes, so the fact of their selection would not stigmatise them as unemployable. The overall success of YTS may partly depend on the relative scale of the primary tier within the scheme, which in turn depends on the extent to which YTS is integrated with employers' routine practices for the recruitment and training of young workers.

The best hope for the secondary-tier schemes may be for the distinction between themselves and the primary tier to become blurred, so that they may ride on the coat tails of the latter's reputation. The more complex (and less visible) the differentiation within YTS, the more likely this may be. It is, however, unrealistic to expect that secondary-tier schemes can break the vicious circle outlined above merely through improvements in the quality or relevance of their training. Except for highly specific training, employers recruiting in the youth labour market have usually judged education and training courses less on their content or quality than on the types of young people believed to enter them in the first place. Moreover, many employers appear to be sceptical of the foundation-training philosophy embodied in YTS. The success of YTS schemes in both tiers depends less on their content than on their context, and specifically on how they articulate with patterns of educational and occupational differentiation and selection.[17]

The future of YTS remains open. The most pessimistic aspect of the survey's findings is not that they show YTS to have functioned largely as an unemployment-based scheme but that this conclusion will come as no surprise to many people practically involved in the scheme. The main impediment to the success of YTS is that people's expectations of it – based on the experiment of YOP – will be too low.

Notes

1. Classic examples of this tradition are contained in Halsey, Floud and Anderson (1961) and, more recently, Halsey, Heath and Ridge (1980). In Raffe (1984c) the perspective is applied, as in this chapter to the macrosociological analysis of educational change.
2. For discussions and evaluations of the YTS in plan or in operation, see Dutton (1981) and chapter 10), Finn (1983), DES (1984), Ryan (1984b), and reports and commentaries in the *Times Educational Supplement* and *Youthaid Bulletin*.
3. More detailed acounts of the policy options with respect to youth unemployment, and of the origins of YTS, are provided by Raffe (1983) and (1984a) respectively.
4. Full details of the survey are reported by Bryant, Burnhill and Raffe (1985). The contribution of Ian Bryant, Peter Burnhill and other

colleagues in the CES is gratefully acknowledged. Andrew McPherson made helpful comments on an earlier draft of this paper. The survey was funded by the MSC and conducted by the Centre for Educational Sociology at Edinburgh University in conjunction with the Scottish Education Department. The author is responsible for the interpretations and opinions expressed in this paper.

5.   All analyses in this paper use data weighted to compensate for non-response biases associated with sex and school qualifications. Reported sample numbers are unweighted; standard errors are calculated from weighted estimates and unweighted sample numbers.

6.   The 'full-time job' category in Table 11.1, and elsewhere in this chapter includes apprentices not on YTS. It probably also includes many of those young people (1 in 20 of YTS entrants) who were funded under YTS but had employee rather than trainee status. Validation work on the survey suggests that YTS employees recorded themselves as in jobs rather than on YTS; many may not even have known that they were, technically, on the scheme. Not only are the effects of this 'misclassification' numerically small, but arguably these young people should not in any case be included as on YTS for the purposes of the present argument, since they were not subject to the same foundation-training requirements as YTS trainees (Ryan, 1984b, p. 38).

7.   A further reason is that there was an exceptionally high level of school leaver recruitment during the winter of 1982–3. This may have partly resulted from the one-off impact of the winding down of YOP, as jobs that were formerly substituted by YOP came on to the market again. The seasonal pattern of school leaver recruitment in 1980–1 is described in more detail by Main and Raffe (1983c).

8.   The availability of YTS in 1983 appears not to have weakened the link between qualification level and entry to full-time post-school education (table not shown).

9.   The questionnaire item asked if respondents were 'unemployed and looking for work'; respondents were not asked whether or not they were registered unemployed.

10.   The difference between males and females in rates of entry to YTS was not due merely to their different rates of participation in the labour market. Among labour market entrants, 51.5 per cent of males and 46.9 per cent of females had entered YTS.

11.   Significance is calculated on the assumption of simple random sampling (two-tailed tests). This is a conservative assumption; standard error estimates empirically derived from variance across sample replicates (Burnhill and Fisk, 1981) indicate a design effect of less than 1, due largely to stratified sampling. However, because of the incorporation of an experimental design the improvement was least marked in the 1984 survey where numbers are most critical (Bryant, Burnhill and Raffe, 1985).

12.   For none of the attainment groups in Figure 11.4 are the 1982 and 1983 employment estimates significantly different. However, for fourth-year leavers with four or more 'O' Grades the difference only just fails to reach significance at the 5 per cent level, and this failure may reflect the

relatively conservative assumptions underlying the standard error estimates (see note 11 above).

13. The attitude items in Table 11.6 offered only 'Yes' or 'No' responses; many respondents felt unable to express an opinion either way and left the item blank, although the proportions doing so were similar in 1981 and 1984. In some versions of the 1984 questionnaire the items were redesigned to allow respondents to say that they were 'not sure'. Up to a third did so, indicating either ignorance or a suspension of judgement by many school leavers. The two new items (described in the text) were included in these versions.

14. In this respect our prediction, based on the experience of YOP, was wrong (Main and Raffe, 1983c, p. 67). In contrast to YOP, YTS appears to offer more (or at least more certain) routes to employment for males than for females.

15. See Raffe (1984a), especially pp. 199–203.

16. An important task for further research is to relate patterns of differentiation within YTS both to patterns of differentiation within the 'ordinary' youth labour market and to variations in the extent and type of competition between adult and youth markets. See for example Ashton, Maguire and Garland (1982).

17. The distinction between content and context is developed in relation to YTS, as well as to developments in Scottish education, in chapters 10 and 11 of Raffe (1984c).

12 The Young Workers' Scheme: A Preliminary Assessment

Amin Rajan[1]

12.1 INTRODUCTION

The object of this chapter is to provide an assessment of the impact of the Young Workers' Scheme (YWS) so far on the youth–adult earnings differential and on youth employment.

The Young Workers' Scheme was introduced in Great Britain in January 1982. Its detailed features are described in two Department of Employment publications (DE, 1982 and 1984). Its aim is to 'price' the young workers into jobs by improving their competitive position in the labour market. Young workers are defined here as those under 18. The scheme involves paying employers a recruitment subsidy. Initially, the subsidy was payable for a year at the rate of £15 per week for eligible young people earning under £40 per week and £7.50 for those earning £40 or more but under £45 per week. These amounts have been revised and consolidated since: the current weekly payment rate is £15 and the earnings threshold £50. The minimal qualifying age has been raised from 16 to 17 years. The inbuilt earnings limit has the potential to widen the difference between the average earnings of young and adult workers – the so-called earnings differential – so as to encourage youth employment. The subsidy has another important feature. It is a flow (as distinct from a stock) subsidy: employers can qualify for it as and when they recruit young workers, irrespective of whether their stock of labour increases or not. It is thus designed to reduce employers' labour costs.

The structure of this chapter broadly follows the objective set out above. Section 12.2 describes the research method and the survey characteristics. Section 12.3 assesses the impact of YWS on the youth–adult earnings differential. Section 12.4 attempts to quantify its employment effect. The final section (12.5) considers the main conclusion. The survey questionnaire and the case study discussion guide are given in the Appendix.

12.2   RESEARCH METHOD

The YWS has now been in operation for under 3 years. Methodologically, its impact so far can be decomposed into two elements: initial (or immediate) effect and cumulative (including initial and lagged) effect. This distinction is important for two reasons. First, the YWS was introduced at a time when the corporate sector was subject to recessionary cost and competitive pressures. For the employers of young workers, it did provide some immediate relief. At the time, the social concern about youth unemployment was also high owing to the civil disturbances in 1981. In theory at least, both these factors argue for an observable initial effect. Second, the prevalence of wage rigidities due to institutional arrangements such as collective bargaining and wages councils mean that the process of 'pricing in' young workers into jobs by widening the youth–adult earnings differentials may take time.

The implication is that a research method designed to assess the impact of the YWS should try to identify the initial as well as the cumulative effect, preferably using a cohort of firms receiving the subsidy from its inception. Accordingly, the method used in this report has two distinct strands: a national *postal survey* designed to identify the initial effect in the first year of the YWS, and a programme of detailed *case studies* designed to identify the cumulative effect. These two elements are described separately below. As Deakin and Pratten (1982) have shown, a two-pronged approach such as this provides more detailed insights into the effectiveness of a subsidy than the standard econometric approach.

Postal Survey

In December 1981, the IMS commissioned a nationally-based postal survey using the questionnaire given in Appendix A. Its purpose, amongst others, was to provide an *ex ante* indication of the employment effect in the first year of the scheme, namely 1982. A total of 719 business organisations across every industry in manufacturing and services participated in the survey.

In March 1983, these 719 companies were approached again, using the same questionnaire. This time round they were asked to provide an *ex post* assessment of the YWS employment effect in 1982. A total of 365 responses was received, again giving a response rate of 51 per cent. The object of this follow-up survey was to obtain a more firm indication of the first-year impact. In this chapter, all the survey-based results are derived from the follow-up survey, referred to hereafter as 'the survey'. In contrast, the first survey is referred to as the 1981 survey.

The 365 respondents from the survey constitute the sample base for this study. Their industrial background is given in Appendix Table 12.A1 (p. 290). It shows that the survey has achieved a very broad coverage: every industry of the 1968 Standard Industrial Classification (SIC) is represented; although the cell frequency in some cases is inevitably small, given that there are 26 industries involved. In aggregate sectoral terms, 67 per cent of the respondents were in manufacturing (covering Orders 3–19); 28 per cent in services (Orders 20–26); and 3 per cent in 'others' (Orders 1 and 2). The remaining 2 per cent are unclassified because of the lack of information. Apart from a broad coverage, the sample also achieved a somewhat disproportionate representation of industries identified by Casson (1979) as being major employers of young workers in Britain – industries such as engineering, textiles, construction, distributive trades and miscellaneous services. Above all, the frequency distribution is similar to the one achieved in the 1981 survey, ruling out the possibility of sampling bias.

That said, it is worth emphasising that the relative predominance of the manufacturing sector in the sample stems from the differences in the choice of reporting units. In manufacturing, each respondent constitutes an individual establishment with its own independent recruitment machinery. In services, on the other hand (owing to increasing centralisation), the individual establishments have few records and much less independence. The service industries responses, as a result, cover whole companies. The sample is thus an amalgam of establishments and companies reflecting the extent of central control in recruitment matters across the two sectors.

Appendix Table 12.A2 (p. 291) gives the employment size characteristics of the sample. About 50 per cent had employment levels of 200 or below; 30 per cent had between 201 and 1000 employees; and about 20 per cent in excess of 1000 employees. The sample has thus achieved a wide representation. In this study, the size bands are deliberately designed to be detailed below 100 employees so as to enable us to find out whether the YWS holds a special appeal for very small organisations.

Finally, that the sample covered the YWS as well as non-users is indicated by the take-up propensity: 36 per cent of the respondents had used the YWS and 64 per cent had not. The latter group was omitted from the case studies (described below). The reasons cited for the non take-up varied between the respondents. Some of them cited more than one reason. These and their percentage distribution (which are not additive because of multiple reasons per respondent) are as follows:

Reasons	%
(a) Do not employ young persons at all	7
(b) Did not recruit young persons in 1982	32
(c) Recruitment plans not principally influenced by wage costs	26
(d) No young persons earn below earnings thresholds	41
(e) Subsidy payment not high enough	9
(f) Payments period not long enough	7
(g) Payments not frequent enough	2

(*N* = 234)

Case Studies

These were carried out in the spring of 1984 and based on the experiences of 20 organisations who had participated in the two postal surveys. Each of them had used the YWS since it was first introduced; and some of them on a substantial scale in absolute and relative terms. They were chosen on the basis of their differing YWS employment impact, and industrial and employment characteristics. These characteristics are summarised in Appendix Table 12.A3 (p. 291).

The main objective of the case studies was to highlight the selected organisations' experiences since 1982 on three principal aspects. First, how has the YWS featured in recruitment decisions. Second, what effect has the YWS had on youth–adult hourly wage differentials. Third, what effect has the YWS had on demand for young workers, directly and indirectly? These and other subsidiary issues were put together in the form of a discussion guide which constituted the basis of the case studies. The guide is given in Appendix B.

12.3 THE YWS AND THE YOUTH–ADULT EARNINGS DIFFERENTIAL

The primary object of the YWS is to improve the competitive position of the relatively inexperienced or untrained young workers in the labour market by encouraging a widening in the youth–adult earnings differential. The underlying logic rests on the view that the high youth unemployment rate since 1978 is caused by (amongst other things) the failure of youth earnings to respond to the excess supply of youth labour. This view is underpinned by some econometric evidence (Marsden and Rajan, 1984). The YWS can therefore be viewed as providing a financial incentive to employers to pay greater attention to excess supply when setting youth pay.

The available econometric evidence is, however, limited in two senses. First, it is too aggregative: it does not allow for the diversity in pay determination that exists in different industries. Second, in terms of time scale, so far it relates to the period ending in 1981 and has little to say on the changing employment practices in the aftermath of the severe economic recession starting in 1979. This section, therefore, examines the question of youth unemployment in a wider and more contemporary context, using the employer-based approach outlined in Section 12.2. Specifically, it attempts to identify the employer perspective on two related aspects: the role of the earnings differential in the demand for young workers and the impact of YWS on the differential since it came into effect in 1982. The object is to highlight the mechanism of job creation at company level and the role of YWS within it. The findings are used as a basis for analysing the initial and cumulative effects of the YWS in section 12.4.

Demand for Young Workers

In Britain, the youth unemployment rate (covering those under 18) increased from approximately 18.5 per cent in 1978 to 25 per cent by 1981 (Wells, 1983). Against the background of this high and rising incidence, employers emphasised the importance of two factors in their demand for youth labour.

First and foremost is the state of demand for their products or services, rehearsing the familiar notion that demand for labour is a derived demand: labour is not wanted for its own sake but to satisfy a market demand. This is neither surprising nor new. However, the unprecedented extent of the economic recession between 1979 and 1981 has induced changes in our case study companies which suggest that the familiar relationship between employment and output (or demand) may have become even more non-linear. The changes that are noteworthy include the introduction of job-saving technologies; reduction in overmanning; and restructuring of organisational design. Under the evolving arrangement, a rising rate of output growth will be needed over time to sustain a given level of employment. In other words, the view that demand is the main influence on the *level* of employment is deemed to be still valid but the nature of the relationship may well have changed as a result of the supply-side changes.

The second factor identified by the employers is relative earnings. The level of product demand has set a limit on the level of employment; but its *composition* is determined by a number of factors one of which is relative earnings between distinct employee groups. So far as young workers are concerned, their earnings relative to adults have influenced their share in employment because of substitutional possibilities within a narrow range of jobs. Companies participating in the case studies singled out two groups which directly competed with young workers who had no experience or training: part-time or 'out' workers, and unskilled full-time adults.

The former group has become increasingly prominent in recent years and lends support to the so-called segmented labour market thesis (see Cain, 1976 and Atkinson, 1984). From the employer's point of view, the group provides flexibility and financial savings. In an uncertain economic climate, manpower adjustments have been more readily achieved through the use of this group. Furthermore, their *per capita* hourly payroll cost is lower because most of them are employed for less than 16 hours a week so that employers' non-wage financial commitments are avoided. In our sample of case studies, the weekly payroll cost for a young worker was between £65 and £75 per week, covering elements such as the National Insurance contribution, statutory sick pay, holidays and pension, apart from basic earnings. Where part time or 'out' workers were used, their full-time equivalent cost varied between £50 and £60 a week. The challenge from part-time workers was most evident in distributive trades and hotel and catering; that from 'out' workers in assembly-type engineering and clothing. These industries are noted for their labour intensity and low-level skill requirements.

The second group, consisting of unskilled adult workers, has competed with young workers in personal service occupations such as porters, waiters, cleaners, hairdressers and other labouring jobs. They are deemed as being more experienced and reliable and the narrowing of the youth–adult earnings differential in the last decade (see, for example, Wells, 1983) has favoured their employment at the expense of young workers.

The case study companies emphasised the link between relative earnings and composition of employment. Those in the distributive trades and personal services (coming under Miscellaneous Services) went even further. They saw the widening of the differentials producing more jobs for young workers over and above the level due to the compositional effect, through two avenues: higher product demand due to competitive prices and better service; and more jobs within the cash limits operating on the payroll budgets.

YWS and the Youth–Adult Earnings Differential

Given the evidence that the earnings differential is a factor in youth employment, the case studies tried to assess the extent to which it has been widened by the YWS since it came into effect in January 1982. There was no agreed definition of 'earnings' between companies in our case studies. Most of them included three elements covered by the national data: basic wage, overtime and other production-related payments.

Since the early 1960s on the basis of aggregate data there has been a steady compression of the differential until the end of the last decade (Wells, 1983). Since then, there has been a reversal in the trend, as can be seen in Table 12.1 which shows the relative earnings of male and female young workers separately. Table 12.2 shows that the reversal has come about as a result of a differential annual growth in weekly earnings, especially in 1983.

In order to assess the contribution of the YWS in this context, it is necessary to establish the size and industrial distribution of its use in the economy. Tables 12.3 and 12.4 provide the data. As usual, much should not be read into individual industry figures in Table 12.4 because the sample proportion covered by each of them is rather small. The figures are, therefore, to be treated as orders of magnitude. Their analysis suggests three observations. First, since it came into effect, the YWS has been claimed for about 100 000 jobs on a rolling basis. This is roughly 14 per cent of all jobs held by workers under the age of 18. Its implied Exchequer cost is less than £75 million per

Table 12.1   Under 18 gross weekly earnings as % of adult average[a]

Year	All Male (%)	All Female (%)
1974	38	58
79	40	58
1980	39	57
81	39	55
82	38	54
83	36	51

Note: [a]   Males over 21, females over 18, full time.
Source: NES, Part A, Tables 10 and 11

Table 12.2   Annual % increases in weekly earnings, all workers[a]

Year	Males		Females	
	Under 18	Adult	Under 18	Adult
1979–80	19.7	22.4	21.5	24.8
1980–81	13.0	13.3	12.2	16.6
81–82	10.0	9.8	5.8	8.3
82–83	1.8	8.3	3.2	9.8

Note: [a]   Including overtime.
Source: NES, Part A, Tables 10 and 11.

annum. The monthly figures in Table 12.3 show some seasonality but the underlying trend appears to be downwards since the end of 1982. Second, in industrial terms, the main recipients of the subsidy have been the distributive trades, construction, miscellaneous services (covering personal services), textiles and clothing, and engineering. Third, once allowance has been made for industry employment size, distributive trades, construction and engineering have the highest proportion of YWS recruits in their labour force – about 1 per cent. Nationally, however, the proportion is well below 1 per cent.

In other words, in the industrial and national context the incidence

Table 12.3   YWS, Number of Young Workers Covered

Month		Nos. covered (000)
1982	January	25
	February	33
	March	41
	April	51
	May	61
	June	71
	July	84
	August	98
	September	113
	October	125
	November	137
	December	130
83	January	110
	February	111
	March	110
	April	108
	May	104
	June	94
	July	94
	August	95
	September	102
	October	107
	November	108
	December	105
84	January	105
	February	106
	March	100
	April	92
	May	83

Source: Department of Employment, press notices.

of the YWS is rather modest. At individual company level, however, the incidence was found to vary between 0.5 and 12 per cent (of the total labour force) amongst those using the YWS, according to our survey.

As regards the YWS impact on earnings differential, amongst the 20 companies participating in our case studies, the pattern of earnings differentials since January 1982 was as follows:

Table 12.4   Distribution of YWS workers and their share in employment[a].

SIC ORDER (revised 1968)		Distribution of YWS workers[b]	Share of YWS workers in total industry employment. (%)
1	Agriculture, forestry, fishing	1.0	1.2
2	Mining and quarrying	0.0	0.0
3	Food, drink and tobacco	3.0	0.2
4	Coal and petroleum products	0.0	0.0
5	Chemicals and allied industries	2.0	0.2
6	Metal manufacture	5.0	0.5
7	Mechanical engineering	6.0	0.1
8	Instrument engineering	3.0	0.2
9	Electrical engineering	4.0	0.2
10	Shipbuilding and marine engineering	1.0	0.0
11	Vehicles	2.0	0.3
12	Metal goods nes	1.0	0.1
13	Textiles	5.0	0.6
14	Leather, leather goods and fur	3.0	0.7
15	Clothing and footwear	7.0	0.9
16	Bricks, pottery, glass, cement, etc.	1.0	0.1
17	Timber, furniture, etc.	1.0	0.1
18	Paper, printing and publishing	2.0	0.3
19	Other manufacturing industries	1.0	0.1
20	Construction	14.0	1.0
21	Gas, electricity and water	1.0	0.1
22	Transport and communication	0.0	0.0
23	Distributive trades	24.0	0.9
24	Insurance, banking and finance	0.0	0.0
25	Professional and scientific services	0.0	0.0
26	Miscellaneous services	12.0	1.0
	Total	100.0	0.5
	of which:		
	Manufacturing	48.0	0.2
	Services	51.0	0.8
	Others	1.0	0.6

Notes:
[a]   All figures are orders of magnitude, rather than precise.
[b]   Rounded to the nearest %.

Group	No. of companies
A Differentials widened	6
B Differentials narrowed	3
C Differentials remaining unchanged	11
Total	20

The distinguishing features of companies in *Group A* were that they were non-unionised and had less than 100 employees. Two of them also had a preponderance of females. Sectorally, two were in manufacturing and four in services. Favouring adult workers, the maximum differential growth in average earnings of youth and adult workers was 5 per cent over two wage rounds. It had occurred as a result of the youth wage increases being at a lower rate which enabled the companies concerned to stay within the earnings thresholds of the YWS. These figures need some qualification, however. In two companies, the differential growth was temporary: the earnings growth of the YWS workers was held back *temporarily* during the period of the subsidy payment, with full restoration after the eligibility ceased. In one company, the differential growth occurred as a result of the adult workers being given special productivity bonuses as a result of increased functional responsibilities.

In *Group B* the narrowing of the differentials had occurred due to three factors, whose importance varied between the companies concerned: union pressure, introduction of special travel allowances for young workers and recognition of the 'equal work, equal pay' principle. The maximum differential growth in average earnings in favour of young workers was 4 per cent in two wage rounds. The companies concerned had no common characteristics.

Finally, *Group C* contained companies who had one or more of the following attributes: they were the largest companies in our case study sample; they had long-established wage structures and relatively strong trade unions; they had a significant proportion of YWS workers in their labour force; and were subject to the wages councils awards under the Wages Councils Act 1979. In some cases, the basic rates set by the wages councils implied a widening of the differential, but a very small one. Industrially, the most conspicuous companies in this group were in the distributive trades and hotel and catering.

Our own sample appears to suggest that the impact of the YWS on differential has so far been modest. Admittedly, our sample size of case studies is rather limited. Even so, the numbers covered by the YWS nationally are not large enough to suggest otherwise. In fact, the settlements independently monitored by IDS (1983) and LRD (1983) suggest that the widening of the differential in 1983 in the national figures may be due to two factors (unrelated to YWS), whose significance will become clearer when the 1984 New Earnings Survey (NES) is published. First, there has been a marked widening of the differential in the public sector, big enough to influence the national figures. Second, the fall in the number of jobs for school leavers has been relatively greater in higher-paid sectors such as engineering, so that lower-paying non-unionised sectors are dictating the trend in average youth pay. The sample base of our case study companies is not so wide to test the validity of these two possible explanations.

YWS and Competitiveness

In the national context, our evidence suggests that the role of the YWS in widening the differential has been modest. At individual company level, however, the subsidy can have a beneficial effect, depending on how it is used. Before attempting an assessment of such an effect in section 12.4, it is useful to highlight the purposes to which the subsidy has been put by our case study companies.

In theory, a recruitment subsidy like the YWS can stimulate supply as well as demand for its recipients' products. On the *supply* side, it can stimulate output through reduction in average labour cost. Cost reduction, in turn, may generate employment through two separate avenues: bringing forward planned increases in jobs, and higher employment within an externally-imposed cash limit on payroll budget. On the *demand* side, the subsidy may stimulate demand by making possible a more competitive price structure or improved quality of product or service.

In practice, the outcome depends on its 'effective incidence': that is, how the subsidy is shifted. Like a tax, subsidy can be shifted 'forward' or 'backward'. Under *forward shifting*, it is passed on to customers in the form of lower prices or better service. Under *backward shifting* it is passed on either to payroll budget to boost employment and earnings, or to corporate profits.

In our case studies, no detailed financial data were available for us to assess the extent of shifting. However, we were able to identify the *direction* of the shift, prompting two generalisations. First, smaller and medium-sized companies (on the whole) have resorted to backward shifting to boost earnings and jobs. One company with 12 per cent of its workforce on the YWS (the sample maximum), had in fact used it entirely to bring forward the increases in employment planned for a year later. Second, larger companies (on the whole) have had a mixed experience. Those in distributive trades have attempted a forward shift by price competition and improved customer services. Those in construction and engineering have had a backward shift into profits, adversely affected by the recession.

Along with its emphasis on the widening of the differential, the foregoing analysis shows that the YWS impact on employment can also come through two forms of effective incidence. The employment effect outlined in section 12.4 has resulted from their combined influence. Of course, in the macroeconomic context it is worth emphasising that this form of the analysis is necessarily partial. It takes no account of interfirm or intraindustry displacement caused by the YWS as recipients of the YWS boost their employment at the expense of the non-recipient competitors. Although such possibilities are real, they are difficult to quantify given the modest annual Exchequer cost of the subsidy at less than £75 million and the rather small number of YWS recruits in each organisation. Furthermore, since some of the companies in our sample are significant exporters, the displacement may have occurred on an international rather than national basis.

12.4 THE YWS AND YOUTH EMPLOYMENT

The last section identified two mechanisms – widening of the earnings differential and effective incidence – through which the YWS has influenced the demand for youth labour. This section attempts to quantify its scale in terms of the initial effect and the cumulative effect outlined in section 12.2.

The YWS has now been in operation for just under 3 years. In that period, a new subsidy called the Youth Training Scheme (YTS) has also come into operation. As the name implies, the YTS is a *training* subsidy. It constitutes the most ambitious measure in the area of youth training and employment in the post-war period. Set at £1950 per trainee, the YTS is more generous than the YWS. In terms of coverage, too, it will be more wide-ranging, since it is targetted at all unemployed school leavers. Until March 1984, the YTS and YWS operated independently and competitively. Since then the YWS eligibility rules have been changed to make them complementary: the minimum age has been raised to 17 so that the YTS trainees can qualify for the YWS after their statutory year of training. This change has added a new dimension to the YWS in its role as a job-creation subsidy.

Accordingly, the employment effects of the YWS are presented in this section under three sub-headings following the distinction developed in section 12.2: the initial effect in the first year of the subsidy; the cumulative effect through earnings differential and effective incidence; and the possible further effect through the interaction with the YTS.

Initial Effect

In this study, the initial effect applies to 1982, the first year of the subsidy. It was estimated from the data collected in the postal survey. Before considering the results, it is necessary to describe the types of employment effect usually associated with a subsidy.

The literature on employment subsidies (see, for example, Deakin and Pratten, 1982) typically identifies four kinds of subsidy-induced effect on employment:

1. *Deadweight effect*, resulting from the subsidy being claimed for jobs which would be created irrespective of the subsidy. It is claimed, in other words, simply 'because it is there', and not specifically for the purpose of creating additional jobs.

2. *Substitution effect*, resulting from the subsidy promoting the employment of the target group but only at the expense of the non-target groups who are not subsidised. This effect usually occurs between firms, through the subsidised firms displacing output and employment of their non-subsidised competitors on account of the subsidy-induced relative price advantage. In this study, however, the emphasis is narrowly focused on intrafirm employment displacement of non-target groups.

3. *Net incremental effect*, otherwise defined here as the 'true' job-creation effect that results from the subsidised labour being employed specifically on account of the subsidy and net of substitution.

4. *Domino effect*, resulting from employers claiming the subsidy in an attempt to minimise the advantage gained by other employers already using it. In our study, this effect is ignored since the emphasis is on intrafirm employment displacement.

It now remains for us to decompose the total anticipated YWS support for employment into the first three components outlined above. From question 4 in the questionnaire (given in Appendix A, p. 286) it is possible to calculate the substitution component directly by aggregating the non-target groups covered by section (d). On the other hand, the deadweight and the net incremental components can be calculated only indirectly by simple manipulations of sections (b), (c) and (d). For an individual respondent, the latter two components can be calculated as follows (with section labels appearing immediately under their respective description):

$$\underset{\text{(b)}}{\text{deadweight}} = \underset{\text{(b)}}{\text{total YWS workers}} - \underset{\text{(c)}}{\text{gross incremental}}$$

$$\underset{\text{(c)}}{\text{net incremental}} = \underset{\text{(c)}}{\text{gross incremental}} - \underset{\text{(d)}}{\text{substitution}}$$

The sum of the three identified components equals the employment effect. For ease of exposition and meaningful comparisons, therefore, the employment effect is decomposed into its three components and the latter are expressed in ratio forms, so that:

$$\frac{\text{deadweight}}{\text{total YWS workers}} + \frac{\text{substitution}}{\text{total YWS workers}} + \frac{\text{net incremental}}{\text{total YWS workers}} = 1$$

In the rest of this chapter, these ratios are expressed as percentages and respectively referred to as the deadweight effect, the substitutional effect and the net incremental effect.

The estimates of the three effects based on the survey data are given in Tables 12.5 and 12.6. They prompt two important conclusions. First, in its first year of operation the YWS net incremental effect was 16 per cent. In other words, of every 100 jobs supported by the YWS, 16 were created directly on account of the subsidy. Of the remaining 84, four came about through substitution of YWS workers for the non-target groups; and 80 would have existed irrespective of the

Table 12.5   'Initial' employment effect of the YWS by industries

	Industrial group[a] (%)			
	Manufacturing	Services	Others	Total
Initial effect				
Decomposed into:				
Deadweight effect	81	78	84	80
Substitution effect	4	8	1	4
Net incremental effect	16	14	15	16
Total	100	100	100	100

Note:
[a]   Only the columns are additive.

subsidy. Second, the size of the incremental effect is inversely related to company size: smaller employers have had a bigger incremental effect than the larger ones. Our subsequent case studies helped to identify the salient features of the three effects.

The *net incremental effect* emanated from two principal sources. First, and foremost, was the employers' perceptions of their social responsibility. According to the case studies, the urban disturbances in 1981 presaging the YWS had heightened the awareness of youth unemployment within the corporate community. For example, one company in our sample took on 120 young workers as supernumaries – surplus to requirements – as a mark of social contribution. This was more evident amongst larger employers in the service industries less affected by the recession. Social responsibility as a factor has also been at work in West Germany in the context of youth training (Marsden and Rajan, 1984). Second, there was some backward shifting into higher employment, mainly amongst the smaller and medium-sized companies. For them the subsidy at the time appeared generous enough to bring forward their plans to increase employment. In none of the companies interviewed in our case studies had the earnings relativity been directly changed to qualify for the YWS or stimulate employment growth in the first year, except in one notable instance where the young workers' standard weekly hours were reduced from 39 to 37 hours so as to stay within the earnings thresholds.

At 4 per cent, the initial *substitution effect* was small and con-

Table 12.6 Initial employment effect of the YWS, by employment size

| | | | | | *Employment size groups[a]* (%) | | | | | |
	1–10	11–25	26–50	51–100	101–200	201–500	501–1000	1001–5000	Over 5000	Total
'Initial' effect Decomposed into:										
Deadweight effect	32	49	54	65	68	80	86	84	90	80
Substitution effect	10	11	10	9	11	3	2	2	1	4
Net incremental effect	58	40	36	26	21	17	12	14	9	16
Total	100	100	100	100	100	100	100	100	100	100

Note:
[a] Only the columns are additive.

founded the fears that the YWS would encourage large-scale substitution of young workers for adults. Our case studies show that such substitution as occurred in the first year did not involve redundancies for the non-target workers, but a reduction in their numbers in replacement recruitment in response to natural wastage. The potential for this form of substitution remains significant, and we return to this point later.

At 80 per cent, the initial *deadweight effect* is notably high. The survey showed that at the start of the subsidy scheme awareness of it was high: 84 per cent of the survey respondents were aware of it. Coupled with the fact that the YWS is a flow (as distinct from a stock) subsidy, employers have claimed it as and when they have recruited young workers, provided the earnings thresholds were observed.

In this context, it is instructive to compare the YWS initial effect with that of two previous youth employment subsidies – the Recruitment Subsidy for School Leavers (RSSL) introduced in 1975 and the Youth Employment Subsidy (YES) introduced in 1976. In the first year, each of them had a deadweight effect of 76 per cent, a substitution effect of 12 per cent and a net incremental effect of 12 per cent (see Layard, 1979). The YWS has thus fared better than its precursors in the initial effect.

Cumulative Effect Through Differentials and Effective Incidence

The further effect since 1982 has been influenced by a number of offsetting factors that have affected the demand for youth labour amongst our case study companies.

On the positive side, we encountered examples of smaller companies with widened differentials; and forward shifting as well as backward shifting (into employment) of the subsidy. This involved three out of 20 companies in our case study sample. We also encountered examples of larger companies in distributive trades and personal services where forward shifting had occurred; although its full effects were slow to materialise because of the time lags between increased product demand and employment. This involved three companies. Altogether, therefore, a beneficial effect (over and above the initial effect) was evident in six out of 20 case study companies (30 per cent). All other things being equal, their experience suggests that by spring 1984 the positive elements may have reduced the overall deadweight effect to 70 per cent amongst the users of the YWS in the economy.

On the negative side, there have been three factors. One of them is the seeming decline in social concern about youth unemployment since 1981. Employers in our case studies were less inclined to create jobs for youths for social reasons. For example, the company that had 120 'supernumaries' in 1982 had none in 1984. The second factor is the introduction of the YTS in 1983. It is a more generous subsidy (£1900 per trainee) and the employers have found it financially more worthwhile to create new opportunities under the 'additionality' provision of the YTS than under the YWS. Finally, as employers have found it difficult to set youth earnings within the YWS thresholds, their take-up rate has declined. This is exemplified by the experience of one case study company. In early 1982, it had 1800 young workers on the YWS; in March 1984, this figure had dropped to 120. This has implications for the effective incidence: companies with a high dead-weight initially have not been able to engage in forward shifting on a significant scale because of the declining intake of YWS workers in the subsequent years. This is most evident in the wages councils industries where the employers have had much less influence on youth pay rates. As such, the thresholds and the seeming inability of the employers to keep youth earnings within them have subdued the beneficial effect through forward shifting. Furthermore, it has also led to a concentration of the YWS into a narrower range of non-career jobs involving clerical, labouring or personal services based work; and reinforcing the labour market segmentation. What Joseph (1983) has argued about women is gradually also coming true of inexperienced and untrained young workers.

When the positive and the negative aspects are taken into account, we estimate that the *net overall YWS cumulative effect* is about 20 per cent; with 15 per cent being the first year net incremental effect, and 5 per cent the lagged effect so far in the life of the subsidy.

This estimate is based on the experience of the companies partici-pating in our survey and the case studies. As we saw in section 12.3, the YWS make-up has covered about 100 000 young workers on a rolling basis. Since the take-up has declined amongst companies who first claimed the subsidy in 1982, in all probability the overall numbers have remained firm because of new companies using the YWS. It is open to argument whether the recent users of the YWS will have, for some unknown reason, a higher incremental effect than their predecessors. On the other hand, if the recent users are mainly smaller companies, then the overall net incremental effect may be higher than 20 per cent owing to the *compositional* change in the take-up rate. If the experience of our case study companies is any guide, it may be as high as 25 per cent.

Further Effects Through YTS–YWS Interaction

Since 1 April 1984, two notable changes have been made in the YWS regime: the dual earnings thresholds have been consolidated and updated to £50 per week and the minimum qualifying age has been revised from 16 to 17 years. In the words of a recent government White Paper, the effect of these changes has been for the YWS 'more closely [to] complement the Youth Training Scheme' (HMSO, 1984).

At the time of the case studies in spring 1984, it was too soon to assess the impact of the proposed complementarity. We were, however, able to obtain employers' initial reactions, which we report here.

In principle (and on the whole), the reactions were favourable. The proposed changes were viewed as constituting a new regime under which the YTS trainees after a year of training will come under the YWS. The combination constituted a package approach, with a tapered element, with the lower YWS payment providing the taper. The package had two merits. First, it explicitly recognised and compensated for the fact that young inexperienced workers have a below-average productivity and required training. Second, it would stimulate the YTS intake and subsequent retention rate of the trainees. We encountered two significant examples where the companies had increased their YTS intake from the planned level in anticipation of qualifying for the YWS when the trainees were offered jobs. This has clear implications for the way the deadweight effect of the YWS is calculated in future: over time YWS may progressively become a *job preservation* subsidy, and increase the cumulative effect.

In practice, however, much would depend on how far companies are able to stay within the new earnings threshold, and how often it is updated. This point was made most forcefully by companies subject to the wages councils awards. In more than two-thirds of the awards in the 1984 wage round, the minimum weekly earnings for 17 year olds were set in excess of the current YWS threshold. The distributive trades industry, for example (which has been the largest user of the YWS so far) now has the weekly rate set at £50.05. None of its current

YTS recruits will qualify for the YWS unless the threshold is uprated before long. One retailer in our case studies had a YTS intake of 1300 in 1983–4, one of the highest in the distributive trades. Its normal intake of young workers was 200. But it recruited YTS trainees beyond the 'additionality' requirement in the expectation of using the YWS when the training period ended. Like other retailers, it has an annual natural wastage rate in excess of 25 per cent. It had planned to retain all the YTS intakes through replacement recruitment and the YWS. Now, it is unable to do so in the light of the recent Wages Council award. In consequence its intake of the YTS in 1984/5 is expected to fall dramatically.

Amongst the case study companies, there was little doubt that unless the YTS–YWS interaction is successful the YWS will be increasingly used for the lowest-grade jobs for young people. A successful interaction, on the other hand, will (through substitution in recruitment) improve the range of jobs and provide access to job ladders. But above all it was expected to distribute employment more equitably between young and adult workers. This form of redistribution would occur through substitution of young workers for adults in the natural wastage. Equity considerations apart, the redistribution was deemed desirable on two grounds. First, being induced by a 'package' of subsidies, it also carried the real possibilities of creating additional jobs through forward and backward shifting. The financial size of the package was deemed large enough to secure a pattern of effective incidence conducive to net job generation. Second, and indirectly, the redistribution may over time weaken at least one of the barriers to new technologies because the young workers are felt to be more readily 'trainable' to handle technical change. For example, a recent study (Rajan, 1984) has found that employers are beginning to rely increasingly on younger workers to operate their new technologies, working alongside adult workers who work the old machines.

12.5 CONCLUSION

This chapter has analysed the impact of the YWS on the youth–adult earnings differential and youth employment. Three conclusions emerge from the analysis. First, the impact on the differential appears to be limited so far because of companies' long-established earnings structures, collective bargaining and statutory awards by the Wages Councils in industries with a preponderance of young workers.

Second, the beneficial employment impact is far from insignificant. Between 20 and 25 per cent of the jobs supported so far by the YWS owe their existence to the scheme. This has resulted from heightened social concern about youth employment, the bringing forward of planned recruitment, widening of the earnings differential, improved trade competitiveness of the YWS users and relief on employers' payroll budgets. Third, the employment impact of the YWS compares favourably with two previous youth employment subsidy schemes. This assessment does not allow for interfirm or intraindustry displacement, caused by the recipients of the YWS boosting their employment at the expense of their non-recipient competitors. Although the displacement possibilities exist, they are unlikely to be significant, given the modest Exchequer cost of the scheme and the small proportion of those recruits in each firm.

Appendixes

Appendix A   Young Workers' Scheme (YWS)

EMPLOYMENT
1. How many people does the organisation currently employ?
   (Please enter total number including part-time employees)

(8–13)

THE YOUNG WORKERS' SCHEME (YWS)
2. Were you aware of the Young Workers' Scheme (YWS) before receiving the attached leaflet?
   (Please tick appropriate box)

YES
NO

(14)

3. Between now and the end of 1982, do you expect to make any claim under YWS for recruitment of a young person (or persons)?
   (Please tick appropriate box)

YES
NO

(15)

> IF YOU ANSWERED 'YES' TO Q3, PLEASE COMPLETE Q4 AND IGNORE Q5: IF YOU ANSWERED 'NO' TO Q3, PLEASE PROCEED TO Q5.

USE OF YWS
4. (a) For how many young persons *already* in your employment are you likely to claim YWS payment?. . . . .
   (Please enter number)

(16–20)

   (b) Between now and the end of 1982, what is the *total* number of young persons for whom you are likely to claim YWS payment?
   (Please enter approximate number)

(21–25)

   (c) Of these, how many young persons would be recruited specifically because of the YWS payment?. . . . .
   (Please enter number; if 'nil' please ignore part (d) below)

(26–30)

   (d) If the young person(s) at (c) were not recruited, would you instead have recruited a different type of person(s) for the same job?
   (Please tick appropriate box)

YES
NO

(31)

   If 'YES', please *estimate* how many of each of the following types of person you would have recruited instead:
   (Please enter approximate number(s) in boxes)

Numbers

   Under 18 but not eligible for YWS . . . .

(32–36)

   Young workers between 18 and 21. . . . .

(37–41)

   Full-time men and women over 21. . . . .

(42–46)

   Part-time men and women over 21. . . . .

(47–51)

(52–56)

Please Turn Over/...

286

REASONS FOR NOT USING YWS

Please indicate why you are unlikely to make use of YWS in
1982.

(Please tick boxes, as appropriate)

a) We *do not* employ young persons (under 18) at all . . . . . ☐ ——(57)

b) We *do* employ young persons, BUT:

(i) we do not expect to recruit in 1982 . . . . ☐ ——(58)

(ii) our recruitment plans are not principally determined
by wage costs . . . . ☐ ——(59)

(iii) we employ none with gross earnings below £45 per
week ☐ ——(60)

c) We *would* employ YWS eligibles:

(i) If the weekly payment was higher than £15 . . . . . . ☐ ——(61)

(ii) if the payments covered a longer period than 12
months ☐ ——(62)

(iii) If the payments were more frequent than quarterly . . ☐ ——(63)

(iv) if other improvements were made *(Please specify)*
. . . . ——(64)
. . . . ——(65)

ANY OTHER COMMENTS

Please use this space for any comments or observations on
YWS.

——(66)

——(67)

——(68)

Thank you for completing this form. It may be necessary to telephone you to elaborate on
your responses. If you are agreeable to that, please enter your name and telephone number
below.

Name . . . .

Tel No. . . . .

Please return this questionnaire in the prepaid envelope provided. Thank you.

Appendix B   Young Workers' Scheme: A Discussion Guide

> *Theme Issues*
>
> I   How long has the YWS featured in recruitment decisions?
>
> II   What are the age and qualification characteristics of the YWS recruits?
>
> III   What effect has YWS had on youth employment?
>
> IV   What effect has YWS had on youth employment?
>
> V   What factors have affected the take-up rate of the YWS?

1   Company Background

   (a)   Main products/services

   (b)   Employment:
      pre- and post-1979
      its youth, adult breakdown
      does breakdown vary between establishments?

   (c)   Degree of unionism

   (d)   Main factors influencing recruitment decision:
      relative cost of labour and machinery
      conditions of local labour markets
      demand
      role of subsidies

   (e)   Experiences of previous subsidies:
      schemes used
      impact on employment and output
      positive and negative features

2   YWS Recruits

   (a)   Numbers since August 1981, and as a percentage of employment

   (b)   Their time profile; continuous or discrete?

   (c)   Sex and education background

   (d)   Normal weekly hours worked by:
      YWS recruits
      others

   (e)   Type of work they do

   (f)   Amount and type of training given

   (g)   What happened when YWS eligibility ceased?
      proportion retained

  Proportion leaving during payment period
  proportion leaving after payment period
(h) Reasons for retention
(i) Reasons for departure

3 YWS and Wage Differentials

(a) Approximate youth–adult wage differentials:
  prior to YWS
  since YWS introduced

(b) Approximate growth in basic wage/earnings since end 1981:
  of YWS recruits
  of others

(c) Assessment of YWS impact on differentials

(d) Reasons for impact:
  wage structure traditionally flexible
  no union opposition
  greater flexibility in youth labour market
  acceptance by adult workers that youth
   unemployment is a special problem
  other

(e) Reasons for non-impact:
  levels of adults too high or youths too low
  too few YWS recruits involved
  wage relatively institutionalised
  union/staff opposition
  changes in working hours
  other

4 YWS Impact on Employment

(a) What proportion would have been recruited without YWS?

(b) Of those recruited under YWS, what was the extent of
  substitution amongst:
  under 18 but not eligable for YWS
  young workers between 18 and 21
  full-time men and woman over 21
  part-time men and women over 21

(c) Evaluation of job-creating element:
  role of earnings differential
  role of competitive effect
  subsidy's job preservation role

5 Reasons for not using YWS

(a) For users, what changes will increase YWS appeal?

(b) For non-users, what are the constraining factors?
  age limit
  earnings thresholds
  size of subsidy
  payment period
  frequency of payment
  recruitment plans not determined
  others

Table 12 A1   Distribution of respondents by SIC orders

SIC Order (revised 1968)		(%)
1	Agriculture, forestry, fishing	1
2	Mining and quarrying	2
3	Food, drink and tobacco	3
4	Coal and petroleum products	2
5	Chemicals and allied industries	5
6	Metal manufacture	6
7	Mechanical engineering	9
8	Instrument engineering	5
9	Electrical engineering	8
10	Shipbuilding and marine engineering	3
11	Vehicles	2
12	Metal goods	4
13	Textiles	4
14	Leather, leather goods and fur	3
15	Clothing and footwear	3
16	Bricks, pottery, glass, cement, etc.	2
17	Timber, furniture, etc.	2
18	Paper, printing and publishing	3
19	Other manufacturing industries	3
20	Construction	7
21	Gas, electricity and water	2
22	Transport and communication	3
23	Distributive trades	7
24	Insurance, banking and finance	3
25	Professional and scientific services	2
26	Miscellaneous services	4
	Unclassified	2
Sub-totals[a]		
a	Manufacturing	67
b	Services	28
c	Others	3
	Unclassified	2
Total		100
		(N = 365)

Note:
[a]   Manufacturing covers Orders 3 – 19; services Orders 20 – 26; and 'others' Orders 1 and 2.

Table 12 A2 Distribution of respondents by employment size

Employment size	(%)
1– 10	7
11– 25	8
26– 50	9
51– 100	12
101– 200	14
201– 500	20
501–1000	10
1001–5000	14
Over 5000	4
Unclassified	2
	100
	(N = 365)

Table 12 A3 Industrial and employment characteristics of the case study companies.

SIC order (revised 1968)		No. of companies	Company employment size				
			0–100	101–200	211–500	501–1000	Over 1000
5	Chemicals	1	1	–	–	–	–
7–11	Engineering and allied industries	6	2	1	1	1	1
13–15	Textiles, clothing and footwear	2	1	1	–	–	–
17	Timber, furniture	1	1	–	–	–	–
20	Construction	3	1	1	–	1	–
23	Distributive trades	5	2	–	–	1	2
26	Miscellaneous services	2	1	1	–	–	–

Bibliography

ABOWD, J., LAYARD R. and NICKELL S. (1981) 'The Demand for Labour by Age and Sex' Centre for Labour Economics, working paper 110 (London: LSE).

ANDERSON, M. and FAIRLEY, J. (1983) 'The Politics of Industrial Training in the United Kingdom', Journal of Public Policy III, pp. 191–208.

ASHENFELTER, O. and LAYARD, P. R. G. (1983) 'Incomes Policy and Wage Differentials', Economica, 50, pp. 127–43.

ASHTON, D. N., MAGUIRE, M. J. and GARLAND, V. (1982) Youth in the Labour Market, research paper 34 (London: Department of Employment).

ATKINSON, A. B., GOMULKA, J., MICKLEWRIGHT, J. and RAU, N. (1984) 'Unemployment Benefits, Duration and Incentives in Britain: How Robust is the Evidence?' Journal of Public Economics, 23, pp. 3–26.

ATKINSON, J. (1982) 'Maintaining Apprentice Intakes: do Public Policies Work?', Manpower Studies Spring, 4, pp. 5–9.

ATKINSON, J. (1984) Flexibility, Uncertainty and Manpower Management (Brighton: Institute of Manpower Studies).

BAIN, G. S. and PRICE, R. (1980) Profiles of Union Growth (Oxford: Basil Blackwell).

BAIN, G. S. and ELIAS, P. (1985) 'Trade Union Membership in Great Britain: An Individual Level Analysis', British Journal of Industrial Relations March, 23, 1, pp. 71–92.

BAXTER, J. L. and McCORMICK, B. L. (1984) 'Seventy per cent of Our Future: the Education, Training and Employment of Young People', National Westminster Bank Review August, pp. 36–44.

BECKER, G. S. (1964) Human Capital: a theoretical and empirical analysis with special reference to education (Chicago: University of Chicago Press).

BRECHLING, F. P. R. (1965) 'The Relationship between Output and Employment in British Manufacturing Industries', Review of Economic Studies 32, pp. 187–216.

BROWN, R., DURBIN, J. and EVANS, J. M. (1975) 'Techniques for Testing the Constancy of Regression Relationships over Time', Journal of the Royal Statistical Society Series B, 37, 2 pp. 149–163.

BRYANT, I., BURNHILL, P. and RAFFE, D. (1985) Report on the 1984 Pilot of the Scottish Young Peoples' Survey, Centre for Educational Sociology (Edinburgh: University of Edinburgh).

BUREAU OF LABOUR MARKET RESEARCH (1983) Youth, Wages, Employment and the Labour Force, research report 3 (Canberra: Australian Government Publishing Service).

BURNHILL, P. and FISK, P. (1981) Standard Errors, Sample Design and Analysis with Standard Statistical Packages: an Overview, Edinburgh Survey Methodology Group (Edinburgh: University of Edinburgh).

CAIN, G. C. (1976) 'The Challenge of Segmented Labour Market Theories to

Orthodox Theory: A Survey', *Journal of Economic Literature*, 14, pp. 1215–57.

CASSON, M. (1979) *Youth Unemployment*, (London: Macmillan).

CBS (1981) 'Het Antaal Minimumloonantrekkers', November 1979, *Sociale Maandstatistiek* April (Netherlands: Centraal Bureau voor de Statistiek) pp. 75–95.

CBS (1983) 'Antaal Minimumlooners', November 1981, *Sociale Maandstatistiek,* April (Netherlands: Centraal Bureau voor de Statistiek) pp. 68–75.

CHILD, J. (1967) *Industrial Relations in the British Printing Industry* (London: George Allen & Unwin).

CLARK, K. and SUMMERS, L. (1979) 'Labor Market Dynamics and Unemployment: A Reconsideration and Discussion', *Brookings Papers on Economic Activity*, 1, January, pp. 13–72.

COCKBURN, C. (1983) 'New Technology in Print: Men's Work and Women's Chances', in G. Winch, *Information Technology in Manufacturing Processes* (London: Rossendale).

COLLIER, P. (1978) 'Crisis in Youth Unemployment?', Manpower Research Group, research paper 33 (Coventry: University of Warwick).

CRAIG, C. *et al.* (1980) 'Labour Market Structure, Industrial Organisation and Low Pay', Department of Applied Economics, occasional paper 53 (Cambridge: Cambridge University Press): see Deakin *et al.* (1982).

CRONE, F. (1986) 'Does Cutting Youth Wages Help Young Workers to find Jobs?' *Social Europe*, Supplement on Youth Pay and Employers' Recruitment Practices for Young People in the Community, pp. 116–28.

CROUCHER, R. (1977) 'Communist Politics and Shop Stewards in Engineering, 1935–46', Ph.D dissertation (Coventry: University of Warwick).

CROUCHER, R. (1982) *Engineers at War* (Manchester: Merlin).

CSO (1982) *Social Trends 1983* 13 (London: HMSO)

CUSACK, S. and ROLL, J. (1985) *Families Rent Apart* (London: Child Poverty Action Group).

DALY, A., HITCHENS, D. M. W. N. and WAGNER, K. (1985) 'Productivity, Machinery and Skills in a Sample of British and German Manufacturing Plant', *National Institute Economic Review*, 111, February, pp. 48–61.

DANIEL, W. W. and STILGOE, E. (1977) *Where are They Now?*, PEP Broadsheet 572 (London: PEP).

DANIEL, W. W. and MILLWARD, N. (1983) *Workplace Industrial Relations in Britain* (London: Heinemann Educational Books).

DEAKIN, B. M. and PRATTEN, C. F. (1982) 'Effects of the Temporary Employment Subsidy', Department of Applied Economics, occasional paper 53 (Cambridge: Cambridge University Press): see Craig *et al.* (1980).

DE (1977) 'Attitude and Personality Lose Young People Jobs', and 'Young People and Work', *Employment Gazette* 85, October pp. 1127, December pp. 1345–47.

DE (1981) *A New Training Initiative: a Programme for Action*, Cmnd. 8455 (London: HMSO)

DE (1982) 'First Employment of Young People', *Employment Gazette* 90, March, pp. 117–120.

DE (1982), (1984) *Young Workers' Scheme*, PL678 and PL742.

DE (1984a) *Training for Jobs*, Cmnd. 9135 (London: HMSO).

DE (1984b) 'First Employment of Young People: 1980 Survey', *Employment Gazette* 92, May, pp. 230–4.

DE (1984c) 'First Employment of Young People', *Employment Gazette*, 92, October, pp. 445–8.

DES (1983) *Report by HM Inspectors on the Youth Training Scheme in Further Education: An HMI Survey* (London: HMSO).

DEX, S. (1982) 'Discrimination and Job Search Theories for Black British Young Men', *Applied Economics*, 14, pp. 533–44.

DHSS (1984) *Social Security Statistics 1984* (London: HMSO).

DOERINGER, P. B. and PIORE, M. J. (1971) *Internal Labour Markets and Manpower Analysis Studies in Social and Economic Process* (Lexington, Mass: Heath Lexington Books).

DONOVAN, T. N. (Baron) (1968) Royal Commission on Trade Unions and Employers' Associations, *Report*, Cmnd. 3623 (London: HMSO).

DOUGAN, D. (1975) *The Shipwrights* (Newcastle: Frank Graham).

DUTTON, P. A. (1981), 'The New Training Initiative: What are its chances?' *Managerial Law*, XXIII, 4, pp. 1–9.

DUTTON, P. A. (1984) 'YTS – Training for the Future', *Public Administration* 62, Winter, pp. 483–94.

EDDING COMMISSION (1974) Sachverstaendingungskommission: *Kostenund Finanzierung der beruflichen Bildung*, Bundestagdrucksache 7/1811, v. 14. 3. 1974.

FINN, D. (1983) 'The Youth Training Scheme: a New Deal?' *Youth and Policy* I, pp. 16–24.

FLINN, C. and HECKMAN, J. (1982) 'Models for the Analysis of Labour Force Dynamics', pp. 33–95 in *Advances in Econometrics I* (Greenwich, CT: JAI Press).

FOURCANS, A. (1980) 'L'impact du SMIC sur le Chômage: les leçons de l'experience', *Revue d'Economie Politique* 90 Année, 6, November–December.

FRANZ, W. (1982) *Youth Unemployment in the Federal Republic of Germany*, (Tuebingen: J. C. B. Mohr, Paul Siebeck).

FREEMAN, R. B. and WISE, D. A. (eds) (1982) *The Youth Labor Market Problem: its Nature, Causes and Consequences*, NBER conference report (Chicago: University of Chicago Press).

FROW, E. and FROW, R. (1983) *Manchester's Big House in Trafford Park* (Manchester: Working Class Movement Library).

GARBADE, K. (1977) 'Two Methods for Examining the Stability of Regression Coefficients', *Journal of the American Statistical Association*, 72, March, pp. 54–63.

GMWU (1982) *YOPS: A Guide for GMWU Negotiators* (Esher, Surrey: GMWU).

GOLLAN, J. (1937) *Youth in British Industry* (London: Gollancz).

GREENWOOD, W. (1933) *Love on the Dole* (London: Jonathan Cape).

GRONAU, R. (1974) 'Wage Comparisons – A Selectivity Bias' *Journal of Political Economy* 82, 6, pp. 1119–43.

HALSEY, A. H., FLOUD, J. and ANDERSON, C. A. (Eds) (1961) *Education, Economy and Society* (New York: Free Press).

HALSEY, A. H., HEATH, A. F. and RIDGE, J. M. (1980) *Origins and Destinations* (Oxford: Clarendon Press).

HAMERMESH, D. S. (1985) 'Substitution Between Different Categories of Labour Relative Wages and Youth Unemployment', *OECD Economic Studies*, 5, Autumn, pp. 57–85.

HARCOURT, G. C. (1977) *Microeconomic Foundations of Macroeconomics* (London: Macmillan).

HART, P. E. (1984) 'Youth Unemployment and Relative Wages in the UK: a Survey of Recent Econometric Evidence', NIESR, discussion paper 70 (London: NIESR).

HAZLEDINE, T. (1981) 'Employment Functions and the Demand for Labour in the Short Run', in Zmira Hornstein, Joseph Grice and Alfred Webb (eds), *The Economics of the Labour Market* (London: HMSO).

HECKMAN, J. (1974) 'Shadow Prices, Market Wages, and Labour Supply', *Econometrica* 42, pp. 679–94.

HECKMAN, J. (1976) 'The Common Structure of Statistical Models of Truncation, Sample Selection and Limited Dependent Variables and a Simple Estimator for Such Models' *Annals of Economic and Social Measurement* 5, pp. 475–92.

HECKMAN, J. (1979) 'Sample Selection Bias as a Specification Error', *Econometrica* 47, pp. 153–61.

HECKMAN, J. and BORJAS, G. (1980) 'Does Unemployment Cause Future Unemployment? Definitions, Questions and Answers from a Continuous Time Model of Heterogeneity and State Dependence', *Economica*, 47, 187, August, pp. 247–83.

HMSO (1984) *Training for Jobs*, Cmnd. 9135 (London: HMSO).

HUMPHRIES, J. and RUBERY, J. (1984) 'The Reconstitution of the Supply Side of the Labour Market: the Relative Autonomy of Social Reproduction', *Cambridge Journal of Economics*, December, 8, 4, pp. 331–46.

HUTCHINSON, G., BARR, N. A. and DROBNY, A. (1984) 'The Employment of Young Males in a Segmented Labour Market: the case of Great Britain', *Applied Economics* 16, 2: pp. 187–204.

IDS (1983). *Young Workers' Pay*, IDS study 291, June (London: IDS).

IDS (1985) *Young Workers' Pay*, IDS study 339, June (London: IDS).

IER (1983) R. M. Lindley and J. D. Whitley (eds) *Review of the Economy and Employment*, Summer (Coventry: IER, University of Warwick).

IRRR (1985) IRRR study 350, August (London.)

JEFFREYS, J. B. (1946) *The Story of the Engineers* (London: Lawrence and Wishart).

JONES, I. (1982) 'The New Training Initiative – an Evaluation', *National Institute Economic Review*, 99, February: pp. 68–74.

JONES, I. (1985) 'Skill Formation and Pay Relativities', in GDN Worswick (ed.) *Education and Economic Performance* (London: Gower).

JONES, I. and HOLLENSTEIN, H. (1983) 'Trainee Wages and Training Deficiencies: An Economic Analysis of a "British Problem"', discussion paper 58, June (London: NIESR).

JONES, P. (1983) 'Effects of Rising Unemployment on School Leavers', *Employment Gazette,* January pp. 13–16.

JONES, P. (1984) *What Opportunities for Youth?*, occasional paper 4 (London: Youthaid).

JOSEPH, G. (1983) *Women at Work* (London: George Joseph).

JUNANKAR, P. N. (1981) 'An Econometric Analysis of Unemployment in Great Britain, 1952–75, *Oxford Economic Papers*, 33, 3, November, pp. 387–400.

JUNANKAR, P. N. (1984) 'Youth Unemployment and Youth Crime: a Preliminary Analysis', Australian National University, Centre for Economic Policy Research, discussion paper 106.

JUNANKAR, P. N. (1986) 'Social Costs of Unemployment', discussion paper 292, July (University of Essex).

JUNANKAR, P. N. (1987) 'The British Youth Labour Market in Crisis', *International Review of Applied Economics* 1, 1, January, pp. 48–71.

JUNANKAR, P. N. and PRICE, S. (1984) 'The Dynamics of Unemployment: Structural Change and Unemployment Flows', *Economic Journal*, conference papers supplement 94, March, pp. 158–65.

KEEP, E. (1984) *The Youth Training Scheme–Some First Thoughts on its Inception*, Industrial Relations Research Unit, internal paper (Coventry: IRRU, University of Warwick).

KEIFER, N. (1980) 'A Note on Regime Classification in Disequilibrium Models', *Review of Economic Studies* 47, 3, pp. 637–9.

KILLINGSWORTH, M. R. (1983) *Labour Supply* (Cambridge: Cambridge University Press).

LAYARD, P. R. G. (1979) 'The Costs and Benefits of Selective Employment Policies: The British Case', *British Journal of Industrial Relations*, 17, July, pp. 187–204.

LAYARD, P. R. G. (1982) 'Youth Unemployment in Britain and the United States Compared', Chapter 15 in Freeman and Wise (eds) (1982).

LEE, D. J. (1979) 'Craft Unions and the Force of Tradition: the Case of Apprenticeship', *British Journal of Industrial Relations*, 17, 1, March, pp. 34–49.

LEIGHTON, L. and MINCER, J. (1982) 'Labor Turnover and Youth Unemployment', Chapter 8 in Freeman and Wise (eds) (1982).

LEWIS, H. G. (1974) 'Comments on Selectivity Biases in Wage Comparisons', *Journal of Political Economy* 82, 6, pp. 1145–55.

LINDLEY, R. M. (1983) 'Active Manpower Policy', in G. Bain (ed.) *Industrial Relations in Britain* (Oxford: Basil Blackwell).

LRD (1983) Bargaining report 30, December (London: LRD).

LYNCH, L. M. (1983) 'Job Search and Youth Unemployment', *Oxford Economic Papers* 35, November, pp. 595–606.

LYNCH, L. M. (1985) 'State dependency in Youth Unemployment: A Lost Generation?' *Journal of Econometrics:* Annals of Applied Econometrics, 28, 1, July, pp. 71–84.

LYNCH, L. M. and RICHARDSON, R. (1982) 'Unemployment of Young Workers in Britain', *British Journal of Industrial Relations* 20, 3, November, pp. 362–72.

MACLEOD, A., MAIN, B. and RAFFE, D. (1983) 'Labour Market for Young People in Scotland', *Employment Gazette*, 91, March, pp. 96–101.

MADDALA, G. S. (1983) *Limited-Dependent and Qualitative Variables in Econometrics* (Cambridge: Cambridge University Press).

MADDALA, G. S. and NELSON, F. (1974) 'Maximum Likelihood Methods for Models in Disequilibrium', *Econometrica* 42, 6, pp. 1013–30.

MAIN, B. G. M. (1985) 'School-leaver Unemployment and the Youth Opportunities Programme in Scotland', *Oxford Economic Papers* 37, 3, November, pp. 426–47.

MAIN, B. G. M. and RAFFE, D. (1983a) 'Determinants of Employment and Unemployment among School Leavers: Evidence from the 1979 Survey of Scottish School Leavers', *Scottish Journal of Political Economy*, 30, 1, February, pp. 1–17.

MAIN, B. G. M. and RAFFE, D. (1983b) 'The Industrial Destinations of Scottish School Leavers 1977–1981', *Fraser of Allander Institute Quarterly Economic Commentary*, 8, 3 February, pp. 37–49.

MAIN, B. G. M. and RAFFE, D. (1983c) 'The Transition from School to Work in 1980/81: a Dynamic Account', *British Educational Research Journal* IX, pp. 57–70.

MAKEHAM, P. (1980) 'Youth Unemployment. An Examination of the Evidence on Youth Unemployment Using National Statistics', Department of Employment, research paper 10, March (London: HMSO).

MAKEHAM, P. (1981) 'Youth Unemployment: Further Analysis', Department of Employment technical note (London: HMSO).

MAKI, D. R. and Spindler, Z. A. (1975) 'The Effect of Unemployment Compensation on the Rate of Unemployment in Great Britain', *Oxford Economic Papers* 27, 3, November, pp. 440–54.

MARIANI, I. F. (1986) 'Youth Pay and Employers' Recruiting Practices: the Italian Experience', *Social Europe*, supplement on Youth Pay and Employers' Recruitment Practices for Young People in the Community pp. 135–43.

MARSDEN, D. W. (with the assistance of L. Redlbacher) (1980) *Study of Changes in the Wage Structure of Manual Workers in Industry in Six Community Countries since 1966*, report for the Statistical Office of the European Communities, Eurostat/C2/80032 (Luxembourg).

MARSDEN, D. W. (1981a) 'Training and Internal Labour Markets in Britain and West Germany', *Manpower Studies*, Spring.

MARSDEN, D. W. (1981b) 'Vive la Différence: Pay Differentials in Britain, West Germany, France and Italy', *Employment Gazette*, 89, 7, July.

MARSDEN, D. W. (1983) 'Youth Pay in France, FR Germany, and the United Kingdom since 1966 (with comparisons with the United States), paper prepared for the OECD (Paris: OECD).

MARSDEN, D. W. (1984) *Guide to Sources of Wages Statistics in EEC Countries*, Eurostat (Luxembourg).

MARSDEN, D. W. (1985) 'Occupational Pay in Some Major OECD Countries since 1972', paper prepared for the OECD (Paris: OECD) (mimeo).

MARSDEN, D. W. and RAJAN, A. (1984) *Young Workers' Pay and their Employment* (Brussels: EEC).

MARSDEN, D. W. and RYAN, P. (1986) 'Where do Young Workers Work? Employment by Industry in various European Economies', *British Journal of Industrial Relations*, 24, 7, March, pp. 83–102.

MARTIN, J. P. (1983) *Effects of the Minimum Wage on the Youth Labour Market in North America and France*, OECD, occasional paper, June (Paris: OECD).

MARX, K. (1906) *Capital* 1 (New York: Kerr).

MEADE, J. (1982) *Wage-Fixing* (London: George Allen & Unwin).

MERRILEES, W. J. and WILSON, R. A. (1979) 'Disequilibrium in the Labour Market for Young People in Great Britain', Manpower Research Group, discussion paper 10, September (Coventry: University of Warwick).

METCALF, D. (1979) 'Unemployment in Great Britain: An Analysis of Area Unemployment and Youth Unemployment', *International Institute of Management Papers*, November (Berlin: Wissenschaft Zentrum).

MEYER, R. and WISE, D. (1982) 'High School Preparation and Early Labour Force Experience', chapter 9 in Freeman and Wise (1982).

MINCER, J. (1974) *Schooling, Experience and Earnings*, NBER (New York: Columbia University Press).

MORTIMER, J. E. (1973) *History of the Boilermakers Society*, 1 (London: George Allen & Unwin).

MSC (1977) *Young People and Work* (London: MSC)

MSC (1979) *Review of the First Year of Special Programmes* (London: MSC)

MSC (1981a) *New Training Initiative: A Consultative Document*, May (London: MSC)

MSC (1981b) *New Training Initiative: An Agenda for Action* (London: MSC).

MSC (1982) *Youth Task Group Report*, April (Sheffield: MSC).

MSC (1984a) *Survey of YTS Schemes* (Sheffield: MSC).

MSC (1984b) *Sample Survey of YTS Start Certificates (November 1983)*, Youth Training Board, July, YTB/84/N6 (Sheffield: MSC).

MSC (1984c) *Results of the Follow-up Survey of YTS Early Leavers*, note by TESB, EG/84/7 (Sheffield: MSC).

MSC (1984d) *Youth Training Scheme Review 1984*, a report by the Youth Training Board to the Manpower Services Commission, September, YTS L60 (Sheffield: MSC).

MSC (1984e) *YTS Leavers*, Youth Training Directorate, October, (Sheffield: MSC).

MSC (1984f) *Annual Report 1983/1984* (Sheffield: MSC).

NADIRI, M. I. and ROSEN, S. (1969) 'Interrelated Factor Demand Functions', *American Economic Review*, 59, 4, pp. 457–71.

NARENDRANATHAN, W., NICKELL, S., and STERN, J. (1985) 'Unemployment Benefits Revisited', *Economic Journal*, 95, 378, pp. 307–29.

EDC (1984) *Competence and Competition. Training and Education in the Federal Republic of Germany, the United States and Japan*, a report prepared by the Institute of Manpower Studies, University of Sussex, for the NEDC and the MSC (London: NEDO).

NICKELL, S. (1977) 'Estimating the Probability of Leaving Unemployment', *Econometrica*, 47, 5, pp. 1249–66.

NOLL, I., BEICHT, U., BOELL, G., MALCHER, W., and WIEDER-HOLD-FRITZ, S. (1983) *Nettokosten der betrieblichen Berufsausbildung* Schriften zur Berufsbildungsforschung 63, Bundesinstitut fuer Berufsausbildung (Berlin: Beuth Verlag).

NYEC (1956–75) Triennial reports on the work of the Youth Employment Service (London: HMSO).

OECD (1980) *Youth Unemployment: The Causes and Consequences* (Paris: OECD)

OECD (1983) 'The Nature of Youth–Adult Unemployment Differentials', chapter VI in *Employment Outlook*, September, (Paris: OECD), pp. 73–80.

OECD (1984) 'Do Relative Wage Levels Affect Youth Employment?' chapter V in OECD *Employment Outlook*, September (Paris: OECD), pp. 69–86.

OECD (1985) 'Moving in and out of Unemployment: The Incidence and Patterns of Recurrent Unemployment in Selected OECD Countries', chapter VI in OECD *Employment Outlook*, September (Paris: OECD) pp. 99–114).

OKUN, A. M. (1981) *Prices and Quantities* (Oxford: Basil Blackwell).

OSTERMAN, P. (1980) *Getting Started: the Youth Labour Market* (Cambridge, Mass: MIT)

PAYNE, J. (1984) 'Changes in the Youth Labour Market', Department of Social and Administrative Studies (Oxford: University of Oxford).

PHELPS, E. S. (ed.) (1971) *Microeconomic Foundations of Employment and Inflation Theory* (London: Macmillan).

PIKE, M. (1984) 'The Employment Response to Equal Pay Legislation', Labour Economics Unit, working paper 2, May (Hull: University of Hull).

PRAIS, S. J. (1981) 'Vocational Qualifications of the Labour Force in Britain and Germany', *National Institute Economic Review*, 98, November, pp. 47–59.

PRICE, R., and BAIN, G. S. (1983) 'Union Growth in Britain: Retrospect and Prospect', *British Journal of Industrial Relations*, March, 21, 1, pp. 46–68.

RAFFE, D. (1983) 'Can There Be an Effective Youth Unemployment Policy?', in R. Fiddy (ed.) *In Place of Work: Policy and Provision for the Young Unemployed* (Lewes: Falmer).

RAFFE, D. (1984a) 'Youth Unemployment and the MSC: 1977–1983', in D. McCrone (ed.) *Scottish Government Yearbook 1984*, Unit for the Study of Government in Scotland, (Edinburgh: University of Edinburgh).

RAFFE, D. (1984b) 'The Transition from School to Work and the Recession, 1977–83: Evidence from the Scottish School Leavers' Surveys', *British Journal of Sociology of Education*, V, 3, pp. 247–65.

RAFFE, D. (ed.) (1984c) *Fourteen to Eighteen: the Changing Pattern of Schooling in Scotland* (Aberdeen: Aberdeen University Press).

RAFFE, D. (1984d) 'The Effects of Industrial Change on School-Leaver Employment in Scotland: a Quasi-Shift-Share Analysis', Centre for Educational Sociology, May (Edinburgh: University of Edinburgh) (mimeo).

RAINBIRD, H. and GRANT, W. (1985) *Employers' Associations and Training Policy. Industrial Training Arrangements in Four Industrial Sectors; Food Processing, Chemicals, Machine Tools and Construction*, research report (Coventry: IER, University of Warwick).

RAJAN, A. (1984) *Training and Recruitment Effects of Technical Change* (Aldershot: Gower).

REES, A. and GRAY, W. (1982) 'Family Effects in Youth Unemployment', chapter 13 in Freeman and Wise (1982).

REYNAUD, J. D., DASSA, S., DASSSA, J., and MACLOUF, P. (1971) 'Les évènements de mai et juin 1968 and le système français de relations professionelles', *Sociologie du Travail* 13, 1, January–March, pp. 77–97.

RICE, P. G. (1986) 'Juvenile Unemployment, Relative Wages and Social Security in Great Britain', *Economic Journal* 96, 382, pp. 352–74.

RICHARDSON, R. (1982) 'Unemployment and the Inner City – a Study of School Leavers', Department of Industrial Relations, June (London: LSE) (mimeo).

ROBERTS, K., DUGGAN, J. and NOBLE, M. (1981a) 'Ignoring the Sign: Young, Unemployed and Unregistered', *Employment Gazette*, August, pp. 353–6.

ROBERTS, K., DUGGAN, J., and NOBLE, M. (1981b) *Unregistered Youth Unemployment and Outreach Careers Work*, Department of Employment, research paper 31, November (London: HMSO).

ROSEN, H. S. and QUANDT, R. (1978) 'Estimation of a Disequilibrium Aggregate Labour Market', *Review of Economics and Statistics* 60, 3, pp. 371–9.

ROTTENBERG, S. (1961) 'The Irrelevance of Union Apprentice/Journeyman Ratios', *Journal of Business*, July, 34, pp. 384–6.

RYAN, P. (1980) 'The Costs of Job Training for a Transferable Skill', *British Journal of Industrial Relations*, November 18, 3, pp. 334–52.

RYAN, P. (1983) 'Youth Labour, Trade Unionism and State Policy in Contemporary Britain', paper presented to Fifth Conference of the International Working Group on Labour Market Segmentation, July (Aix-en-Provence).

RYAN, P. (1984a) 'Job Training, Employment Practices and the Large Enterprise', pp. 191–230 in P. Osterman (ed.) *Internal Labour Markets*, (Cambridge, Mass: MIT).

RYAN, P. (1984b) 'The New Training Initiative after Two Years', *Lloyds Bank Review*, 152, April, pp. 31–45.

SAUNDERS, C. T. and MARSDEN, D. W. (1981) *Pay Inequalities in the European Community* (London: Butterworths).

SCULLION, H. (1981) 'The Skilled Revolt against General Unionism; the Case of the BL Toolroom Committee', *Industrial Relations Journal*, May, 12, 3, pp. 15–27.

SMITH, J. P. (ed.) (1980) *Female Labor Supply: Theory and Estimation* (Princeton, N. J.: Princeton University Press).

STERN, J. (1981) 'Choice of Pressure of Demand Variables for the Cohort Study of the Unemployed', Centre for Labour Economics, working paper 236, January (London: LSE).

STERN, J. (1982) 'Unemployment Inflow Rates for Autumn 1978', Centre for Labour Economics, discussion paper 129, June (London: LSE).

STERN, J. (1984). 'Repeat Unemployment Spells: The Effect of Unemployment Benefits on Unemployment Entry', Centre for Labour Economics discussion paper 192, March (London: LSE).

TAYLOR, M. E. (1981) *Education and Work in the Federal Republic of Germany* (London: Anglo–German Foundation for the Study of Industrial Society).

TOBIN, J. (1972) 'Inflation and Unemployment', *American Economic Review*, 62, 1, March, pp. 1–18.

TUCKETT, A. (1974) *The Blacksmiths' History* (London: Lawrence and Wishart).

TURNER, H. A. T. (1952) 'Trade Unions, Differentials and the Levelling of Wages', *Manchester School,* September XX, 3, pp. 227–82.

WEBB, S. and WEBB, B. (1920) *Industrial Democracy* (London: Longmans).

WELLS, W. (1983) *The Relative Pay and Employment of Young People*, Department of Employment research paper 42 (London: HMSO).

WIGHAM, E. (1973) *The Power to Manage* (London: Macmillan).

WIRTSCHAFT UND STATISTIK (1981) Bildung und Kultur: Auszubildende 1980, *Wirtschaft und Statistik*, 9, pp. 679–86.

WRAY, J. V. C. (1959) 'Trade Unions and Young Workers in Great Britain', *International Labour Review*, April, 75, 4, pp. 304–18.

ZABALZA, A and TZANNATOS, Z. (1983) 'The Effect of Britain's Anti-Discriminatory Legislation on Relative Pay and Employment', Centre for Labour Economics, working paper 155 (London: LSE).

ZELLNER, A. (1962) 'An Efficient Method of Estimating Seemingly Unrelated Regressions and Tests for Aggregation Bias', *Journal of the American Statistical Association*, 57, pp. 348–68.

Index

Page numbers in *italics* refer to Figures. (T) following a page number indicates a Table.